# ENGLISH

## THE Easy Way

## THIRD EDITION

**Harriet Diamond, M.A.**
President, Diamond Associates,
Multi-Faceted Training & Development
Westfield, New Jersey
and
**Phyllis Dutwin, M.A.**
President, Dutwin Associates,
Training and Development Programs
Wickford, Rhode Island

## BARRON'S

This book is dedicated to those adults committed to lifelong learning: the students and their teachers.

ACKNOWLEDGMENTS

We wish to express our appreciation to Walter Hauck, former director of the New Jersey State Department of Education's Office of High School Completion, for his encouragement and assistance.

Thanks to Harry Linkin, former director of Adult and Continuing Education at the Union County Regional Adult School, to Wayne Hemingway, former director of the High School Equivalency Program and Ted Gnagey, former director of Adult Education at the South Orange-Maplewood Adult School, for providing the teaching atmospheres that allowed us to work creatively and develop our material.

Finally, we would like to thank our families for their patience and encouragement.

Portion of material adapted from Russell Baker's "Backwards Wheels the Mind," *The New York Times,* July 1, 1973. © 1973 by The New York Times Company. Reprinted by permission.

Quote from Richard Bach's *Jonathan Livingston Seagull.* © 1970, Macmillan Publishing Co., Inc. Reprinted by permission.

Paragraph from *A Civil Tongue* by Edwin Newman. © 1976 by Edwin Newman.

Portions of Chapter 22 adapted from *Writing the Easy Way* by Harriet Diamond and Phyllis Dutwin. © 1991 by Barron's Educational Series, Inc.

*All inquiries should be addressed to:*
Barron's Educational Series, Inc.
250 Wireless Boulevard
Hauppauge, New York 11788

*Library of Congress Catalog Card No. 88-6301*
International Standard Book No. 0-8120-9142-6

**Library of Congress Cataloging in Publication Data**

Diamond, Harriet.
   English the easy way.

   1. English language—Grammar—1950—
2. English language—Usage I. Dutwin, Phyllis.
II. Title.
PE1112.D47      1988  428.2      88-6301
ISBN 0-8120-9142-6

PRINTED IN THE UNITED STATES OF AMERICA
**19 18 17 16 15 14**

# Table of Contents

# Introduction

In traditional grammar programs, students are often baffled by the necessity of memorizing numerous definitions of grammatical terminology, none of which has any practical meaning in terms of day-to-day speech and writing. The confusion that results is often detrimental; the student's frustration ultimately overcomes his or her desire to learn.

*English The Easy Way* is designed to encourage, not frustrate, the student. Written specifically for adult students who want an all-inclusive self-help program in grammar, *English The Easy Way* also serves as an invaluable tool for all English language improvement programs.

Its main feature is a common sense approach to language study. Recognizing that traditional grammar is not easy for everyone to master, *English The Easy Way* emphasizes language structure. Thus, the main purpose of this format is to motivate by showing how much the student already knows about the language.

*English The Easy Way* builds upon the student's basic understanding in an organized way. Beginning with the basic sentence pattern—performer-action—the book continues until all essential elements are introduced. Ample practice material follows each newly introduced concept. Because of the manner of presentation of the instructional material, *English The Easy Way* lends itself easily either to group or individualized classroom instruction or to independent study.

# Effective Use of This Book

Because *English The Easy Way* is a cumulative study, we recommend beginning with Chapter 1 and continuing consecutively. There are two chapters that do not fit into the consecutive pattern of the book: "Spelling" and "Word Usage." Spelling rules can be summarized in one chapter, but they cannot be learned in one lesson. The same is true of word usage. The authors, therefore, recommend that students begin studying these chapters early in their program and continue on a regular basis.

Guard against skimming over instructional material. Skipping instructional material, in order to complete practices quickly, will result in unnecessary errors and time lost. Before attempting a Cumulative Review, the authors recommend reviewing the major concepts presented in the chapters that precede it.

---

**Consistent use of the *Answer Key* is essential to proper study.** The authors recommend that students check each practice exercise with the *Answer Key* before going on to the next section. By checking answers after each exercise, students can avoid repeating errors. Cumulative Reviews should be considered tests and should be taken in their entirety before checking answers. Students should note the kinds of errors made in Cumulative Reviews (these answers have been keyed to the applicable review chapters) and return to the appropriate chapters for reinforcement of the correct concepts.

# CHAPTER 1

# THE SIMPLEST COMPLETE THOUGHT

> "Twas brillig and the slithy toves
>    Did gyre and gimble in the wabe;
> All mimsy were the borogroves,
>    All the mome raths outgrabe.
>
> "Beware the Jabberwock, my son!
>    The jaws that bite, the claws that catch!
> Beware the Jubjub bird, and shun
>    The frumious Bandersnatch!"
>                    —Lewis Carroll
>                    "Jabberwocky"

## A Word With You . . .

"Jabberwocky," the most famous nonsense poem ever written, can be enjoyed on several levels. Literary detectives have tried to find hidden meanings in the made up words, while others have been amused by the poet's cleverness with sounds and rhythms.

Although Lewis Carroll never heard of "the flink glopped," it is a phrase he might have approved of—especially in the way it is used in the chapter you are about to read.

## What You've Always Known

The flink glopped.

What is the above sentence about? What action is taking place in this sentence? Who is performing this action? You are able to understand the nonsense sentence because you are familiar with that sentence pattern: a person or thing performing an action.

Performer Action
(The) flink glopped.

You frequently see this pattern written, and you hear it spoken.

1

Another clue in this sentence is a clue to time. Is the action past, present, or future? What was the clue? Yes, the *-ed* ending is the clue to time. The action occurred in the past.

Notice the word endings in the following sentences:

The flin<u>k</u> glo<u>ps</u>.
Two flin<u>ks</u> glo<u>p</u>.

When the performer (*flink*) is <u>*singular*</u>, an <u>s</u> is added to the present action. When the performer (*flinks*) is *plural* (more than one), no <u>s</u> is added to the present action.

This simple pattern may have *more than one performer*:

The *flink and his brother* *glop.*

There may be one performer and *more than one action:*

The *flink* *glops* and *glarks*.

There may also be *more than one performer and more than one action:*

The *flink and his brother* *glop* and *glark*.

Now, let's examine some real sentences that use the same pattern: a person or thing performing an action and the action. As you read the following sentences, think about who or what is performing the action, what the action is, and when the action occurs (present, past, or future). Next, write the performer, the action, and the times in the spaces provided. The first sentence is done for you.

|  | Performer | Action | (present, past, future) Time |
|---|---|---|---|
| 1. The law student completed the difficult exam. | student | completed | past |
| 2. Mrs. Smith sings in the church choir each Sunday. |  |  |  |
| 3. The plane raced across the sky. |  |  |  |
| 4. They will speak at the November meeting. |  |  |  |

|  | Performer | Action | (present, past, future) Time |
|---|---|---|---|
| 5. The interviewer listened attentively. | | | |
| 6. A cashier always counts the change. | | | |
| 7. Star Cleaners picks up and delivers cleaning. | | | |
| 8. The woman and her children crossed the street. | | | |
| 9. The gardener rakes the leaves and cuts the grass. | | | |
| 10. Diane and Joe dined at the tavern and attended the theater. | | | |

PRACTICE
I

_Directions:_   Complete the pattern in each of the following sentences by adding either the person or thing performing the action or the action.

1. The children _____ into the street.
2. _____ barked at the mailman.
3. _____ will signal at the light.
4. The choir _____ last Sunday.
5. _____ hesitated in the doorway.

PRACTICE
II

_Directions:_   Draw a line from the people or things in the left column to the actions in the right column to make complete sentences.

| Performers | Actions |
|---|---|
| The jury | travel. |
| An accident | will attend. |
| A salesman and his assistant | occurred. |
| A motorcycle | convened and concurred. |
| We | backfires. |

PRACTICE
III

*Directions:*  Write three sentences of your own using the sentence pattern you have just studied: a person or thing performing an action and an action.

| Performer | Action |
| --- | --- |
| 1. | |
| 2. | |
| 3. | |

PRACTICE
IV

*Directions:*  In each of the following sentences, one word is underlined. If the underlined word is the person or thing performing the action, blacken number 1. If the underlined word is the action word, blacken number 2.

1. The *manager* shouted at the salesman.            ① ②
2. A large delivery *truck* approached the intersection.            ① ②
3. We *celebrated* her graduation.            ① ②
4. The *mayor* proclaimed a clean-up week.            ① ②
5. The members *contributed* large sums of money.            ① ②
6. The huge *machine* sputtered menacingly.            ① ②
7. A committee *will convene* within the week.            ① ②
8. The *union* struck after much negotiation.            ① ②
9. The checkbook *balances* for the first time.            ① ②
10. A soprano *will sing* this part of the opera.            ① ②

PRACTICE
V

*Directions:*  Blacken number 1 if a sentence has one performer and one action; blacken number 2 if a sentence has more than one performer and one action; blacken number 3 if a sentence has one performer and two actions; blacken number 4 if a sentence has more than one performer and two actions.

1. This candidate addresses the issues.            ① ② ③ ④
2. His opponent evades difficult questions.            ① ② ③ ④
3. Meditation relaxes many people.            ① ② ③ ④
4. Mr. Valdez proposed several good ideas.            ① ② ③ ④
5. Six team members shouted at the coach.            ① ② ③ ④
6. Maria and Julia sold their pottery.            ① ② ③ ④
7. The electrician and his assistant stopped and rested.            ① ② ③ ④

8.  The audience cheered and applauded.  ① ② ③ ④
9.  Batman always wins.  ① ② ③ ④
10.  I asked a searching question.  ① ② ③ ④

## Recognizing Complete and Incomplete Thoughts

You are ready now to add another element to your understanding of complete thoughts.

*Example:*   When you arrive.

The above sentence has a performer *(you)* and an action *(arrive)*; yet, it is not a complete thought. Because the sentence begins with the word *when,* the thought is not complete as it stands.

---

Any sentence that begins with such words as *when, after, because, as soon as, before,* or *since* needs to have a completing thought.

---

Possible thought completions for *When you arrive* are:

a.  When you arrive, *relax.*
b.  When you arrive, *call me.*
c.  When you arrive, *I will leave.*

*Example:*  The tall figure walking hurriedly through the park.

The above sentence has a performer *(figure)*, but the action *(walking)* is incomplete. It would be correct to say the figure *was walking* or the figure *is walking.*

Possible thought completions for *The tall figure walking hurriedly through the park* are:

a.  The tall figure *is walking hurriedly through the park.*
b.  The tall figure *was walking hurriedly through the park.*
c.  The tall figure *walked hurriedly through the park.*

PRACTICE
VI

*Directions:* Blacken the circle that corresponds to the number of the incomplete sentence in each group. If there is no error, blacken number 5.

1. (1) After McCarthy's defeat, he retired from public office.
   (2) Bring me a cup of coffee, please.
   (3) When Richard called his office.
   (4) The two truckers arrived at the delivery depot at the same time.
   (5) No error

   ① ② ③ ④ ⑤

2. (1) The man in the blue suit and the lady in the tan coat walking.
   (2) The legislature meets daily.
   (3) I did not buy enough yarn for the sweater.
   (4) A large delivery truck reached the intersection.
   (5) No error

   ① ② ③ ④ ⑤

3. (1) The nervous waitress spilled the coffee in the celebrity's lap.
   (2) The fumbling, bumbling clown dancing.
   (3) The county official faced the angry crowd.
   (4) The women in the community organized a boycott against Sam's Market.
   (5) No error

   ① ② ③ ④ ⑤

4. (1) A favorite history question involves the causative factors of the Civil War.
   (2) Federal spending cuts will cause much discussion.
   (3) The winning pitcher threw a fast ball.
   (4) Her considerate husband brought a dozen roses for their anniversary.
   (5) No error

   ① ② ③ ④ ⑤

5. (1) The students studied and reviewed.
   (2) Flour, sugar, and three eggs blending.
   (3) The book fell suddenly from the shelf.
   (4) The mayor proclaimed a clean-up week.
   (5) No error

   ① ② ③ ④ ⑤

6. (1) Leona working harder than any other lawyer in the firm.  ① ② ③ ④ ⑤
   (2) A soprano will sing this part in the opera.
   (3) Robert and Chico prepare the finest paella.
   (4) The candidate spoke the truth.
   (5) No error

7. (1) The man threw away the garbage.  ① ② ③ ④ ⑤
   (2) The soldiers walked quietly.
   (3) When I have finished dusting and vacuuming and washing, I will relax.
   (4) The mayor commended the members of the local rescue squad.
   (5) No error

## Action Words: Special Problems

Many action words undergo simple changes to show changes in time. *For example:*

| Present | Past | Action words used with helping words, such as has, had, have, is, etc. |
|---|---|---|
| kick | kicked | kicked |
| plan | planned | planned |
| cheer | cheered | cheered |

The simplest change is the addition of an *-ed* ending.

1. I *kick* the ball 200 yards each time. (Present)
2. The tenants' association *planned* a victory party. (Past)
3. The overzealous Viking fans *had cheered* before they realized that the Eagle quarterback was really injured. (Past with helping word, *had*)

Many action words use entirely different forms to show these same changes. *For example:*

| Present | Past | Action words used with helping words, such as has, had, have, is, etc. |
| --- | --- | --- |
| break | broke | broken |

1. Anna never *breaks* a promise.
2. Rosemary *broke* several promises to Anna.
3. Rosemary *has broken* her last promise.

Following is a list of commonly used action words that change their forms to show time changes.

| Present | Past | Action words used with helping words, such as has, had, have, is, etc. |
| --- | --- | --- |
| begin | began | begun |
| blow | blew | blown |
| break | broke | broken |
| bring | brought | brought |
| build | built | built |
| burst | burst | burst |
| choose | chose | chosen |
| dive | dived *or* dove | dived |
| do | did | done |
| draw | drew | drawn |
| drink | drank | drunk |
| drive | drove | driven |
| eat | ate | eaten |
| fall | fell | fallen |
| flee | fled | fled |
| fly | flew | flown |
| forbid | forbade | forbidden |
| freeze | froze | frozen |
| get | got | gotten *or* got |
| give | gave | given |
| go | went | gone |
| grow | grew | grown |
| have, has | had | had |
| know | knew | known |
| lay (place) | laid | laid |
| lead | led | led |
| leave (depart) | left | left |
| lie (recline) | lay | lain |

| Present | Past | Action words used with helping words, such as has, had, have, is, etc. |
|---------|------|------------------------------------------------------------------------|
| pay | paid | paid |
| raise (elevate) | raised | raised |
| ride | rode | ridden |
| ring | rang | rung |
| rise (ascend) | rose | risen |
| run | ran | run |
| see | saw | seen |
| shake | shook | shaken |
| shine | shone, shined | shone, shined |
| shoot | shot | shot |
| shrink | shrank, shrunk | shrunk |
| sing | sang | sung |
| sit | sat | sat |
| slay | slew | slain |
| speak | spoke | spoken |
| spring | sprang | sprung |
| steal | stole | stolen |
| sting | stung | stung |
| swear | swore | sworn |
| swing | swung | swung |
| swim | swam | swum |
| take | took | taken |
| tear | tore | torn |
| throw | threw | thrown |
| wake | waked *or* woke | waked |
| wear | wore | worn |
| write | wrote | written |

**PRACTICE VII**

*Directions:*  Choose an action word in the parentheses to complete each sentence. Find the correct form of the word in the list above.

1. The employee entered the correct code and the gate (rose, rise). (Hint: Choose the word that means *goes up*, or, *ascends.*)
2. I bought new running shoes because the heels had (worn, wore) down in the old ones.
3. If we had (knew, known) how long the movie was, we wouldn't have rented it.

4. The laundry had (shrinked, shrunk) my only good shirt just before the awards dinner.

5. The children always have (lain, laid) the money on the counter when they arrived, but today it was not there. (Hint: Choose the word that means *to place*.)

PRACTICE
VIII

*Directions:*  Blacken the circle that corresponds to the number of the sentence with the incorrect action word in each group. If there is no error, blacken number 5. (Note: Refer to the preceding list to find the correct form of the action word.)

1. (1) Marigolds always have <u>grown</u> well in that sunny spot.     ① ② ③ ④ ⑤
   (2) I have <u>rang</u> her doorbell several times today.
   (3) After we had <u>set</u> the bowl of flowers on the table, the room looked complete.
   (4) Having <u>ridden</u> for hours, the sightseers were ready to check into a motel.
   (5) No error

2. (1) Angela <u>led</u> the church choir.     ① ② ③ ④ ⑤
   (2) Last year, Marlene <u>lead</u> the church choir.
   (3) I never <u>have led</u> a church choir.
   (4) Have you ever <u>led</u> a church choir?
   (5) No error

3. (1) I <u>swear</u> that I told the truth.     ① ② ③ ④ ⑤
   (2) The defendant <u>swore</u> to tell the truth.
   (3) The plaintiff <u>swore</u> to tell the truth.
   (4) All of the witnesses have been <u>sworn</u> in.
   (5) No error

4. (1) Martina Navratilova has <u>swung</u> many tennis rackets in her time.     ① ② ③ ④ ⑤
   (2) I, on the other hand, have never <u>swung</u> a tennis racket quite like she did during that decisive game.
   (3) I wonder if Joani <u>swings</u> a golf club incorrectly.
   (4) He <u>swinged</u> a tennis racket fairly well.
   (5) No error

5. (1) The opinionated Mr. Dobbs never had _run_ for office himself.    ① ② ③ ④ ⑤
   (2) Colonel Adams has _run_ for mayor several times.
   (3) I have _ran_ for public office once.
   (4) Mrs. Diaz plans to _run_ next year.
   (5) No error

6. (1) Did you _write_ to Mattie about your promotion?    ① ② ③ ④ ⑤
   (2) Arthur _wrote_ to her several times.
   (3) I had not _written_ before the summer ended.
   (4) Mrs. Scott has always _written_ excellent business letters.
   (5) No error

7. (1) Mother had _threw_ out my favorite old sneakers before I could stop her.    ① ② ③ ④ ⑤
   (2) I wouldn't _throw_ out someone else's sneakers.
   (3) I saved those sneakers from being _thrown_ out several times.
   (4) This time, they were _thrown_ out for the last time.
   (5) No error

PRACTICE
IX

_Directions:_    Blacken the circle that corresponds to the number of the incorrect word in each sentence. If there is no error, blacken number 5.

1. The injured bird _flew_ to the ground, _letting_ his    ① ② ③ ④ ⑤
              1                                2
   _broken_ wing _lay_ at his side. _No error_
   3              4                  5

2. Upon seeing the young child _fall_ into the lake,    ① ② ③ ④ ⑤
                                  1
   Eric _sprung_ to his feet, _ran_, and _dived_. _No error_
        2                      3          4          5

3. Because Teddy had frequently _fallen_ asleep on    ① ② ③ ④ ⑤
                                  1
   the job, he was not _payed_ the full _amount_ that
                        2                 3
   had been _written_ into his contract. _No error_
            4                              5

4. If you *choose* to *rise* within the company, you    ① ② ③ ④ ⑤
         1        2

    *must* *raise* your level of work. *No error*
     3    4              5

5. The guest *arrived* unexpectedly, *shaked* every-    ① ② ③ ④ ⑤
             1                2

    one's hand, *ate*, and *left* as unexpectedly as he
               3       4

    had arrived. *No error*
            5

6. We *seen* the lights that *shined* in the distance,    ① ② ③ ④ ⑤
       1             2

    and we *began* to *walk* toward them. *No error*
          3      4            5

7. Because I had *forgotten* my driver's license,    ① ② ③ ④ ⑤
             1

    the policeman *forbidded* me to *drive* any
               2          3

    *farther*. *No error*
      4       5

8. Once their leader had *fallen*, the young sol-    ① ② ③ ④ ⑤
                 1

    diers did not *know* how to continue, so they
               2

    *fleed* in many directions and were never *seen*
     3                         4

    again. *No error*
        5

9. The *armed* man *slayed* the innocent victim,    ① ② ③ ④ ⑤
       1        2

    *stole* his watch, and *ran* down the alley. *No error*
     3             4             5

10. Maxine *waked* me early this morning, and I    ① ② ③ ④ ⑤
         1

    *ate* my eggs, *drunk* my juice, and *left*. *No error*
     2          3             4    5

# Chapter 1  The Simplest Complete Thought

| Performer | Action | Time |
|---|---|---|
| 1. student | completed | past |
| 2. Mrs. Smith | sings | present |
| 3. plane | raced | past |
| 4. they | will speak | future |
| 5. interviewer | listened | past |
| 6. cashier | counts | present |
| 7. Star Cleaners | picks up, delivers | present |
| 8. woman, children | crossed | past |
| 9. gardener | rakes, cuts | present |
| 10. Diane, Joe | dined, attended | past |

**Practice I** *Page 3.*

Answers will vary. *Sample* answers:

1. The children *ran* into the street.
2. *The dog* barked at the mailman.
3. *Henry* will signal at the light.
4. The choir *sang* last Sunday.
5. *Susan* hesitated in the doorway.

**Practice II** *Page 3.*

1. The jury convened and concurred.
2. An accident occurred.
3. A salesman and his assistant travel.
4. A motorcycle backfires.
5. We will attend.

**Practice III** *Page 4.*

Answers will vary. *Sample* answers:

1. *John cashed* a check at the bank.
2. The *roses bloomed* early this year.
3. My *mother-in-law calls* every Friday.

**Practice IV** *Page 4.*

| Performer | Action |
|---|---|
| 1. **(1)** manager | |
| 2. **(1)** truck | |
| 3. **(2)** | celebrated |
| 4. **(1)** mayor | |
| 5. **(2)** | contributed |
| 6. **(1)** machine | |
| 7. **(2)** | will convene |
| 8. **(1)** union | |
| 9. **(2)** | balances |
| 10. **(2)** | will sing |

**Practice V** *Page 4.*

| Performer | Action |
|---|---|
| 1. **(1)** candidate | addresses |
| 2. **(1)** opponent | evades |
| 3. **(1)** meditation | relaxes |
| 4. **(1)** Mr. Valdez | proposed |
| 5. **(2)** members | shouted |
| 6. **(2)** Maria and Julia | sold |
| 7. **(4)** electrician and assistant | stopped and rested |
| 8. **(3)** audience | cheered and applauded |
| 9. **(1)** Batman | wins |
| 10. **(1)** I | asked |

**Practice VI** *Page 6.*

Possible Corrections:

1. **(3)** a. When Richard called his office, the phone rang unanswered.

   b. Richard called his office.

2. **(1)** a. The man in the blue suit and the lady in the tan coat walk.

   b. The man in the blue suit and the lady in the tan coat, walking along the street, were stopped by a stranger.

3. **(2)** a. The fumbling, bumbling clown danced.

   b. The fumbling, bumbling clown dancing makes the children laugh.

4. **(5)** No error

5. **(2)** a. Blend flour, sugar, and three eggs.

   b. Flour, sugar, and three eggs blending completes the recipe.

6. **(1)** a. Leona worked harder than any other lawyer in the firm.

   b. Leona, working harder than any other lawyer in the firm, was promoted to vice president.

7. **(5)** No error

**Practice VII** *Page 9.*

1. Use *rose* (the past form of the action word that means *to ascend*).

2. Use *worn* with the helping word *had*.

3. Use *known* with the helping word *had*.

4. Use *shrunk* with the helping word *had*.

5. Use *laid* (the action word that means *to place*) with the helping word *have*.

**Practice VIII** *Page 10.*

1. **(2)** have *rung*

   Use *rung* with the helping word *have*.

2. **(2)** *led*

   *Lead* is present; *led* is past.

3. **(5)** No error

   *Swear* is present; *swore* is past; *sworn* is used with *have been*.

4. **(4)** *swung*

   *Swinged* is not a word.

5. **(3)** have *run*

   Use *run* with the helping word *have*.

6. **(5)** No error

   *Write* is present; *wrote* is past; *written* is used with *has*.

7. **(1)** *thrown*

   Use *thrown* with the helping word *had.*

**Practice IX** *Page 11.*

1. **(5)** No error

2. **(2)** sprang

   *Sprung* is used only with helping words such as *has*, *have* or *had*.

3. **(2)** paid

   *Payed* is not a word.

4. **(5)** No error

5. **(2)** shook

   *Shaked* is not a word.

6. **(1)** saw

   *Seen* is used only with helping words such as *has*, *have* or *had*.

7. **(2)** forbade

   *Forbidded* is not a word.

8. **(3)** fled

   *Fleed* is not a word.

9. **(2)** slew

   *Slayed* is not a word.

10. **(3)** drank

    *Drunk* is used only with helping words such as *has*, *have* or *had*.

# CHAPTER 2

# PERFORMER AND ACTION: UNDERSTANDING TIME AND NUMBER

> Every so often, Mr. Spector called on Vinnie to answer, and that was when English 117 really came to life.
>
> "So I says to Angie . . ."
>
> "No, Vinnie," interjected Mr. Spector, "you didn't '*says*' to Angie, you '*said*' to him."
>
> "That's right," continued Vinnie, "I *says* to Angie . . ."
>
> "Go on," Mr. Spector replied wearily; "You *says* to Angie . . ."
>
> "That's what I *said*, man," snorted Vinnie. "Can't a guy tell a story without bein' interrupted?"
>
> —Roger Talifiero
> *Our Little Red Schoolhouse*

## *A Word With You . . .*

Mr. Spector's English class was a lively place because the teacher encouraged free and open discussion. At times, however, Mr. Spector's classical training set his teeth on edge when he saw a misspelling or a failure to capitalize.

In this excerpt, his student, Vinnie, was confused about different forms of the action word *to say*. After you read Chapter 2, you should know why Mr. Spector often needed an aspirin after English 117.

## Understanding Time

As you learned in Chapter 1, actions occur at different times.

John walks. (*present*)
John walked. (*past*)
John will walk. (*future*)

PRACTICE

I   *Directions:*   Use *work, worked,* or *will work* in each of the following sentences.

1. Willie Farris _____ overtime last week.
2. We must _____ a certain number of hours each day.
3. Four employees _____ overtime next week.

It is easy to determine the time of the action word in a single sentence. When sentences appear in paragraph form, however, the time of each action is more difficult to determine. *The time of all action words in a paragraph must be the same.* The action word in the first sentence sets the time for the paragraph. For example:

INCORRECT:   John *entered* the library. He *speaks* to the librarian. He *walked* from stack to stack looking for something in particular. Finally, John *chooses* a book.

CORRECT:   John *entered* the library. He *spoke* to the librarian. He *walked* from stack to stack looking for something in particular. Finally, John *chose* a book.

Because *entered* is in the past, *spoke, walked,* and *chose* must be in the past, too.

PRACTICE

II   *Directions:*   For each underlined action word, blacken circle number 1 if the time is correct and circle number 2 if the time is incorrect. Remember that the action word *filed* sets the time for the other action words in the paragraph.

The crowd filed into the meeting room. The      (1)      ① ②

chairman *raps* his gavel. An angry murmur      (2)      ① ②
       1

*continued* in the room. The chairman *will rap*      (3)      ① ②
  2                3

his gavel a second time. Quiet finally *settles*      (4)      ① ②
                              4

over the room. The chairman *began* his port.      (5)      ① ②
                          5

# Understanding Number

When we talk about a performer's *number*, we are talking about whether it is singular or plural.

*Example:*
PERFORMER-Singular
Sometimes the *appliance* works.

*Example:*
PERFORMER-Plural
Sometimes the *appliances* don't work.

A plural performer may be expressed in one word that ends in <u>s</u> (girls) or in one word that does not end in <u>s</u> (children). A plural performer also may be expressed in more than one word (a pad, a pen, and a book), none of which ends in <u>s</u>.

*Example:* PERFORMER-Plural
*Diets* often result in temporary weight loss.

*Example:*
PERFORMER-Plural
*Diet and exercise* keep the weight off.

*Example:*
PERFORMER-Plural
We take the *children* to day care four times a week.

PRACTICE
III

*Directions:*   In each of the following sentences, underline the performer or performers. Write an *S* over the word if the performer is singular. Write a *P* over the word or words if the performer is plural.

S
*Example:*       <u>Mr. Warner</u> knows everyone in town.

1. The women work well together.
2. Mr. Smith and his son address the Cub Scouts.
3. Flour, sugar, and milk complete this recipe.
4. Connie Martine understands community relations.
5. Mr. Luchner's grandchildren often visit him.

As you are beginning to see, the performer and action words *work together* (grammarians say they *agree*) to show that they are singular or plural.

*Example:*       Singular   Singular
Performer   Action Word
Our *relative* *comes* to dinner every Sunday.

*Example:*

Plural        Plural
Performer   Action Word

Our <u>relatives</u> <u>come</u> to dinner every Sunday.

Did you notice anything surprising? You are probably saying to your-self, as you did when you read Chapter 1, "Why is there an <u>s</u> at the end of a singular action word (travel<u>s</u>)? An <u>s</u> means the word is plural, does-n't it?" Well, yes—and no. An <u>s</u> at the end of the performer (relative<u>s</u>) shows that it is plural. On the other hand, an <u>s</u> at the end of an action word (come<u>s</u>) shows that the action word is singular and should be used with a singular performer.

*Example:*

Singular      Singular
Performer   Action Word

That <u>car</u> <u>travels</u> at top speed.

*Example:*

Plural        Plural
Performer   Action Word

Those <u>cars</u> <u>travel</u> at top speed.

*Example:*

Singular Performer

The <u>house</u> stand<u>s</u> on a hill.

*Example:*

Plural Performer

The <u>houses</u> stan<u>d</u> on a hill.

**PRACTICE IV**

*Directions:*   Correct the number error in each underlined action word.

1. Today, companies <u>*focuses*</u> on their customers._____
2. The machine <u>*make*</u> 300 gallons of pure water._____
3. Beautifully wrapped presents <u>*does*</u> not stay that way for very long._____
4. Today, many businesses <u>*manages*</u> offices all over the world. _____
5. That agency <u>*give*</u> the kind of advice I need._____

You have been working with performers in the present time: *comes, travels, stands,* etc. Now we've come to the easier part—performers in past time. Why easier? You will see that although the performer changes in number, the action word remains the same. For example, we can select the action word *ride* and use it in its past form, *rode.* Now, when we change the performer in every sentence below so that there are both singular and plural performers, what happens to the word *rode*? Nothing. *Rode* remains the same.

I *rode* the subway.
You *rode* the subway.

(He)　　　　　　　David *rode* the subway.
(She)　　　　　　Pam *rode* the subway.
　　　　　　　　Who *rode* the subway?
(We)　　　　David and I *rode* the subway.
　　　　　　You and Pam *rode* the subway.
(They)　　Ellen and Linda *rode* the subway.

In the following sentences, the time is present. Notice that the form of the action word changes for singular and plural performers. You see that an *s* is added to the action word when the performer is *singular*—except when the performer is *I* or *you*.

*Example:*　　　　The studen**t** ride**s** the subway.
　　　　　　　　The student**s** rid**e** the subway.

I *ride* the subway.
You *ride* the subway.
(He)　　　　　　　David *rides* the subway.
(She)　　　　　　Pam *rides* the subway.
　　　　　　　　Who *rides* the subway?
(We)　　　　David and I *ride* the subway.
　　　　　　You and Pam *ride* the subway.
(They)　　Ellen and Linda *ride* the subway.

---

PRACTICE
V

*Directions:*　Blacken the circle that corresponds to the number of the incorrect action word in each group of sentences. If there is no error, blacken number 5.

1. A shopping trip *makes* me angry. Prices *soar*　　① ② ③ ④ ⑤
　　　　　　　1　　　　　　　　　　　　2
each week. Meat prices *changes* almost daily.
　　　　　　　　　　3
Oranges, apples, and bananas *cost* more than
　　　　　　　　　　　　　　4
ever. A shopper needs more and more money

each week. *No error*
　　　　5

2. Tom *jogs* each morning. Macon and Gary *join*
    1                                    2

   him on Mondays and Thursdays. The Robinson

   twins *likes* jogging too. Jogging now *replaces*
           3                               4

   basketball as the neighborhood pastime.

   *No error*
    5

① ② ③ ④ ⑤

3. Each year local artists *participate* in an art
                               1

   show. The Community Center *offers* a perfect
                                 2

   gallery. One artist *wins* in each of five categories.
                      3

   The winning artists *displays* their works in the
                      4

   Town Hall. *No error*
            5

① ② ③ ④ ⑤

---

The above paragraphs had errors in *number*. In the following exercise, look for errors in *time* and *number*.

**PRACTICE VI**

*Directions:*   Blacken the circle that corresponds to the number of the incorrect word in each group of sentences. If there is no error, blacken number 5.

1. In the spring, the honeysuckle *droops* over the
                             1

   hillside. Its sweet *smell* *hangs* heavily in the
                     2     3

   air outside. It floats into the room when the

   doors *are open*. *No error*
         4        5

① ② ③ ④ ⑤

2. A hummingbird *dives* daily in and out of the          ① ② ③ ④ ⑤
                  1

   honeysuckle. He *bombs* *past* the doors with
                   2      3

   his heavy load and *balanced* on a branch of
                       4

   the little olive tree. *No error*
                          5

3. A teenage driver *causes* one out of every          ① ② ③ ④ ⑤
                    1

   three  automobile  accidents.  Many  *accuse*
                                        2

   teen  drivers  of  not  concentrating  on  the

   road.  Three  out  of  six  parents  *interviewed*
                                         3

   *fears* for their children's safety. *No error*
    4                                    5

4. The  farmer  and  his  hired  men  *gathers*  the          ① ② ③ ④ ⑤
                                      1

   corn.  The  farmer,  along  with  his  hired  men,

   *harvests* the wheat.  Neither  the  corn  nor  the
    2

   wheat  is  *neglected*.  The  farmer's  wife  and
                3

   daughter *argue* a great deal. *No error*
            4                    5

# Chapter 2    Performer and Action: Understanding Time and Number

**Practice I** *Page 16.*

1. Willie Farris _worked_ overtime last week.
2. We must _work_ a certain number of hours each day.
3. Four employees _will work_ overtime next week.

**Practice II** *Page 16.*

Remember *filed* set the time (past) for the other action words in the paragraph. The crowd *filed* into the meeting room.

1. **(2)** The chairman _rapped_ his gavel.
   1
2. **(1)** An angry murmur _continued_ in the
   2
3. **(2)** room. The chairman _rapped_ his
   3
   gavel a second time. Quiet finally
4. **(2)** _settled_ over the room. The chairman
   4
5. **(1)** _began_ his report.
   5

**Practice III** *Page 17.*

    P
1. women
        P
2. Mr. Smith and his son
        P
3. Flour, sugar, and milk
    S
4. Connie Martine
    P
5. grandchildren

**Practice IV** *Page 18.*

1. focus — Use the plural form of the action word (_focus_) when the performer is plural (_companies_).
2. makes — Use the singular form of the action word (_makes_) when the performer is singular (_machine_).
3. do — Use the plural form of the action word (_do_) when the performer is plural (_presents_).
4. manage — Use the plural form of the action word (_manage_) when the performer is plural (_businesses_).
5. gives — Use the singular form of the action word (_gives_) when the performer is singular (_agency_).

**Practice V** *Page 19.*

1. **(3)** change
   _Change_ is the plural form of the action word that agrees in number with the performer, _prices_.
2. **(3)** like
   _Like_ is the plural form of the action word that agrees in number with the performer, _twins_.
3. **(4)** display
   _Display_ is the plural form of the action word that agrees in number with the performer, _artists_.

**Practice VI** *Page 20.*

1. **(5)** No error

   All of the action words in the paragraph are in the *present time*.

2. **(4)** balances

   All of the action words in the paragraph are in the *present time*.

3. **(4)** fear

   *Fear* is the plural form of the action word that agrees with *parents*.

4. **(1)** gather

   *Gather* is the plural form of the action word that agrees with *farmer and his hired men*.

# CHAPTER 3

# ADDING DESCRIPTIVE WORDS

| | |
|---|---|
| Vic: | We have to advertise, Charley. No wonder no one comes into our store. |
| Charley: | I hate all those phoney ads where they hit you in the head with one lie after another. |
| Vic: | We don't have to lie. The truth will bring the suckers in. |
| Charley: | This is a fruit store—that's it, a fruit store. What else can we say about it? |
| Vic: | Use your head, Charles, my boy. Our fruit isn't just fruit, it's *delectable* fruit; we've got *golden* bananas, our cherries are *heavenly delicious*, the *sugar-sweet* pears would kill a diabetic. |
| Charley: | I dunno, to me fruit is fruit. |

—L. I. Meyers
*A Lovely Bunch of Coconuts*

## A Word With You . . .

Vic and Charley, the owners of Plaza Fruit, appear in a one-act play called *A Lovely Bunch of Coconuts*. As you can see, their personalities are different. Charley lacks romance—to him an apple is an apple. But Vic has the Madison Avenue approach to glamorizing his product.

Actually, what Vic did in this brief slice from the play is to add meaning by the use of descriptive words. You'll learn more about the technique in the next few pages.

## Descriptive Words: Adding Meaning

You know that an English sentence must have a person or thing performing an action and the action itself. You might say that these words are the core of every sentence. But we don't speak in such simple sentences: *He ran. She jumped.* Other words are added to the core to make a sentence more meaningful and interesting. These words may tell you more about the performer, or they may tell you more about the action. Look at the following example:

Performer   Action
The beautiful swan swam quickly.

The performer is *swan* and the action is *swam*. Note the words *the, beautiful,* and *quickly*. These are descriptive words. *The* tells which swan; *beautiful* tells you more about the performer, *swan,* and *quickly* tells you more about *swam,* the action.

Performer   Action
The beautiful swan swam quickly.
descriptive words

Now study the two sentences below. Label the performer, action, and descriptive words in each sentence.

A large apple fell suddenly.

*Large* describes *apple*.     *Suddenly* describes *fell*.

The decaying tooth throbbed painfully.

*Decaying* describes *tooth*.     *Painfully* describes *throbbed*.

PRACTICE
I

*Directions:*   Complete the pattern in each of the following sentences by adding a descriptive word.

1. A _____ man entered the store.
2. _____ music annoys me.
3. The cat jumped _____.
4. The _____ book slipped to the floor.
5. Dolores Bremmer walked _____ from the room.

PRACTICE
II

*Directions:*   Write five sentences of your own. Use descriptive words to tell more about the performer, the action, or both.

1. _____
2. _____
3. _____
4. _____
5. _____

PRACTICE
III

*Directions:* In each of the following sentences, one word is underlined. If the underlined word is the performer, blacken number 1. If the underlined word is the action, blacken number 2. If the underlined word describes the performer, blacken number 3. If the underlined word describes the action, blacken number 4.

1. The <u>gooey</u> candy stuck to the seat of the unsuspecting moviegoer's pants. ① ② ③ ④

2. Mr. McCarthy strode <u>away</u> angrily. ① ② ③ ④

3. The sweet old man <u>winked</u>. ① ② ③ ④

4. My <u>friend</u> cooks well. ① ② ③ ④

5. Ricardo <u>gave</u> me a good suggestion. ① ② ③ ④

6. We <u>sat</u> down beneath some trees. ① ② ③ ④

7. Four hungry <u>children</u> arrived for lunch. ① ② ③ ④

8. <u>Northern</u> merchants paid little for raw materials. ① ② ③ ④

9. Rita came <u>directly</u> home after work. ① ② ③ ④

10. A <u>violent</u> storm of controversy raged at our council meeting. ① ② ③ ④

PRACTICE
IV

*Directions:* The descriptive words in the following sentences are underlined. In each sentence, draw an arrow from the descriptive word to the word that it describes.

*Example:* The subway lurched *wildly*.

1. The telephone rang <u>unexpectedly</u>.
2. A <u>heavy</u> rain ruined our picnic.
3. The <u>talented</u> fingers knit the sweater.
4. The speeding truck swerved <u>abruptly</u>.
5. The <u>soft</u> snow fell <u>gently</u>.

PRACTICE
V

*Directions:* Blacken the circle that corresponds to the number of the action word in each sentence.

1. <u>Barbra Streisand</u> *sings* *emotionally* charged *songs*. ① ② ③ ④
    1        2     3        4

2. The *rumbling* truck *sped* *down* the *highway*. ① ② ③ ④
    1       2  3    4

3. A *monotonous* *tapping* *annoyed* the *students*. ① ② ③ ④
    1      2     3      4

4. My foreman, Roy, <u>*bought*</u> beer for <u>*all*</u> the men <u>*on*</u>    ① ② ③ ④
             1            2        3

    the <u>*shift*</u>.
       4

5. The <u>*President of the United States*</u> <u>*walked*</u> <u>*slowly*</u>    ① ② ③ ④
                     1            2    3

    <u>*toward*</u> the microphone.
      4

PRACTICE
VI

*Directions:*   Draw an arrow from each descriptive word to the word that it describes.

1. Mr. Hudson displays a cheerful disposition.
2. The dull day passed slowly.
3. The fast car raced quickly.
4. The cool, clear water shimmered.
5. A hungry seagull greedily grabbed the fish.

## Descriptive Words: Special Problems

Many words that are used to describe performers must add *-ly* in order to describe actions. *For example:*

The <u>*nice*</u> woman spoke at the meeting.
The woman spoke <u>nice*ly*</u> at the meeting.

In the above sentences, *nice* and *nicely* do two very different jobs. *Nice* describes the performer, *woman*. *Nicely* describes the action *spoke*. You would never say, "The *nicely* woman spoke at the meeting." However, a common error is, "The woman spoke *nice*." You can avoid that common error by recognizing that most words that describe actions end in *-ly*.

- *Well* describes actions, unless referring to a state of health. *Good* never describes an action.

My neighbor paints *well*.
My neighbor is a *good* painter.
I don't feel *well* today.

- *Real* describes a person, place, or thing.

> The shoes were made of *real* leather.
> I prefer *real* butter to imitation.
> His loyalty makes him a *real* friend.

- *Really* describes another descriptive word.

> Many of the events in our history are *really* exciting.
> His story was not *really* believable.
> Jan's shoes were *really* too small.

- *Very* describes another descriptive word.

> The basketball game was *very* exciting.
> The members of this community work *very* well together.
> The guitarist played *very* quickly.

PRACTICE VII

*Directions:* Choose the word that best completes each sentence and draw an arrow from this word to the word it describes.

1. My brother adds (quick, quickly).
2 That neighbor's (loud, loudly) radio annoys me.
3. He behaved (polite, politely) toward me.
4. The old dog walked (lazy, lazily) down the street.
5. I'll give you a (quick, quickly) call when I need you.
6. He plays the piano too (loud, loudly).
7. I don't like (soft, softly) music.
8. The (delicate, delicately) bird hovered in the sky.
9. Maria (sincere, sincerely) apologized for her error in bookkeeping.
10. The dancer balanced (delicate, delicately) on one foot.
11. You have my (sincere, sincerely) apology.
12. Stanley answered (immediate, immediately).
13. This problem requires your (immediate, immediately) attention.
14. Rosemary sings (good, well).
15. A (good, well) singer remains calm.

# Chapter 3   Adding Descriptive Words

*Page 25.*

Performer   Action

A large apple fell suddenly.

Descriptive Words

Performer   Action

The decaying tooth throbbed painfully.

Descriptive Word

## Practice I *Page 25.*

Answers may vary.

*Sample answers:*

1. A *tall* man entered the store.
2. *Loud* music annoys me.
3. The cat jumped *suddenly*.
4. The *heavy* book slipped to the floor.
5. Dolores Bremmer walked *quickly* from the room.

## Practice II *Page 25.*

Answers may vary.

*Sample answers:*

The shy girl spoke softly.

The delicate jonquils announced spring.

## Practice III *Page 26.*

1. **(3)** *gooey* describes candy, the performer.
2. **(4)** *away* describes strode, the action.
3. **(2)** *winked* is the action.
4. **(1)** *friend* is the performer.
5. **(2)** *gave* is the action.
6. **(2)** *sat* is the action.
7. **(1)** *children* is the performer.
8. **(3)** *northern* describes merchants, the performers.
9. **(4)** *directly* describes came, the action.
10. **(3)** *violent* describes storm, the performer.

## Practice IV *Page 26.*

1. rang       *unexpectedly* describes rang.
2. rain       *heavy* describes rain.
3. fingers    *talented* describes fingers.
4. swerved    *abruptly* describes swerved.
5. snow, fell   *soft* describes snow, *gently* describes fell.

## Practice V *Page 26.*

1. **(2)** sings
2. **(2)** sped
3. **(3)** annoyed
4. **(1)** bought
5. **(2)** walked

## Practice VI *Page 27.*

1. *cheerful* describes disposition.
2. *dull* describes day, *slowly* describes passed.
3. *fast* describes car, *quickly* describes raced.
4. *cool* describes water, *clear* describes water.
5. *hungry* describes seagull, *greedily* describes grabbed.

**Practice VII** *Page 28.*

1. My brother adds *quickly*.
2. That neighbor's *loud* radio annoys me.
3. He behaved *politely* toward me.
4. The old dog walked *lazily* down the street.
5. I'll give you a *quick* call when I need you.
6. He plays the piano too *loudly*.
7. I don't like *soft* music.
8. The *delicate* bird hovered in the sky.
9. Maria *sincerely* apologized for her error in bookkeeping.
10. The dancer balanced *delicately* on one foot.
11. You have my *sincere* apology.
12. Stanley answered *immediately*.
13. The problem requires your *immediate* attention.
14. Rosemary *sings* well.
15. A *good* singer remains calm.

# CHAPTER 4

# USING DESCRIPTIVE WORDS CORRECTLY

Maury Wills has described a player as having good running speed. "I knew it was hit good," said Mike Schmidt of the Philadelphia Phillies, "but the ball doesn't carry good in the Astrodome." It carries bad. When James J. Braddock died, there were stories about the fight in which he lost his heavyweight championship to Joe Louis. In the first round Braddock knocked Louis down. Louis got up. Braddock: "I thought if I hit him good, he'll stay down." It did not work out that way. Braddock was a brave man, a light-heavyweight, really, who returned to fighting when he was unemployed and on relief and went on to win the heavyweight championship. He was a longshoreman and uneducated. Tom Seaver of the New York Mets is a college graduate: "Cedeno hit the ball pretty good." Budd Schulberg is a novelist. Said he, after the Ali-Foreman fight, "The fight turned out pretty good."

—Edwin Newman
*A Civil Tongue*

## *A Word With You . . .*

Obviously, many people's use of *good* isn't their *best* grammar. The notables quoted by Edwin Newman are not alone in their misuse of that common adjective. Remember, no matter how *good* a player you are, you *play well*. This chapter will help you *use* descriptive words *well*.

## Descriptive Words: Using Comparison

Many descriptive words follow this pattern:

Mr. Smith built a *tall* fence.
Mr. Jones built a *taller* fence.
Mr. White built the *tallest* fence *of the three*.

Why is the fence in sentence 1 described as *tall*, the fence in sentence 2 described as *taller*, and the fence in sentence 3 described as *tallest*? *Tall* is a descriptive word that describes *fence*. *Taller* is a descriptive word that describes and compares *two fences*. *Tallest* is a descriptive word that compares *more than two fences*.

As you have seen in the above sentences, *-er* is added to a descriptive word to show a comparison between two people or things; *-est* is added to a descriptive word to show a comparison among more than two people or things. This is the general rule for comparison of descriptive words. *Study the examples below:*

| Description | Comparison of Two | Comparison of More than Two |
|---|---|---|
| pretty | prettier | prettiest |
| small | smaller | smallest |
| fast | faster | fastest |
| near | nearer | nearest |
| soon | sooner | soonest |
| rude | ruder | rudest |
| shrewd | shrewder | shrewdest |
| spicy | spicier | spiciest |
| green | greener | greenest |
| stout | stouter | stoutest |

Many descriptive words sound awkward when *-er* or *-est* is added. These words use <u>more</u> instead of *-er* and <u>most</u> instead of *-est* when making a comparison. *Study the examples below:*

| Description | Comparison of Two | Comparison of More than Two |
|---|---|---|
| beautiful | more beautiful | most beautiful |
| tenacious | more tenacious | most tenacious |
| enormous | more enormous | most enormous |
| quickly | more quickly | most quickly |
| torrid | more torrid | most torrid |
| valuable | more valuable | most valuable |
| legible | more legible | most legible |
| difficult | more difficult | most difficult |
| wonderful | more wonderful | most wonderful |
| sympathetic | more sympathetic | most sympathetic |

Some descriptive words have entirely different forms to express different degrees of comparison. *Study the examples below:*

| Description | Comparison of Two | Comparison of More than Two |
|---|---|---|
| good | better | best |
| bad | worse | worst |

**PRACTICE I**

*Directions:*   Complete the pattern in each of the following sentences by adding the *proper form* of one of the descriptive words below.

boring     magnificent     long     high     good

1. This is the _____ meeting I've ever attended.
2. We chose the _____ day of the summer for our office picnic.
3. Mr. Valdez is one of the _____ people I know.
4. Ricky works _____ than anyone else in the plant.
5. Our plants grew _____ this year than last year.

**PRACTICE II**

*Directions:*   Blacken the circle that corresponds to the number of the incorrect sentence in each group.

1. (1) This week's show was more funnier than last week's show.      ① ② ③
   (2) A tiny, delicate bird flew quietly away.
   (3) That loud noise is very irritating.

2. (1) The nervous woman seemed very impatient.      ① ② ③
   (2) Only close relatives visited the very old man.
   (3) John received the job because he was the efficientest competitor.

3. (1) Seven of the candidates competed vigorously for the local mayoralty.      ① ② ③
   (2) This dinner is the most delicious I've ever had.
   (3) Willie is the better basketball player of the three.

4. (1) Harry Truman read continually.      ① ② ③
   (2) Of the two, Freddie runs quicker.
   (3) The delightful aroma drifted across the room.

5. (1) Ed suggests a better solution.  ① ② ③
   (2) This coffee pot makes the baddest coffee I've ever had.
   (3) He handled the bus more skillfully than any other driver.

6. (1) The worst damage occurred in the rear.  ① ② ③
   (2) Of the two books I like this one most.
   (3) This is the shortest of the three books.

7. (1) I like Indian sand paintings better than modern art.  ① ② ③
   (2) The corner market always has the best cheese.
   (3) I chose the evergreen because it is the beautifulest of the three.

8. (1) Navajo artwork is more elaborate than Pueblo artwork.  ① ② ③
   (2) The morning trains are slower than the afternoon trains.
   (3) This horse wins frequentlyer than any other.

9. (1) We liked this movie more better than any other.  ① ② ③
   (2) Our team was the best in the league.
   (3) Colonel Eden was a better officer than anyone else in the brigade.

10. (1) He lost his composure during the worse battle of the war.  ① ② ③
    (2) The science teacher carefully explained that this was the best technique.
    (3) The record showed that their team was stronger than any other in the conference.

PRACTICE
III

*Directions:*   The following paragraph has four descriptive words or phrases. On the lines below, correct those that are incorrect.

The department meeting this month was the <u>boringest</u> one yet. Each
                                                                                                                    1

speaker was <u>most difficult</u> to understand than the next. The meeting
                                  2

notes were <u>difficult</u> to read, and the refreshments were <u>the worse</u> I've
                                  3                                                                                4

ever had.

1. _____

2. _____

3. _____

4. _____

# Chapter 4　Using Descriptive Words Correctly

**Practice I** *Page 33.*

Answers may vary.

　*Sample answers:*

1. longest
   most boring
   best
2. best
   most magnificent
3. most boring
   most magnificent
   best
4. better
   longer
5. higher
   better

**Practice II** *Page 33.*

1. **(1)** This week's show was *funnier* than last week's show. Do not use *more* with a descriptive word that ends in *-er*.
2. **(3)** John received the job because he was the *most efficient* competitor. Use *most* rather than *-est* with *efficient*.
3. **(3)** Willie is the *best* basketball player of the three. Use *best* when comparing three or more.
4. **(2)** Of the two, Freddie runs *more quickly*. Quickly describes run; therefore, *more quickly* compares how *two* people run.

5. **(2)** This coffee pot makes the *worst* coffee I've ever had. *Worst* is the form of *bad* used when comparing three or more.
6. **(2)** Of the two books, I like this one *more*. Use more to compare two items.
7. **(3)** I chose the evergreen because it is the *most beautiful* of the three. Use *most* rather than *-est* with *beautiful*.
8. **(3)** This horse wins *more frequently* than any other. Use *more* with *frequently* rather than *-er*.
9. **(1)** We liked this movie *better* than any other. Do not use *more* with better.
10. **(1)** He lost his composure during the *worst* battle of the war. *Worst* is the form of *bad* used when comparing three or more.

**Practice III** *Page 35.*

1. most boring
2. more difficult
3. correct as is
4. the worst

# CHAPTER 5

# ADDING DESCRIPTIVE PHRASES

"I spoke to Jerry at the office party about his need to
get more education," said Mr. Grogan.

"You mean that there was an office party just to
consider Jerry's lack of education," Mrs. Grogan
sweetly replied. "Maybe Jerry should ask you to go
back to school if you use sentences like that."

Mrs. Grogan ducked as the pillow came sailing at
her head. Lions don't like to have their tails tugged.

—Les Camhi
*V.I.P. at I.B.M.*

## *A Word With You . . .*

Mrs. Grogan was having some fun at her husband's expense because he had been
tarred with his own brush. Instead of coming across as the friendly vice-president who
points out a weakness to his employee, he had the tables turned on him by the clever
Mrs. Grogan, who spotted an error in her husband's sentence structure.

Do you see the mistake? In Chapter 5 you will learn how to avoid it.

## Descriptive Phrases: Adding Meaning

You have just been working with descriptive words that help to make
the sentence more meaningful and interesting. Frequently, one descriptive word is not enough. We need a group of words (a phrase) to
expand the meaning.

*Example:* The coffee cup fell *on the floor.*

Before you look for descriptive phrases, you must be sure that you
understand the core of the sentence. Ask yourself these questions:

1. What is the action word in the sentence?
   Fell.

2. What is performing the action?
Cup.
3. What do *the* and *coffee* describe?
Cup.
4. Finally, what does *on the floor* describe?
Fell.

*Example:*    *Jurassic Park,* the movie *at our local theater,*
terrifies audiences.

1. What is the action word in the sentence?
Terrifies.
2. Who or what is performing the action?
*Jurassic Park.*
3. What does *movie* describe?
*Jurassic Park.*
4. Finally, what does *at our local theater* describe?
Movie.

PRACTICE
I

*Directions:*    Each of the sentences below contains at least one descriptive phrase. Draw an arrow from each descriptive phrase to the word it describes. The first one is done for you.

1. The company solved its financial problems through efficiency techniques.
2. The musicians at the club played into the night.
3. The dentist's ultrasonic cleaner sped along the surfaces of his patient's teeth.
4. Maria put a wallpaper border around the kitchen.
5. A contestant with an electric guitar won the talent competition.
6. During the training session, the recruits crawled under the fence.
7. A lonely figure waited on the bridge.
8. Everyone except him cheered.
9. The dealer divided the cards among the four players.
10. An argument raged between the two teams.

PRACTICE
II    <u>*Directions:*</u>   These words frequently begin descriptive phrases. Choose from among them to complete the following sentences. More than one answer may be correct.

| of | at | between | after | under | on |
| in | from | through | beside | over | before |
| to | into | around | except | off | along |
| for | among | by | alongside | up | with |

1. A brief summary of World War I is _____ the first chapter.
2. A large crowd walked _____ the stairs in the historic building.
3. Surprised by the house owner's return, the intruder hurried _____ the door.
4. The unseasoned traveler put his hand _____ his pocket in search of the proper coin.
5. The book _____ the top shelf belongs _____ Ada.
6. _____ more peaceful methods had failed, the government seized control of the newspapers and radio stations.
7. Combined _____ the bank's interoffice banking service is their policy of all-day, all-night depositing.
8. In dull winter weather, African violets will bloom _____ 100 watt grow lights.
9. Sitting _____ me was a man who laughed and clapped loudly.
10. The unfortunate children were scattered _____ many homes.

# Descriptive Phrases: Correct Placement

A descriptive phrase should be placed next to the word that it describes. Misplacement of a descriptive phrase results in confused meaning.

*Example 1:*   The congressman made an unfavorable comment at a White House reception *about rising prices.*

The reception was not *about rising prices;* the congressman's comment was *about rising prices.* The sentence should read:

The congressman made an unfavorable comment *about rising prices* at a White House reception.

*Example 2:* *After completing his report,* Jerry's laptop computer shut down automatically.

The computer did not complete his report, Jerry did. The sentence should read:

*After Jerry completed his report,* his laptop computer shut down automatically.

PRACTICE
III

*Directions:* The underlined descriptive phrase in each of the following sentences is correctly placed. Draw an arrow from each descriptive phrase to the word that it describes. The first one is done for you.

1. The American way *of life* changes constantly.
2. Serious budget cuts will increase <u>through the 1990s</u>.
3. This course *of action* is intolerable.
4. The prosecutor spoke <u>to Steve</u>.
5. John Canady writes <u>about art</u>.
6. Several angry commuters walked <u>to the bus stop</u>.
7. Representatives <u>of the different factions</u> spoke.
8. The actors dine <u>after the show</u>.
9. The panelist <u>at the end</u> of the table spoke decisively.
10. Mr. Simmons spoke <u>at length</u>.

Notice that each descriptive phrase is next to the word that it describes. In the following exercise, each descriptive phrase is incorrectly placed.

PRACTICE
IV

*Directions:* On the line provided, rewrite each sentence so that each descriptive phrase is next to the word that it describes.

1. The man ran down the stairs in a blue coat.

2. That gentleman often walks to the corner in the trenchcoat.

3. Tom did not see across the street the accident.

4. Show Ella in the baggy pants the clown.

 

5. That boy runs around the track in the sweatsuit each day.

 

6. The dog belongs to that child with the brown spots.

 

All of the above sentences had simple placement errors. Each incorrectly placed phrase began with a clue word such as: of, in, to, at, from, with, across, etc.

**PRACTICE V**

*Directions:* One sentence in each group has a placement error in it. Blacken the circle that corresponds to the number of the incorrect sentence.

1. (1) The man in the tweed suit ran toward the departing bus.
   (2) A woman in a raincoat hailed a passing taxi.
   (3) The man in the drawer found his handkerchief.
   ① ② ③

2. (1) The grateful veteran relaxed after years of battle in his living room.
   (2) The battery in my car died.
   (3) The woman on the park bench smiled warmly.
   ① ② ③

3. (1) Cher sang as she sauntered across the stage.
   (2) Michael Jordan will play in next Tuesday's game.
   (3) Mrs. Smith hung on the wall her favorite painting.
   ① ② ③

4. (1) The car drove 7,000 miles in the driveway.
   (2) The new sports car in the parking lot was stolen.
   (3) The man in the moon winked at the astronauts.
   ① ② ③

5. (1) The registration desk was located in the gymnasium.
   (2) Voter registration took place at three o'clock.
   (3) The voters on the table completed the forms.
   ① ② ③

Frequently, a descriptive phrase separates the performer and the action. You must remember that *the action agrees in number with the performer.*

*Examples:*      The *man walks* slowly.
         The *man* in the blue coat *walks* slowly.
         The *man* in the blue boots *walks* slowly.

Notice that the action word remains *walks* in each sentence. The number of that word is not affected by any word in the descriptive phrase. The action word, *walks,* agrees with *man* in each sentence. It does not, for example, change to agree with *boots.*

PRACTICE
VI

*Directions:*   For each sentence below, blacken circle number 1 if the performer and action agree. If the performer and action do not agree, blacken number 2.

1. Russell Baker writes excellent satire.  ① ②
2. The girl in the blue overalls builds skyscrapers.  ① ②
3. The clouds in the sky drifts by.  ① ②
4. The problem of too many cooks create chaos.  ① ②
5. One of the men in our office works late every night.  ① ②
6. The latest machine in the line features a self-cleaning device.  ① ②
7. Some of the most unusual animals lives at the Bronx Zoo.  ① ②
8. The rollers in her hair detracts from her beauty.  ① ②
9. One out of three employees stays with the company after the first year.  ① ②
10. A catalog of publications arrive at our office monthly.  ① ②

# Chapter 5   Adding Descriptive Phrases

**Practice 1** *Page 38.*

1. *through efficiency techniques* describes solved.
2. *at the club* describes musicians.
   *into the night* describes played.
3. *along the surfaces* describes sped.
4. *around the kitchen* describes wallpaper border.
5. *with an electric guitar* describes contestant.
6. *under the fence* describes crawled.
7. *on the bridge* describes waited.
8. *except him* describes everyone.
9. *among the four players* describes divided.
10. *between the two teams* describes raged.

**Practice II** *Page 39.*

Answers will vary.

   *Sample answers:*

1. in, after, before
2. up
3. through, to, from
4. into
5. on, to
6. After, Before
7. with
8. under
9. beside
10. among

**Practice III** *Page 40.*

1. *of life* describes way.
2. *through the 1990s* describes increased.
3. *of action* describes course.
4. *to Steve* describes spoke.

5. *about art* describes writes.
6. *to the bus stop* describes walked.
7. *of the different factions* describes representatives.
8. *after the show* describes dine.
9. *at the end* describes panelist; *of the table* describes end.
10. *at length* describes spoke.

**Practice IV** *Page 40.*

1. The man in a blue coat ran down the stairs.
2. That gentleman in the trenchcoat often walks to the corner.
3. Tom did not see the accident across the street.
4. Show Ella the clown in the baggy pants.
5. That boy in the sweatsuit runs around the track each day.
6. The dog with the brown spots belongs to that child.

**Practice V** *Page 41.*

1. (3) The man found his handkerchief in the drawer.
2. (1) The grateful veteran relaxed in his living room after years of battle.
3. (3) Mrs. Smith hung her favorite painting on the wall.
4. (1) The car in the driveway drove 7,000 miles.
5. (3) The voters completed the forms on the table.

**Practice VI** *Page 42.*

The descriptive phrases in these sentences
have been set off with parentheses so that
you can clearly see the *performer* and *action*
in each sentence.

1. **(1)** Russell Baker writes
2. **(1)** girl (in the blue overalls) builds
3. **(2)** clouds (in the sky) drift
4. **(2)** problem (of too many cooks) creates
5. **(1)** one (of the men in our office) works
6. **(1)** machine (in the line) features
7. **(2)** some (of the most unusual animals) live
8. **(2)** rollers (in her hair) detract
9. **(1)** one (out of three employees) stays
10. **(2)** catalogue (of publications) arrives

# CUMULATIVE REVIEW

This review covers:

- Performer and Action: Agreement in Number
- Action Words: Agreement in Time
- Correct Use of Descriptive Words

After completing the Cumulative Review exercises, evaluate your ability using the SUMMARY OF RESULTS chart on page 50. Acceptable scores for each practice are given.

To learn your areas for skill improvement, find the question numbers you answered incorrectly on the SKILLS ANALYSIS table. The table will show which of your skills need improvement and the necessary chapters to review.

## Practice Exercises

PRACTICE
I

_Directions:_  Blacken the circle that corresponds to the number of the error in each sentence. If there is no error, blacken number 5.

1. The delegate and _his_ alternate _votes_ at _each_     ① ② ③ ④ ⑤
                  1                 2      3

   _monthly_ meeting. _No error_
      4              5

2. If a person _maintains_ a _good_ historical per-     ① ② ③ ④ ⑤
                1        2

   spective, he _understands_ the present and
                    3

   _predicted_ the future. _No error_
      4                5

3. Although I _cannot_ _see_ you, I can _hear_ you     ① ② ③ ④ ⑤
                 1   2             3

   _good_. _No error_
     4     5

4. The _plumbers_ union, along with _several_ other   ① ② ③ ④ ⑤
      1                                    2
   unions in the area, _choose_ not to _work_ on
                        3              4
   Saturdays. _No error_
               5

5. We _spent_ a perfect day at the beach because   ① ② ③ ④ ⑤
        1
   the ocean was _real_ calm and the sun _wasn't_
                    2                       3
   _too_ hot. _No error_
    4          5

6. Before anyone _makes_ a decision, he _weighs_   ① ② ③ ④ ⑤
                   1                      2
   all of the alternatives and _chose_ the _best_.
                                 3        4

   _No error_
      5

7. Because _she enjoys_ the exercise, Patricia, _along_   ① ② ③ ④ ⑤
            1    2                                3
   with several of her friends, _skates_ every Friday
                                  4
   evening. _No error_
              5

8. Because _less_ money is available, we are _faced_   ① ② ③ ④ ⑤
            1                                 2
   with the problem of providing _better_ educa-
                                  3
   tion at _lower_ cost. _No error_
            4            5

9. The _more_ they _grapple_ with the problem, the   ① ② ③ ④ ⑤
        1          2
   _less_ the members of the legislature _understands_
    3                                     4
   it. _No error_
        5

10. Of _all_ the _downtown_ merchants, I _like_ Mr.   ① ② ③ ④ ⑤
        1        2                       3
    Mitchell _more_. _No error_
              4        5

PRACTICE
II

*Directions:*    Blacken the circle that corresponds to the number of the error in each sentence. If there is no error, blacken number 5.

1. The electrician and his assistant <u>*always*</u> <u>*shuts*</u>    ① ② ③ ④ ⑤
                                        1          2
   off  the  electricity  <u>*before*</u>  beginning  <u>*work*</u>.
                             3                          4
   <u>No error</u>
   5

2. The late Louis Braille, <u>*inventor*</u> of the Braille    ① ② ③ ④ ⑤
                              1
   alphabet, <u>*pioneered*</u>  in  his  own  right  and
                2
   <u>*contributes*</u>  to  <u>*aids*</u>  for  the  handicapped.
      3                    4
   <u>No error</u>
   5

3. As  food  prices  continue  to  <u>*rise*</u>,  more  and    ① ② ③ ④ ⑤
                                      1
   <u>*more*</u>  people  turn  to  farming  and  <u>*most*</u>  of
      2                                            3
   them <u>*enjoy*</u> it. <u>No error</u>
          4              5

4. Some of the finest modern artists cannot <u>*sketch*</u>    ① ② ③ ④ ⑤
                                               1
   <u>*accurate*</u> or <u>*reproduce*</u> a likeness <u>*well*</u>. <u>No error</u>
      2              3                    4          5

5. Robert Pace <u>*designed*</u> a unique method of piano    ① ② ③ ④ ⑤
                  1
   instruction  that  <u>*combines*</u>  <u>*classical*</u>,  <u>*romantic*</u>,
                         2              3              4
   and contemporary music. <u>No error</u>
                              5

6. During the <u>*recent*</u> blackout, <u>*many*</u> refrigera-    ① ② ③ ④ ⑤
                 1                       2
   tors <u>*defrosted*</u> and the food <u>*spoils*</u>. <u>No error</u>
          3                            4          5

7. Maria and her _best_ friend, Lucy, _goes_ to _adult_    ① ② ③ ④ ⑤
           1                  2       3

   school twice each week and _study_ together.
                              4

   _No error_
      5

8. The tools _in_ the storage chest _accomplishes_    ① ② ③ ④ ⑤
           1                         2

   _most_ of the _necessary_ tasks. _No error_
      3           4           5

9. The _tiles_ in the bathroom _shows_ _signs_ of _wear_.    ① ② ③ ④ ⑤
        1                     2      3      4

   _No error_
      5

10. Of all the people I _know_, Manuel _works_ _most_    ① ② ③ ④ ⑤
                    1            2      3

   _efficient_. _No error_
      4        5

**PRACTICE III**

_Directions:_   Blacken the circle that corresponds to the number of the error in each sentence. If there is no error, blacken number 5.

1. Martin and his brother _walks_ to _work_ _each_    ① ② ③ ④ ⑤
                        1        2     3

   morning and _take_ the bus home each evening.
               4

   _No error_
      5

2. _One_ of those packages _belong_ to the _tall_ man    ① ② ③ ④ ⑤
    1                    2           3

   at the end of the _long_ line. _No error_
                 4         5

3. A book of food _stamps_ _fell_ _onto_ the counter    ① ② ③ ④ ⑤
                   1     2    3

   in the supermarket and several people

   _reached_ for it. _No error_
      4           5

4. The superintendent and his wife _argues_    ① ② ③ ④ ⑤
                                           1

   _frequently_ and the neighbors _listen_ _attentively._
      2                        3     4

   _No error_
     5

5. The team _played_ _clumsy_ and, therefore, _lost_    ① ② ③ ④ ⑤
             1     2                   3

   the _game_. _No error_
      4     5

6. Perry _enters_ the _crowded_ movie theater, _buys_    ① ② ③ ④ ⑤
         1         2                3

   popcorn, and _looked_ for a seat. _No error_
               4           5

7. Don't _rise_ your hand at the meeting unless you    ① ② ③ ④ ⑤
       1

   _plan_ to _speak_ in _favor_ of the proposal. _No error_
    2     3     4              5

8. _Please_ _bring_ the _tape_ recorder with you and    ① ② ③ ④ ⑤
     1     2     3

   tape the evening's _discussion_. _No error_
                4      5

9. A carton of eggs _smash_ on the floor at _least_    ① ② ③ ④ ⑤
              1                   2

   _once_ a week in _that_ store. _No error_
    3         4      5

10. The radio and the TV _play_ so _loud_ that I _have_    ① ② ③ ④ ⑤
                 1      2       3

   trouble _reading_. _No error_
         4      5

11. I would not _have_ _rang_ your doorbell if I didn't    ① ② ③ ④ ⑤
          1    2

   _have_ an _important_ message. _No error_
    3     4         5

12. Mr. Ricardi _played_ basketball _so_ _good_ that the    ① ② ③ ④ ⑤
          1                2  3

   men _asked_ him to be the center on the
       4

   neighborhood team. _No error_
        5

13. Several doses of that medicine <u>*makes*</u> me <u>*feel*</u>    ① ② ③ ④ ⑤
                                 1                 2

      tired and <u>*react*</u> <u>*slowly*</u>. <u>*No error*</u>
                   3     4      5

14. Buddy <u>*listens*</u> to instructions <u>*attentively*</u>, but    ① ② ③ ④ ⑤
             1                      2

      cannot <u>*remember*</u> them <u>*clear*</u>. <u>*No error*</u>
                 3       4    5

15. One of the women <u>*on*</u> the bus <u>*talk*</u> <u>*incessantly*</u>    ① ② ③ ④ ⑤
                        1         2    3

      and <u>*annoys*</u> the driver. <u>*No error*</u>
         4              5

---

After reviewing the Answer Key on page 52, chart your scores below for each practice exercise.

**SUMMARY OF RESULTS**

| Practice Number | Number Correct | Number Incorrect *(Including Omissions)* | Acceptable Score |
|---|---|---|---|
| I | | | 7 correct |
| II | | | 7 correct |
| III | | | 11 correct |

To identify your areas for skill improvement, locate the questions you answered incorrectly and circle the numbers on this Skills Analysis chart. Wherever you have circled errors, review the chapters listed in the last column.

**SKILLS ANALYSIS**

| Skill | Question Number | Review Chapter |
|---|---|---|
| **Practice I** | | |
| Performer and Action: Agreement in Number | 1, 4, 7, 9 | 2 |
| Action Words: Agreement in Time | 2, 6 | 2 |
| Correct Use of Descriptive Words . | 3, 5, 8 | 3 |
| Correct Use of Descriptive Words: Comparison | 10 | 4 |
| **Practice II** | | |
| Performer and Action: Agreement in Number | 1, 7, 8, 9 | 2 |
| Action Words: Agreement in Time | 2, 5, 6 | 2 |
| Correct Use of Descriptive Words | 3, 4, 10 | 2 |
| **Practice III** | | |
| Performer and Action: Agreement in Number | 1, 2, 4, 9, 13, 15 | 2 |
| Correct Use of Descriptive Words | 5, 10, 12, 14 | 3 |
| Performer and Action: Agreement in Time | 6 | 2 |
| Action Words: Special Problems | 7, 11 | 1 |

# Chapter 6   Cumulative Review

**Practice I** *Page 45.*

1. **(2)** *Vote* agrees with the plural performer, *The delegate and his alternate.*

2. **(4)** *Predicts* agrees in time with the action words, *maintains* and *understands.*

3. **(4)** *Well* describes the action word, *hear.*

4. **(3)** *Chooses* agrees with the singular performer, *union.*

5. **(2)** *Really* describes the descriptive word, *calm.*

6. **(3)** *Chooses* agrees in time with the action words *makes* and *weighs.*

7. **(5)** No error. *Enjoys* and *skates* agree.

8. **(5)** No error. *Faced* and *is* agree in time.

9. **(4)** *Understand* agrees in number with the plural performer, *members.*

10. **(4)** Use *most* to compare three or more groups of people, as indicated in, "Of *all* the downtown *merchants* . . ."

**Practice II** *Page 47.*

1. **(2)** *Shut* agrees with the plural performer, *the electrician and his assistant.*

2. **(3)** *Contributed* agrees in time with the action word, *pioneered.*

3. **(5)** No error

4. **(2)** *Accurately* describes the action word, *sketch.*

5. **(5)** No error

6. **(4)** *Spoiled* agrees in time with the action word, *defrosted.*

7. **(2)** *Go* agrees with the plural performer, *Maria and her best friend, Lucy.*

8. **(2)** *Accomplish* agrees with the plural performer, *tools.*

9. **(2)** *Show* agrees with the plural performer, *tiles.*

10. **(4)** *Efficiently* describes the action word, *works.*

**Practice III** *Page 48.*

1. **(1)** *Walk* agrees with the plural performer, *Martin and his brother.*

2. **(2)** *Belongs* agrees with the singular performer, *one* (*of those packages* describes one).

3. **(5)** No error

4. **(1)** *Argue* agrees with the plural performer, *superintendent and his wife.*

5. **(2)** *Clumsily* describes the action, *played.* Clumsy would describe a person or thing.

6. **(4)** *Looks* agrees in time with *enters* and *buys.*

7. **(1)** *Raise* means *lift;* rise means get up.

8. **(5)** No error

9. **(1)** *Smashes* agrees with the singular performer, *carton.*

10. **(2)** *Loudly* describes the action, *play.* Loud would describe a person or thing.

11. **(2)** *Rung* is used with the helping word, *have.*

12. **(3)** *Well* describes the action, *played.* Good would describe a person or thing.

13. **(1)** *Make* agrees with the plural performer, *doses*.

14. **(4)** *Clearly* describes the action, *remember*. Clear would describe a person or thing.

15. **(2)** *Talks* agrees with the singular performer, *one*.

# LINKING WORDS

"The murderer is . . ."

"Yes, yes," exclaimed Colonel Van Raalte, speaking for everyone in the living room. "Tell us who it is."

Detective Ling went on: "The murderer is . . . a real villain."

"We don't need any genius of a Chinese detective to tell us that," sneered the Colonel. "You might just twist that sentence around and tell us that 'the real villain is . . . a murderer.' It makes just as much sense—or stupidity!"

"Patience, my friend, patience," said Ling. "Before the evening is much older, I will point my finger in the direction of the killer."

—Stillwell Kee
*The Inscrutable Detective Ling*

## *A Word With You . . .*

The murderer is a villain.

A villain is the murderer.

Colonel Van Raalte was right in that he didn't learn anything from Detective Ling's statement.

You, however, are going to learn what a *linking word* is, why certain sentences can be reversed without changing their meanings—and you might even discover who killed Mrs. Van Raalte.

## The Flink Is Pretty: The Subject Is *Being,* Not *Doing*

You have been working with the simplest complete thought: a performer and an action.

Performer      Action
The huge Super Bus swerved unexpectedly.

Another simple, complete thought in the English language is one in which a person or thing is *being* something rather than *doing* something.

*Example:*     The Super Bus is huge.

As you see, the phrase Super Bus in this sentence cannot be called the performer since it is not performing any action (swerving, flying, landing, departing). It is actually being described (huge). *Huge* describes *Super Bus. Is* links the descriptive word *huge* to the subject *Super Bus.* The subject is the word *Super Bus* which the sentence is about.

linking word

*Example:*     The Super Bus is huge.

subject          descriptive word

The word *is* is not an action word; it is a *linking word.* Study these examples of linking words:

linking word

The apple tastes rotten.

subject          descriptive word

linking word

Alaskan oil seems abundant.

subject          descriptive word

Sometimes *is* links the subject with another word which equals the subject.

linking word

*Example:*     Columbo is a detective.

subject          subject

It is interesting to note that whenever the word linked with the subject *equals* the subject, the sentence can be reversed without changing its meaning. The reversed sentences may sound awkward; however, the meaning remains clear.

linking word

*Examples:*     A detective is Columbo.

subject          subject

linking word

Columbo is a detective.

subject          subject

linking word

Gerald Ford was the United States' first nonelected president.

subject                                                              subject

linking word
The United States' first non-elected president was Gerald Ford.
subject              subject

linking word
The Statue of Liberty is a remarkable sight.
subject              subject

linking word
The remarkable sight is the Statue of Liberty.
subject              subject

---

### Linking Words

| appear | remain | become | seem |
|--------|--------|--------|------|
| feel   | smell  | grow   | sound |
| look   | taste  | be     | is   |
| are    | am     | was    | were |

---

**PRACTICE I**

*Directions:*   Complete each sentence using the correct form of a linking word from the above list. Several words may be appropriate. Choose one.

1. After the Knicks game, the players _____ tired.
2. The labor representative _____ angry during the extensive negotiations.
3. The late Dwight Eisenhower _____ once a general.
4. The watchman _____ restless.
5. While shooting hoops, the teens never _____ exhausted.

**PRACTICE II**

*Directions:*   Locate the subject in each sentence, and label it. Then underline the linking word that connects the subject and the descriptive word. Draw an arrow from the descriptive word to the subject.

subject
*Example:*      An extensive renovation *seems* wasteful.

1. The entire class felt more ambitious after the coffee break.
3. The lilacs in the park are breathtaking.
3. Seven noisy children suddenly grew still.
4. Ronald Reagan had been president of the United States for eight years.
5. The smoke in the kitchen became unbearable.

PRACTICE
III

*Directions:*  Each of the sentences below contains either an action word or a linking word. If the sentence contains an action word, blacken the circle 1. If the sentence contains a linking word, blacken circle 2.

1.  The snowmobile raced down the hill. ① ②
2.  The tone of the meeting became threatening. ① ②
3.  That candidate was our favorite. ① ②
4.  We eat only organic foods. ① ②
5.  Our day at the lake was pleasant. ① ②
6.  Maximum individual choice is the democratic ideal. ① ②
7.  Alvin Toffler, author of *Future Shock,* conjures up a bleak picture of the future. ① ②
8.  People turn to a variety of experts. ① ②
9.  The situation appeared uncomfortable. ① ②
10. Most people do not consider their own lives as typical of particular life styles. ① ②
11. It was I at the door. ① ②

Use the descriptive word correctly in the *Subject-linking Word Descriptive Word* pattern.

> Never use a descriptive word that ends in *-ly* to describe the subject of the sentence. Descriptive words that end in *-ly* are reserved for describing actions.

CORRECT:  The child *is* adorable. (linking word)

INCORRECT: The child is adorably.

CORRECT:  She *speaks* too softly. (action)

INCORRECT: She speaks too soft.

PRACTICE
IV

*Directions:*  Blacken the circle that corresponds to the number of the incorrect sentence in each group. If all the sentences in a group are correct, blacken number 5.

1. (1) The delicate bird is graceful. ① ② ③ ④ ⑤
   (2) The graceful bird seems delicate.
   (3) The bird is graceful and delicate.
   (4) The bird flies graceful.
   (5) No error

2. (1) Mr. Jackson plays piano loud.　　　　① ② ③ ④ ⑤
   (2) Mr. Jackson's piano is loud.
   (3) Mr. Jackson, along with his piano, is loud.
   (4) Mr. Jackson plays piano loudly.
   (5) No error

3. (1) Floyd reads quickly.　　　　① ② ③ ④ ⑤
   (2) Angelo is the quickest sorter in the mailroom.
   (3) Floyd reads more quick than Harvey.
   (4) Alex seems very quick.
   (5) No error

4. (1) Annemarie seems nicely.　　　　① ② ③ ④ ⑤
   (2) Carmen seems nice.
   (3) Annemarie seems nicer than Cathy.
   (4) Raymond's nice sister is Georgia.
   (5) No error

5. (1) Good butter tastes sweet.　　　　① ② ③ ④ ⑤
   (2) Taste the good butter.
   (3) The butter tastes well.
   (4) This butter tastes good!
   (5) No error

6. (1) Rudy feels badly about the argument.　　　　① ② ③ ④ ⑤
   (2) That dress looks bad on Vera.
   (3) That was a bad choice.
   (4) Since she had the flu, Carla has felt bad.
   (5) No error

## Subject and Linking Word: Agreement in Number

You have already studied agreement of performer and action in number. The same concept applies to the subject and the linking word. For example, look at the following incorrect sentences:

1. *All* of our relatives *is* coming to dinner.
2. Those *cars appears* fast.
3. The *house are* on a hill.

Of course, these sentences sound awkward. Look at the same sentences written correctly. What changes have been made?

1. *All* of our relatives *are* coming to dinner.
2. Those *cars appear* fast.
3. The *house is* on a hill.

*You see that a singular subject needs a singular linking word, and a plural subject needs a plural linking word.*

> Every linking word must agree with its subject in time and number.

Notice that agreement in the past is easier to achieve than agreement in the present. For example:

## LINKING WORD: *APPEAR*
### *Present Time, Singular and Plural*

|        | I appear nervous. |
|--------|-------------------|
|        | You appear confident. |
| (He)   | David appears belligerent. |
| (She)  | Pam appears calm. |
| (It)   | The dog appears ill. |
|        | Who appears contented? |
| (We)   | Michael and I appear relaxed. |
| (You)  | You and Marcel appear tired. |
| (They) | Ellen and Linda appear friendly. |

### *Past Time, Singular and Plural*

|        | I appeared nervous. |
|--------|---------------------|
|        | You appeared confident. |
| (He)   | David appeared belligerent. |
| (She)  | Pam appeared calm. |
| (It)   | The dog appeared ill. |
|        | Who appeared contented? |
| (We)   | Michael and I appeared relaxed. |
| (You)  | You and Marcel appeared tired. |
| (They) | Ellen and Linda appeared friendly. |

### LINKING WORD: *BE*

*Be* is a difficult word to understand. *Be* is used when preceded by *to*, *will*, *can*, *could*, *would*, or *should*. *Examples:*

The policeman wants *to be* helpful.

Next time, I *will be* more thoughtful.

Crowded supermarkets *can be* annoying.

This *could be* one chance in a lifetime.

The supervisor *would be* grateful if you could work late.

World peace *should be* everyone's goal.

Other forms of *be* are used in sentences that do not have the helping words *to*, *will*, *can*, *could*, *would*, or *should*. You already are familiar with these forms: *am, is, are, was, were.* The following lists show you the proper use of these words.

### *Present Time, Singular and Plural*

|        |                                       |
|--------|---------------------------------------|
|        | I am a nurse.                         |
|        | You are a policeman.                  |
| (He)   | David is a crossing guard.            |
| (She)  | Pam is a teacher.                     |
| (It)   | The dog is a collie.                  |
|        | Who is that lady?                     |
| (We)   | Bill and I are co-chairmen.           |
| (You)  | You and your brother are partners.    |
|        | Who are those ladies?                 |
| (They) | Ellen and Linda are sisters.          |

### *Past Time, Singular and Plural*

|        |                                       |
|--------|---------------------------------------|
|        | I was a nurse.                        |
|        | You were a policeman.                 |
| (He)   | David was a crossing guard.           |
| (She)  | Pam was a teacher.                    |
| (It)   | The dog was a collie.                 |
|        | Who was that lady?                    |
| (We)   | Bill and I were co-chairmen.          |
| (You)  | You and your brother were partners.   |
|        | Who were those ladies?                |
| (They) | Ellen and Linda were sisters.         |

PRACTICE
V

*Directions:*   Use *is, are, was,* or *were* in each of the following sentences.

1. Fritz _____ always late.
2. The Murphys _____ home from their vacation.
3. The woman and her child _____ in the park.
4. The books _____ interesting.
5. He _____ a member of the group when it was first formed.

PRACTICE
VI

*Directions:*   Use the *correct form* of one of the following linking words to complete each of the following sentences. Use at least one form of each word.

*be*     *grow*     *become*     *appear*     *feel*

1. The soldiers _____ weary after the long march.
2. The crowd _____ angry.
3. The child quickly _____ tired of his new toy.
4. Mr. and Mrs. Smith _____ elated after winning the lottery.
5. The football players _____ traded.

PRACTICE
VII

*Directions:*   Blacken the circle that corresponds to the number of the error in each passage. If there is no error, blacken number 5.

1. Ecology *is emerging* into an exact science. At last,     ① ② ③ ④ ⑤
        1     2

   the function of waste products *are being* discov-
                                    3     4

   ered. *No error*
        5

2. Glass, plastic, and paper finally *has been*     ① ② ③ ④ ⑤
                                        1     2

   *recognized* as reusable and *are* being recycled.
        3                        4

   *No error*
        5

3. Now, as their multiple functions _are_ gradually      ① ② ③ ④ ⑤

                                                    1

_being_ _studied,_ their importance _is_ more apparent

  2       3                    4

than ever before. _No error_

               5

4. Finally, man's _belief_ that his own actions, at least      ① ② ③ ④ ⑤

                1

in part, _control_ his destiny _are_ _being_ justified.

          2              3    4

_No error_

  5

5. Each local ecology group through its efforts,      ① ② ③ ④ ⑤

_have_ _been_ instrumental, in recent years, in

 1    2

_identifying_ and _solving_ solid waste problems.

    3           4

_No error_

  5

6. The chairman of one local organization _believes_      ① ② ③ ④ ⑤

                                 1

that the advent of recycling waste products _are_

                                2

just beginning. The same _is_ true of non-polluting

                       3

detergents, which _may_ perhaps be even more

                  4

important. _No error_

        5

# The Missing Link(ing Word)

Often, a linking word is combined with another word. In combining, the initial letters of the linking word are dropped and replaced by an apostrophe.

_Example:_        _There is_ one answer to that question.
                     _There's_ one answer to that question.

                There is = There's

## COMMON MISSING LINK(ING WORD) COMBINATIONS:

| | |
|---|---|
| he is = he's | *He's* the most forward-looking senator. |
| she is = she's | *She's* the strongest voice in Congress. |
| we are = we're | *We're* eager to hear your proposal. |
| you are = you're | *You're* one of the few people I trust. |
| they are = they're | *They're* determined to interfere. |
| here is = here's | *Here's* your hat. |
| it is = it's | *It's* an active committee. |

NOTE: *Its* without the apostrophe indicates possession.

*Example:*  The committee concluded *its* hearing.

## MISSING LINK COMBINATIONS WITH *NOT:*

| | |
|---|---|
| is not = isn't | Destruction *isn't* my idea of fun. |
| are not = aren't | The striking workers *aren't* going to settle for less pay. |
| were not = weren't | Lou and Toby *weren't* on the train. |
| was not = wasn't | I *wasn't* prepared for the crowd at the bus stop. |

**PRACTICE VIII**

*Directions:*  In each of the following sentences, there is an underlined phrase. Make a missing link combination from each underlined phrase and write it on the line provided.

*Example:*  If it is convenient for Lucy, the bowling team will meet at 6 P.M. it's

1. They are the best approaches to the problem. _____
2. If you can understand management-labor relations, you are a better businessman than I. _____
3. Agreement is not as important as understanding. _____
4. We did not realize that the job action had ended. _____
5. Here is the name of an excellent mechanic. _____
6. The legislators were not expecting such a strong consumer lobby.

   _____

7. He is the least competent programmer in the company.

   _____

8. There is only one best product in each line of merchandise.

   _____

# Chapter 7    Linking Words

**Practice I** *Page 55.*

Answers may vary.

> *Sample answers:*

1. appeared, felt, looked
2. seemed, became, grew
3. was
4. became, grew, is, was
5. were, seemed

**Practice II** *Page 55.*

1. The entire class *felt* more ambitious after the coffee break.

2. The lilacs in the park *are* breathtaking.

3. Seven noisy children suddenly *grew* still.

4. Ronald Reagan *had been* President of the United States for eight years.

5. The smoke in the kitchen *became* unbearable.

**Practice III** *Page 56.*

1. **(1)** raced
2. **(2)** became
3. **(2)** was
4. **(1)** eat
5. **(2)** was
6. **(2)** is
7. **(1)** conjures
8. **(1)** turn
9. **(2)** appeared
10. **(1)** consider
11. **(2)** was

**Practice IV** *Page 57.*

1. **(4)** The bird flies gracefully.
2. **(1)** Mr. Jackson plays piano loudly.
3. **(3)** Floyd reads more quickly than Harvey.
4. **(1)** Annemarie seems nice.
5. **(3)** The butter tastes good.
6. **(1)** Rudy feels bad about the argument.

**Practice V** *Page 60.*

Answers may vary.

> *Sample answers:*

1. is, was
2. are, were
3. are, were
4. are, were
5. was

**Practice VI** *Page 60.*

Answers may vary.

> *Sample answers:*

1. were, grew, became, appeared, felt, are, become, grow, appear, feel
2. was, grew, became, appeared, appears, becomes, grows, is
3. grew, became, is, grows, becomes
4. were, appeared, felt, are, appear, feel
5. were, are

**Practice VII** *Page 60.*

1. **(3)** At last, the function (of waste products) *is* being discovered.

   *Is* agrees in number with the singular subject, *function*.

2. **(1)** Glass, plastic, and paper finally
<br>*linking word*
*have been* recognized as reusable. *Have been* agrees in number with the plural subject, *glass, plastic, and paper.*

3. **(5)** No error

4. **(3)** Finally, man's belief (that his own actions at least in part, control his
<br>*linking word*
destiny) *is* being justified . . .
<br>*Is* agrees in number with the singular subject, *belief.*

5. **(1)** Each local ecology group (through its
<br>*linking word*
efforts,) *has been* instrumental . . .
<br>*Has been* agrees in number with the singular subject, *group.*

6. **(2)** The chairman of one local organization believes that the advent (of recycling waste products) *is* just beginning.
<br>*Is* agrees in number with the singular word, *advent.*

**Practice VIII** *Page 63.*

1. They're
2. you're
3. isn't
4. didn't
5. Here's
6. weren't
7. He's
8. There's

# CHAPTER 8

# AGREEMENT: SPECIAL PROBLEMS

*Each* of the veterinary surgeons gathered around
Ruffian knew *his* job. *Neither* the doctors *nor* Mr.
Janney *was* willing to give up on the magnificent
filly, but despite *everyone's* desire00 to do *his* best,
it became necessary to put the horse to sleep.

—Murray Bromberg
*The Great Match Race*

## A Word With You . . .

The scene from the book took place in the early hours of Monday morning, July 7, 1975, as the veterinarians tried to save the life of a great horse whose leg had been shattered.

Our chief interest, however, is in the italicized words:

each—his
neither . . . nor—was
everyone's—his

Some people might not see the reason for using these word combinations. Their relationships will be made clear in the following pages.

You know that an action word must *agree* with its performer in number, and with the sentence or paragraph in time.

The jury *enters* the courtroom. A hush *falls* over the crowd.
The judge *asks* for the verdict.

You know that a linking word must agree with its subject in number and with the sentence or paragraph in time.

Court *is* in session. Please *remain* silent.
The defendant *seems* apprehensive. The prosecutor *appears* angry.

# Rules Concerning Special Problems of Agreement

### EACH

*Each* is singular when it is the performer or subject of the sentence.
*Example:*

Performer   Action
<u>Each</u> *shows* promise.

PRACTICE

I   <u>*Directions:*</u>   Underline either the singular or plural action word or linking word that correctly completes each sentence.

1. Each (gives, give) a lecture.
2. Each of the teachers (gives, give) a lecture.
3. They each (gives, give) a lecture.
4. Each (is, are) a good candidate.

### EITHER-OR

When using *either-or,* you are choosing *one* or the *other.* The action or linking word is *singular* if the performer or subject closest to it is singular.

*Example:*       <u>Either</u> Tom <u>or</u> Bill drives to school.

*Drives* agrees with the singular performer, *Bill.*

The action or linking word is *plural* if the performer or subject closest to it is plural.

*Example*:       <u>Either</u> Tom <u>or</u> his friends drive to school.

*Drive* agrees with the plural performer, *friends.*

PRACTICE

II   <u>*Directions:*</u>   Underline either the singular or plural linking word that correctly completes each sentence.

1. Either the coach or the captain (is, are) late.
2. Either the coach or the players (is, are) late.
3. Either the players or the coach (is, are) late.
4. Either these players or those players (is, are) late.

## ANY

*Any* is singular. It is used when a choice involves *three* or more. *Either* is used for a choice between *two*.

*Example*:          <u>*Any*</u> of the <u>*three*</u> movies suits me.

*Directions:*    Underline either the singular or plural action or linking word that correctly completes each sentence.

1. Any of the sandwiches (is, are) fine.
2. Any of the four records (sounds, sound) good.
3. (Any, either) of the three books (serves, serve) well.

## HERE AND THERE

In sentences that begin with *here* or *there*, the action or linking word must agree with the performer or subject. *Here* and *there* are never performers or subjects.

*Example:*                Here (is, are) my coat.

   (WHAT is here? COAT. COAT is the SUBJECT.) *Coat* is singular; therefore, the singular linking word *is* correctly completes the sentence.

*Directions:*    Locate the performer or subject in each sentence. Underline the action or linking word that correctly completes each sentence.

1. There (is, are) my boots.
2. There (is, are) two sides to the argument.
3. Here (goes, go) my last chance.
4. There (is, are) no way out.

## WHO AND THAT

You are familiar with the following sentence structures:

performer   action
The woman attends every meeting.

action                      performer
Woman is singular; attends agrees with woman.

performer          action

One (of those women) attends every meeting.

       action        performer

*One* is singular: *attends* agrees with *one*.

The following example is significantly different from the above.

*One* (of those women) *who* ATTEND every meeting seldom SPEAKS.

Ready?

     performer    action

"One seldom speaks" is the *core* of the sentence.

*One* is singular: *speaks* agrees with *one*.

"Of those women who attend every meeting" describes
or tells more about, *one*.

*Who* might be singular or plural. How do we decide? We look at the word to which *who* refers. In this case, that word is *women*. *Women* is plural; therefore, *who* is plural. Within the descriptive group of words, "of those women who attend every meeting," *attend* must agree with *who*. *Who* is plural; *attend* agrees with *who*.

This rule also applies to *that*.

        performer   action

*Examples*:      The *ruler belongs* to me.

One (of those rulers) belongs to me.

*One* (of those rulers) *that* ARE on the desk BELONGS to me.

PRACTICE
V

*Directions:*   Underline either the singular or plural action or linking word that correctly completes each sentence.

1. One of the musicians (plays, play) better than the others.
2. Several of those pencils (belongs, belong) in this container.
3. John Kennedy was one of those leaders who (has, have) charisma.
4. One of those underdeveloped nations that (counts, count) upon outside sources for food will inevitably be disappointed.
5. One of those vocations that (has, have) always appealed to me (is, are) radio announcing.

## SURPRISINGLY SINGULAR SUBJECTS

Some words seem to refer to more than one person. In fact, they do not. They are singular. These include:

| | |
|---|---|
| *Everybody* | means every *single* body. |
| *Somebody* | means some *one* body. |
| *Anybody* | means any *one* body. |
| *None* | means no *one*. |
| *Everyone* | means every *one*. |

## SOME PLURAL SUBJECTS

Six words that take plural action or linking words are:

all     few     several     both     many     some

PRACTICE
VI

*Directions:* Underline the action word that correctly completes each sentence.

1. Everybody (hear, hears) a different drummer.
2. Somebody (call, calls) our office at 5:05 each day.
3. Anybody who (want, wants) to can join our cooperative supermarket.
4. None of the scout leaders (shirk, shirks) his responsibility.

| To Do | | |
|---|---|---|
| I do | | we do |
| you do | | you do |
| **he, she, it does** | | they do |

## REVIEW EXERCISES

PRACTICE
VII

*Directions:* Underline the action or linking word that agrees with the performer or subject in each of the following sentences.

*Example:* The coat (<u>is</u>, are) too large.

1. The books (is, are) on the shelf.
2. Each (selects, select) his own menu.
3. Each of the students (is, are) registered for ten weeks.
4. Any of the six choices (is, are) suitable.
5. Everybody (does, do) his job.
6. This kind of movie (is, are) boring.
7. Those kinds of flowers (seems, seem) delicate.
8. None of the candidates (speaks, speak) well.
9. There (was, were) several good items on the menu.
10. Neither the meats nor the vegetables (is, are) fresh.
11. Either the children or the babysitter (drinks, drink) the milk.
12. He (doesn't, don't) speak well.
13. She is one of those women who never (says, say) what they mean.
14. One of those tractors (is, are) broken.

## *TO DO* STATEMENTS

**She works** with Allen.
  *Works* agrees with *she.*

**She does** work with Allen.
  *Does* agrees with *she; work* is used in the "to work" form.
  (*Does* would be used in this sentence for emphasis or clarification.)

**They work** with Allen.
  *Works* agrees with *they.*

**They do** work with Allen.
  *Do* agrees with *they; work* is used in the "to work" form.

## *TO DO* QUESTIONS

**Does she** work with Allen?
  *Does* agrees with *she; work* is used in the "to work" form.
  In a typical question, the subject (*she*) follows *does.*

**Do they** work with Allen?

  When using a negative, *not* follows *do* or *does:*

**Doesn't she** work with Allen?

**Don't they** work with Allen?

PRACTICE
VIII

*Directions:* If the action or linking word in each sentence agrees with the subject, blacken circle 1. If the action or linking word does not agree with the subject, blacken circle 2.

1. There were two planes outside the hangar. ① ②
2. Macaroni or potatoes go with this dinner. ① ②
3. Any of these dips are great with crackers. ① ②
4. Ten minutes of my time is all that I can offer. ① ②
5. Don't she know your address? ① ②
6. My son or my daughter are coming for me. ① ②
7. There's two overseas routes to Europe. ① ②
8. One of the most recent discoveries are in regard to aging. ① ②
9. Doesn't any famous politician ever arrive on time? ① ②
10. Here's Joanna's friends. ① ②
11. One of those library books is lost. ① ②
12. Either the coach or the players argue with the manager every week. ① ②
13. Oprah Winfrey is one of those people who says what she means. ① ②

PRACTICE
IX

*Directions:* Blacken the circle that corresponds to the number of the incorrect sentence in each group. If there is no error, blacken number 5.

1. (1) Each of the projects is interesting. ① ② ③ ④ ⑤
   (2) There's my two favorite magazines.
   (3) Here's the best seat in the house.
   (4) Any of those concerts would please me.
   (5) No error

2. (1) Neither of us is really qualified for that job. ① ② ③ ④ ⑤
   (2) Those kinds of personalities are most difficult to live with.
   (3) Everybody shirks their responsibility occasionally.
   (4) Nelson Mandela is one of the most interesting people I know about.
   (5) No error

3. (1) Any of those arrangements is a suitable centerpiece.   ① ② ③ ④ ⑤
   (2) Either Mr. Hanns or his assistants write the weekly reports.
   (3) The men each take a turn nailing the paneling.
   (4) Either of the two plants enhances that corner.
   (5) No error

4. (1) The Jones sisters are among those people who always have time to listen.   ① ② ③ ④ ⑤
   (2) One of those books is mine.
   (3) Each of those buildings have to be painted.
   (4) Here are my choices.
   (5) No error

5. (1) Don't he ever get to work on time?   ① ② ③ ④ ⑤
   (2) One of these records belongs to the library.
   (3) There's the only gifted writer I know.
   (4) Carmen is one of those people who speak constantly.
   (5) No error

6. (1) Every day seems busier than the day before.   ① ② ③ ④ ⑤
   (2) Either the stewardesses or their captain make the necessary announcements.
   (3) Neither the lemons nor the oranges were fresh.
   (4) Several of his poems are very good.
   (5) No error

7. (1) Any of these coats or dresses suits you well.   ① ② ③ ④ ⑤
   (2) Here's the most authoritative book about the Civil War.
   (3) Doesn't he seem right for the job?
   (4) Each participant is expected to follow the rules.
   (5) No error

8. (1) They each sings in the community choir.  ① ② ③ ④ ⑤
   (2) There's no time to waste.
   (3) Colonel Adams or Major Niles is planning to attend.
   (4) Here's the last of those tapes you ordered.
   (5) No error

9. (1) Doesn't he ever take a day off?  ① ② ③ ④ ⑤
   (2) Each of my children visits during the holidays.
   (3) Any of these shirts are a bargain.
   (4) Either the grass or the shrubs need tending.
   (5) No error

10. (1) Any one of those mountain trails is the same as the others.  ① ② ③ ④ ⑤
    (2) Don't Angie look pretty?
    (3) Four days is long enough for this type of project.
    (4) One of the biggest problems is a lack of honesty.
    (5) No error

---

Do you remember the paragraph that introduced this chapter?

*Each* of the veterinary surgeons gathered around Ruffian knew *his* job. *Neither* the doctors *nor* Mr. Janney *was* willing to give up on the magnificent filly, but despite *everyone's* desire to do *his* best, it became necessary to put the horse to sleep.

Look at these agreement examples:

1. *Each* of the veterinary surgeons gathered around Ruffian knew *his* job.
2. Neither the doctors nor *Mr. Janney was* willing . . .
3. . . . but despite *everyone's* desire to do *his* best, . . .

These relationships should be clear to you after studying Chapter 8.

# Chapter 8  Agreement: Special Problems

**Practice I** *Page 67.*

1. Each *gives*

   *Gives* agrees with the singular performer, *each.*

2. Each *gives*

   *Gives* agrees with the singular performer, *each.*

3. They *give*

   *Give* agrees with the plural performer, *they.*

4. Each *is*

   *Is* agrees with the singular subject, *each.*

**Practice II** *Page 67.*

1. captain *is*

   *Is* agrees with the singular subject, *captain.*

2. players *are*

   *Are* agrees with the plural subject, *players.*

3. coach *is*

   *Is* agrees with the singular subject, *coach.*

4. players *are*

   *Are* agrees with the plural subject, *players.*

**Practice III** *Page 68.*

Linking Word

1. Any (of the sandwiches) *is* fine.

   *Is* agrees with the singular subject, *any.*

Linking Word

2. Any (of the four records) *sounds* good.

   *Sounds* agrees with the singular subject, *any.*

Action Word

3. Any (of the three books) *serves* well.

   *Serves* agrees with the singular performer, *any.*

**Practice IV** *Page 68.*

1. There *are* my boots.

   *Are* agrees with the plural subject *boots.*

2. There *are* two sides to the argument.

   *Are* agrees with the plural subject *sides.*

3. Here *goes* my last chance.

   *Goes* agrees with the singular performer *chance.*

4. There *is* no way out.

   *Is* agrees with the singular subject *way.*

**Practice V** *Page 69.*

1. One of the musicians *plays* . . .

   *Plays* agrees with the singular subject *One.*

2. Several of those pencils *belong* . . .

   *Belong* agrees with the plural subject *several.*

3. John Kennedy was one of those leaders who *have* charisma.

   *Have* agrees with its subject, *who,* which refers to the plural word *leaders.*

4. One of those underdeveloped nations that *count* . . .

   *Count* agrees with its subject *that,* which refers to the plural word *nations.*

5. One of those vocations that *have* . . . always appealed to me *is* . . .

   *Have* agrees with its subject *that,* which refers to the plural word *vocations; is* agrees with the singular subject *One.*

**Practice VI** *Page 70.*

1. Everybody *hears* a different drummer.
2. Somebody *calls* our office at 5:05 each day.
3. Anybody who *wants* to can join our co-operative supermarket.
4. None of the scout leaders *shirks* his responsibility.

The performer in each sentence is singular and requires a singular action word.

**Practice VII** *Page 71.*

The correct action or linking word in each sentence is underlined twice. The subject in each sentence is underlined once.

1. The books are on the shelf.
2. Each selects his own menu.
3. Each (of the students) is registered for ten weeks.
4. Any (of the six choices) is suitable.
5. Everybody does his job.
6. This kind (of movie) is boring.
7. Those kinds (of flowers) seem delicate.
8. None (of the candidates) speaks well.
9. There were several good items on the menu.
10. Neither the meats nor the vegetables are fresh.
11. Either the children or the babysitter drinks the milk.
12. He doesn't speak well.
13. She is one of those women who never say what they mean.
14. One (of those tractors) is broken.

**Practice VIII** *Page 72.*

1. **(1)** planes were there

   *Were* agrees with the plural subject, *planes.*

2. **(1)** potatoes go

   *Go* agrees with the plural subject, *potatoes.*

3. **(2)** any (of these dips) is

   *Is* agrees with the singular subject, *any.*

4. **(1)** ten minutes (as a *unit* of time ) is

   *Is* agrees with the singular subject, *ten minutes.*

5. **(2)** doesn't she know

   *Doesn't* agrees with the singular performer, *she.*

6. **(2)** my daughter is

   *Is* agrees with the singular subject, *daughter.*

7. **(2)** two routes are there

   *Are* agrees with the plural subject, *routes.*

8. **(2)** one (of the most recent discoveries) is

   *Is* agrees with the singular subject, *one.*

9. **(1)** doesn't any famous politician ever arrive

   *Doesn't* agrees with the singular performer, *any.*

10. **(2)** Joanna's friends are here

    *Are* agrees with the plural subject, *friends.*

11. **(1)** One (of those library books) is

    *Is* agrees with the singular subject, *one.*

12. **(1)** players argue

    *Argue* agrees with the plural performer, *players.*

13. **(2)** people who say what they mean.

    *Who* must agree with the plural *people.* *Say* agrees with the plural performer, *who.* *They* agrees with the plural performer, *who.* *Mean* agrees with *they.*

**Practice IX** *Page 72.*

1. **(2)** There *are* my two favorite magazines.

   The plural linking word *are* agrees with the plural *subject,* magazines.

2. **(3)** Everybody shirks *his* or *her* responsibility occasionally.

   The singular word *his* or *her* agrees with the singular performer, *everybody.*

3. **(5)** No error. (1) any . . . is, (2) assistants write, (3) men . . . take, (4) each . . . enhances

4. **(3)** Each of those buildings *has* to be painted.

   The singular action word *has* agrees with the singular performer, *each.*

5. **(1)** *Doesn't* he ever get to work on time?

   The singular helping word *does* (not) agrees with the singular performer, *he.*

6. **(2)** Either the stewardesses or their captain *makes* the necessary announcements.

   The action word *makes* is singular because the performer that is closest to it, *captain,* is singular.

7. **(5)** No error. (1) any . . . suits, (2) here is, (3) he does(n't), (4) participant is

8. **(1)** They each *sing* in the community choir.

   The plural action word, *sing,* agrees with the plural performer, *they.*

9. **(3)** Any of these shirts *is* a bargain.

   The singular linking word *is* agrees with the singular subject, *any.*

10. **(2)** *Doesn't* Angie look pretty?

    The singular helping word *does* (not) agrees with the singular subject, *Angie.*

# CHAPTER 9

# TIME: SPECIAL PROBLEMS

Eddie's father insisted that he pay attention. If Dad was going to give up a half hour of Archie Bunker in order to help Eddie with his homework, he wanted to make sure that Eddie was all ears.

"Now, there are the *present perfect*, the *past perfect*, and the *future perfect*," explained Eddie's father. "Why can't you understand that?"

"Well, nobody's perfect, Dad," quipped Eddie.

"Okay, wise guy," his father said. "Just listen to this example of the *future perfect tense*: 'By next week, you *will have discovered* a decrease in your allowance.'"

—Carol Lehrer
*Tenting Out in the Suburbs*

## A Word With You . . .

It might not be fair to cut a youngster's allowance because he had trouble with tenses (time), but Eddie's father seemed to know what he was doing in grammar, as well as in child rearing.

The hapless Eddie was not concentrating—but you will, we are sure. Fortunately, you won't have to grapple with the "perfect" terms.

You know that sentences express time. For instance,

PRESENT ACTION: I commute to work each day.

PAST ACTION: I commuted to work each day.

FUTURE ACTION: I will commute to work each day.

Occasionally, time is more complicated than the simple expression of past or future.

Sometimes an action that began in the past continues into the present.

*Examples*:     I *have commuted* to work for six years.
                     Marie *has commuted* to work for five years.
The addition of the helping word *have* or *has* expresses the idea of
an action that began in the past, but is continuing into the present. In
the above examples, the helping words, *have* and *has*, are in the present and the action word, *commuted*, is in the past.


## Common Misuses of *Has* and *Have*

a. I *commuted* to work for six years and I am tired of commuting.
b. I *commuted* to work for six years and I have been tired of commuting.

The only correct use of the helping word *have* in these examples:

I *have commuted* to work for six years and I am tired of commuting.

PRACTICE
I

*Directions:*    Blacken the circle that corresponds to the number of the
incorrect sentence in each group.

1. (1)  I have lived in this community for ten years.          ① ② ③ ④
   (2)  Ellen has been climbing trees since she was six
        years old.
   (3)  Eric was the last in line since he began school.
   (4)  Liz and Paula have known each other for six
        years.

2. (1)  You and she have worked together for years.          ① ② ③ ④
   (2)  Shirley has spoken highly of you always.
   (3)  Andrea did not visit us for the past several days.
   (4)  Wendy and Karen have babysat for us since we
        moved here.

Sometimes a past action has occurred before another past action.

*Example*:      I *had commuted* for two hours each way
                    before I *moved* to the city.

Even though both actions occurred in the past (*commuted, moved*),
one happened before the other. You need to make clear which past

action occurred first (further in the past). The addition of the helping word *had* shows that the *commuting* occurred in the past before the *moving* occurred (also in the past).

*Example:*　　　William had *resisted* working on a team
　　　　　　　 before he *attended* the training seminar.

The addition of the helping word *had* shows that William *resisted* even before he *attended* the training session (also in the past).

## Common Misuses of *Had*

　　a. I *had commuted* two hours each way before I *had moved* to the city.

　　b. I *commuted* two hours each way before I *had moved* to the city.

The only correct use of the helping word *had* in this sentence:

I *had commuted* two hours each way before I *moved* to the city.

PRACTICE
II　　*Directions:*　　Blacken the circle that corresponds to the number of the incorrect sentence in each group.

1. (1) John Milton had become immortalized before　　① ② ③ ④
Ernest Hemingway was born.
(2) Jean had driven fifteen miles before she had realized that she was going north instead of south.
(3) Prior to our purchasing a new one, our old refrigerator had needed repair every six to eight weeks.
(4) Since environmental care has become a public concern, paper and glass recycling are common in many communities.

2. (1) If I had known I could have a paying job, I never    ① ② ③ ④
would have volunteered my services.
(2) If you had planned a thorough outline earlier,
you would not be so rushed to complete your report now.
(3) I had suffered the pain of a sore throat for three
days before I had called a doctor.
(4) After we had bought the large oak table, we saw
the glaring imperfection in it.

---

Sometimes a future action can occur before another future action.

*Example*:    I *will have commuted* four million miles
by the time I retire.

The addition of the helping words *will have* shÔws that the commuting will be completed before the retiring. Notice that when you use the
words *will have*, you are talking about an action that will be completed
in the future *before* another action.

*Example*:    Before the meeting begins, I will have written
and circulated the agenda.

All actions will occur in the future, but the *writing* and *circulating*
will occur *before* the meeting *begins*.

## Common Misuses of *Will Have*

a. I *will have commuted* four million miles by the time I *will have*
*retired*.
b. I *will commute* four million miles by the time I *will have retired*.

The only correct use of *will have* in this sentence:

I *will have commuted* four million miles by the time I *retire*.

*Directions:* Blacken the circle that corresponds to the number of the incorrect sentence in each group.

1. (1) By the time your plane lands in Cleveland, I will have left for Colorado.    ① ② ③ ④
   (2) By the time you call for me, I will have typed our report.
   (3) Before they leave, Mary and Agnes will have instructed the children to go to bed at nine.
   (4) Martin will complete high school by the time his brother begins.

2. (1) Jeannie will have graduated from high school before David enters.    ① ② ③ ④
   (2) By next summer, I will retire from public office.
   (3) By this time next week, I will have seen Paris.
   (4) The meeting will have adjourned before you leave your office.

---

When two actions occur simultaneously, their time must be the same.

*Example:*    As the curtain rises, the audience *applauds*.
As the curtain *rose*, the audience *applauded*.

# Common Errors Regarding Simultaneous Actions

a. As the curtain *rose* to reveal the elaborate set, the enthusiastic audience *had applauded*.
b. As the curtain *had risen* to reveal the elaborate set, the enthusiastic audience *applauded*.

In sentences a and b, the audience applauded *as* the curtain rose. Since both actions occurred *at the same time,* neither action word should be accompanied by *had*.

PRACTICE
IV

*Directions:*    Blacken the circle that corresponds to the number of the incorrect sentence in each group.

1. (1) As the class filed out of the room, David noticed    ① ② ③ ④
the trampled book on the floor.
   (2) When the power failed, all of our food was ruined.
   (3) As soon as you finish rereading the *Pathfinders*, please call me.
   (4) As the fish bit the worm, he had realized his error.

2. (1) As we began our trip in our brand new convertible, gray clouds hovered threateningly above.    ① ② ③ ④
   (2) When the automobile industry's strike ended, our car was delivered.
   (3) When I lifted the papers, I had found Ellen's missing glasses.
   (4) As soon as you gave me your requirements, I shipped the order.

Linking words express time, also. *Has, have,* and *had* are used with linking words in order to clarify time.

*Examples:*        Tom *has been* irritable all morning.
Tom *had been* irritable before he received his promotion.
Tom *will have been* president
for two years, by the time he retires.

PRACTICE
V

*Directions:*    Blacken the circle that corresponds to the number of the incorrect sentence in each group.

1. (1) I have felt tired since my illness.    ① ② ③ ④
   (2) Jules always has been a good sport.
   (3) Before she began working full-time, Erica seemed more relaxed.
   (4) By the time this very long documentary ends, I will have grown bored.

2. (1) The amplifier had sounded distorted for several hours before it stopped working.          ① ② ③ ④

(2) The court claimed that the children had been neglected.

(3) For the past three days, your socks have been in the same place on the floor.

(4) As I looked across the room at the woman who bore an uncanny resemblance to me, I had felt as though I were looking into a mirror.

## REVIEW EXERCISES

PRACTICE
VI

*Directions:*   Blacken the circle that corresponds to the number of the incorrect sentence. If there is no error, blacken number 5.

1. (1) Lady Bird Johnson had shown an interest in conservation long before she became the First Lady.          ① ② ③ ④ ⑤

(2) The CIA had overstepped its bounds long before Watergate publicized its far-reaching arm.

(3) As I spoke, I realized my error.

(4) Prior to the election, the candidate promised law and order.

(5) No error

2. (1) I am teaching for twenty years.          ① ② ③ ④ ⑤

(2) Betty Friedan has been a pioneer in the women's movement.

(3) The Thompsons have owned the drug store since 1947.

(4) Before he spoke, he had carefully prepared his speech.

(5) No error

3. (1) In 1974, Richard Nixon resigned.          ① ② ③ ④ ⑤

(2) John had changed jobs. Then the family followed him.

(3) During this decade, elections have been less exciting each year.

(4) We had seen Laura last night.

(5) No error

4. (1) As the car pulled to the curb, a man jumped out.    ① ② ③ ④ ⑤

   (2) Before the phone stopped ringing, Mary had answered it.

   (3) Before the music had stopped, a shot rang out.

   (4) When you arrive, we will begin the discussion.

   (5) No error

5. (1) By next week, the price of lettuce will have doubled.    ① ② ③ ④ ⑤

   (2) Before the doorbell rang, Ida seemed nervous.

   (3) Because he had known the temper of the crowd, he spoke calmly and clearly.

   (4) By the time the repairman arrives, I will have left.

   (5) No error

6. (1) By this time tomorrow, I will have taken the test.    ① ② ③ ④ ⑤

   (2) If you studied, you might have known the answer.

   (3) The historian carefully studied his subject.

   (4) Before boarding the plane, Tom had expressed a fear of flying.

   (5) No error

7. (1) These sentences have been difficult.    ① ② ③ ④ ⑤

   (2) Last week, they would have been impossible.

   (3) By next week, you will have mastered the problem.

   (4) Before he passed the test, the man studied for many hours.

   (5) No error

PRACTICE
VII

*Directions:* Blacken the circle that corresponds to the correct rewriting of the underlined portion of the sentence. Choice 1 is always the same as the underlined portion and is sometimes the right answer.

1. I signed the letter several days after <u>I wrote it.</u>   ① ② ③ ④ ⑤
   (1) I wrote it.
   (2) I writed it.
   (3) it was written.
   (4) I had written it.
   (5) I have written it.

2. By the time the sun comes out, the pool <u>will close</u> for the day.   ① ② ③ ④ ⑤
   (1) will close
   (2) will have closed
   (3) has closed
   (4) will be closed
   (5) would close

3. The telephone <u>rang as my guest entered</u> the room.   ① ② ③ ④ ⑤
   (1) rang as my guest entered
   (2) rang as my guest had entered
   (3) had rung as my guest entered
   (4) had rung as my guest had entered
   (5) rang as my guest has entered

4. Since I began to study music appreciation, I <u>had enjoyed</u> Beethoven.   ① ② ③ ④ ⑤
   (1) had enjoyed
   (2) always had enjoyed
   (3) have enjoyed
   (4) will enjoy
   (5) enjoy

5. On this, his anniversary, Simpson <u>was with the bank</u> for forty years.   ① ② ③ ④ ⑤
   (1) was with the bank
   (2) had been with the bank
   (3) is with the bank
   (4) has been with the bank
   (5) will be with the bank

6. I <u>received a ticket because I parked</u> in a no    ① ② ③ ④ ⑤
   parking zone.
   (1) received a ticket because I parked
   (2) received a ticket because I had parked
   (3) had received a ticket because I parked
   (4) had received a ticket because I had parked
   (5) received a ticket because parking

7. If you arrive after 10, the kitchen <u>will have</u>    ① ② ③ ④ ⑤
   <u>closed</u>.
   (1) will have closed.
   (2) closes.
   (3) will close.
   (4) should close.
   (5) has closed.

8. As soon as the bell rings, the horses <u>will begin</u> to    ① ② ③ ④ ⑤
   run.
   (1) will begin
   (2) shall begin
   (3) have begun
   (4) began
   (5) begin

9. He <u>made the appointment</u> before he con-    ① ② ③ ④ ⑤
   sulted me.
   (1) made the appointment
   (2) made that appointment
   (3) had made the appointment
   (4) has made the appointment
   (5) have made the appointment

10. I <u>was unusually busy</u> for the past two weeks.    ① ② ③ ④ ⑤
    (1) was unusually busy
    (2) will have been unusually busy
    (3) am unusually busy
    (4) have been unusually busy
    (5) had been unusually busy

**PRACTICE VIII**

*Directions:*  Blacken the circle that corresponds to the number of the error in each sentence. If there is no error, blacken number 5.

1. We *had traveled* extensively *before* we *had*  *bought*     ① ② ③ ④ ⑤
       1                     2       3     4

   our summer home. *No error*
                     5

2. We  *traveled*  in  Europe  and  Asia  *before*     ① ② ③ ④ ⑤
          1                           2

   we *went* to *South* America. *No error*
      3      4            5

3. For  the  past  year,  *however*,  we  *were*  *inclined*     ① ② ③ ④ ⑤
                      1         2    3

   *to stay home*. *No error*
       4       5

4. Travel *became* so expensive over the *past* few years     ① ② ③ ④ ⑤
         1                   2

   that we *can* no longer *afford* it. *No error*
         3          4       5

5. Perhaps *by the time* our children *are grown*,     ① ② ③ ④ ⑤
             1                2

   *we will have decided* to *travel* again. *No error*
          3           4        5

6. As  soon  as  they  *become*  independent  of  us,     ① ② ③ ④ ⑤
                      1

   *we will have become* independent of them.
      2     3      4

   *No error*
     5

7. During  the  *past*  *several*  years,  the  children's     ① ② ③ ④ ⑤
              1      2

   *increasing* activities *hampered* our independence.
       3            4

   *No error*
     5

8. Before  we  *started*  a  family,  we  *did  not*     ① ② ③ ④ ⑤
              1                2

   *travel* as  much  as  we  *should have*. *No error*
       3                 4       5

# Chapter 9    Time: Special Problems

**Practice I** *Page 79.*

1. **(3)** Eric *has been* the last in line since he began school.

    The addition of the helping word *has* expresses the idea of an action that began in the past but is continuing into the present.

2. **(3)** Andrea *has not visited* us for the past several days.

    See explanation above.

**Practice II** *Page 80.*

1. **(2)** Jean *had driven* fifteen miles before she *realized* that she was going north instead of south.

    When a sentence contains two past actions, the action that occurred first is accompanied by the helping word *had*.

2. **(3)** I *had suffered* the pain of a sore throat for three days before I *called* a doctor.

    See explanation above.

**Practice III** *Page 82.*

1. **(4)** Martin *will have completed* high school by the time his brother *begins*.

    When a sentence contains two future actions, the action that will occur first is accompanied by the helping words *will have*.

2. **(2)** By next summer, I *will have retired* from public office.

    See explanation above.

**Practice IV** *Page 83.*

1. **(4)** As the fish *bit* the worm, he *realized* his error.

    When two actions occur simultaneously, their forms must be the same. Omit *had* before *realized*.

2. **(3)** When I *lifted* the papers, I *found* Ellen's missing glasses.

    See explanation above. Omit *had* before *found*.

**Practice V** *Page 83.*

1. **(3)** Before she *had begun* working full-time, Erica seemed more relaxed.

    Addition of the helping word *had* shows that *begun* occurred in the past before *seemed*.

2. **(4)** As I looked across the room at the woman who bore an uncanny resemblance to me, I *felt* as though I were looking into a mirror.

    Eliminate *had* before *felt*. *Looked* and *felt* are simultaneous actions.

**REVIEW**

**Practice VI** *Page 84.*

1. **(4)** Prior to the election, the candidate *had promised* law and order.

    The addition of the helping word *had* shows that the promising occurred in the past *before* the election.

2. **(1)** I *have been teaching* for twenty years.

The helping words *have been* show that the teaching began in the past and continues into the present.

3. **(4)** We *saw* Laura last night.

Eliminate the helping word *had* since the seeing did not occur in the past before another action.

4. **(3)** Before the music stopped, a shot *had rung* out.

The helping word *had* shows that *rung* occurred in the past before the music stopped.

5. **(2)** Before the doorbell rang, Ida *had seemed* nervous.

The helping word *had* shows that *seemed* occurred before the doorbell rang.

6. **(2)** If you *had studied*, you might have known the answer.

The helping word *had* shows that *studied* began in the past before the knowing.

7. **(4)** Before he passed the test, the man *had studied* for many hours.

The helping word *had* shows that *studied* began in the past before *passed*.

**Practice VII** *Page 86.*

1. **(4)** I signed the letter several days after *I had written it*.

The helping word *had* shows that the writing occurred in the past *before* the signing.

2. **(2)** By the time the sun comes out, the pool *will have closed* for the day.

The helping words *will have* show that the closing will be completed *before* the sun comes out.

3. **(1)** The telephone *rang as my guest entered* the room.

Since both actions occurred at *the same time*, the same form (past) is used for both action words.

4. **(3)** Since I began to study music appreciation, I *have enjoyed* Beethoven.

The helping word *have* shows that *enjoyed* began in the past and is continuing into the present.

5. **(4)** On this, his anniversary, Simpson *has been with the bank* for forty years.

The helping word *has* shows that Simpson *has been* with the bank in the past and is continuing into the present.

6. **(2)** I *received a ticket because I had parked* in a no parking zone.

The helping word *had* shows that the parking occurred in the past *before* the receiving.

7. **(1)** If you arrive after 10, the kitchen *will have closed*.

The helping words *will have* show that the closing will be completed *before* the arrival.

8. **(5)** As soon as the bell rings, the horses *begin* to run.

Since both actions occur at the *same time*, the *same form* (present) is used for both action words.

9. **(3)** He *had made the appointment* before he consulted me.

The helping word *had* shows that the appointment was made *before* the consulting took place.

10. **(4)** *I have been unusually busy* for the past two weeks.

The helping word *have* shows that I *have been* busy in the past and am continuing into the present.

**Practice VIII** *Page 88.*

1. **(3)** We had traveled extensively before we *bought* our summer home.

2. **(1)** We *had traveled* in Europe and Asia before we went to South America.

3. **(2)** For the past year, however, we *have been* inclined to stay home.

4. **(1)** Travel *has become* so expensive over the past few years that we can no longer afford it.

5. **(5)** No error. The helping words *will have* show that the decision to travel occurred in the past, before the children were grown.

6. **(3)** As soon as they become independent of us, we *will become* independent of them.

7. **(4)** During the past several years, the children's increasing activities *have hampered* our independence.

8. **(2)** Before we started a family, we *had not traveled* as much as we should have.

# PRONOUNS

Years ago when I was just out of graduate school and thought I could remake society by cleaning up slovenly grammar in the media, I sent some naive letters to the networks. Johnny Carson's quiz show should be called "*Whom* Do You Trust?" not "*Who* Do You Trust?" Arthur Godfrey should ask his Talent Scouts, "*Whom* did you bring to the show?" instead of "*Who* . . . ?" and the ABC situation comedy should be "My Sister and *I*" not "My Sister and *Me*."

The networks never made any changes, and now I sing "Ain't Misbehavin'" just like every other former purist.

—Bob Kassell
*Surrounded By Assassins*

## A Word With You . . .

The words of critic Bob Kassell are amusing. There is a serious side to them, however, for students of language. Why are some people more comfortable while using the incorrect form of the language?

You might not find the answer to that question in Chapter 10—but you will learn why "I gave the books to Joe and *her*," "It is *I*," "Just between Edith and *me*," and "It is *we* players who must protest" all illustrate correct pronoun usage.

## Rules Concerning Pronoun Usage

Pronouns are used as performers/subjects or as words that receive action. *For example:*

performer
Lloyd ran home.

performer pronoun
He ran home.

subject
Lloyd is pleasant.

subject pronoun
He is pleasant.

performer
Elana gave a bright smile to Tom.

receives action

performer           pronoun that receives action

Elana gave a bright smile to him.

performer    receives action

Maria gave Tom an icy stare.

performer    pronoun that receives action

Maria gave him an icy stare.

| Perfomer/Subject Pronouns | Pronouns That Receive Action |
|---|---|
| I | me |
| you | you |
| he | him |
| she | her |
| it | it |
| we | us |
| they | them |
| who | whom |

PRACTICE
I

*Directions:* Complete each sentence using a pronoun from the above list. More than one choice may be correct.

1. _____ won the election.
2. _____ campaigned all week.
3. The National Organization for Women gave the citation to _____ _____.
4. The student hitchhiker got a lift from _____.
5. _____ was responsible for legislation providing consumer protection?
6. For _____ did the witness testify?

# Pronoun Clue 1:

Don't be confused by *who* and *whom*. As you can see in the preceding list, *who* is a subject/performer and *whom* is a pronoun that receives action.

IF:     *He* painted the house.

THEN: *Who* painted the house?

IF:     The phone call is for *him*.

THEN:   For *whom* is the phone call?

IF:     Jane hired Crisala (her).

THEN:   Crisala is the woman *whom* Jane hired.

PRACTICE
II

*Directions:*   Underline the pronoun that correctly completes each sentence.

*Example*:          (*Who*-Whom) rang the doorbell?
Clue:                *He* rang the doorbell.

1. (Who - Whom) did you call?
2. (Who - Whom) answered your letter?
3. (Who - Whom) will help with this project?
4. *Consumer Reports* cites manufacturers from (who - whom) we can expect quality products.
5. Mariah Carey is the singer (who - whom) Tony likes best.

# Pronoun Clue 2:

Don't be confused by more than one subject.

IF:     He won the election.

THEN:   Macon and *he* won the election.

*Because* it is incorrect to say:

Him won the election.

It is also incorrect to say:

*Macon* and *him* won the election.

PRACTICE
III

*Directions:*   Underline the pronoun that correctly completes each sentence.

1. Mr. Jones and (he, him) ran the fair.
2. (They, Them) and their father went fishing.
3. My friend and (I, me) are planning a camping trip.
4. (She, her) and (he, him) were delegates to the convention.
5. The Walters and (we, us) go to the shore each summer.
6. (Who, whom), along with Susan, will work on this committee?

# Pronoun Clue 3:

Don't be confused by more than one word receiving the action.

IF: I gave the present to *her*.

THEN: I gave the present to Tom and *her*.

*Because* it is incorrect to say:

I gave the present to *she*.

It is also incorrect to say:

I gave the present to Tom and *she*.

IF: Sam bought her lunch.

THEN: Sam bought Robert and *her* lunch.

*Because* it is incorrect to say:

Sam bought *she* lunch.

It is also incorrect to say:

Sam bought Robert and *she* lunch.

PRACTICE
IV

*Directions:* Underline the pronoun that correctly completes each sentence.

1. When the plans for the new community center are completed, call Mr. Faldez and (I, me).
2. The supermarket manager gave discount coupons to Olga and (she, her).
3. When they question you about the accident, tell Paul and (they, them) the truth.
4. Will you be speaking to Hiroko and (he, him)?
5. The MacDonalds sent regards to Joanna and (we, us).

# Pronoun Clue 4:

Don't be confused by a condensed thought.

IF: Elmer runs more quickly *than I do*.

THEN: Elmer runs more quickly *than I*.

*Because* it is incorrect to say:

Elmer runs more quickly *than me do*.

It is also incorrect to say:

Elmer runs more quickly *than me*.

*Directions:* Underline the pronoun that correctly completes each sentence.

1. Mary is a better cook than (I, me).
2. I sew better than (she, her).
3. You don't feel as sorry as (he, him).
4. The Ortegas are better swimmers than (we, us).
5. Their neighbors don't argue as often as (they, them).

# Pronoun Clue 5:

A sentence in which a linking word is connecting the subject to a word that means the same thing as the subject, is reversible.

IF:   Carl is the mayor.

THEN: The mayor is Carl.

IF:   He is the mayor.

THEN: The mayor is he.

*Because* it is incorrect to say:

*Him* is the mayor.

It is also incorrect to say:

The mayor is *him*.

*Directions:* Underline the pronoun that correctly completes each sentence.

1. My secretary is (she, her).
2. The winner of the contest was (he, him).
3. (Who, whom) seems most likely to get the promotion?
4. The culprits were (they, them).
5. The person who called you was (I, me).
6. If there is a couple who enjoys dancing, it is (we, us).

# Pronoun Clue 6:

Certain pronouns—*my, your, his, her, its, our, their*—may be used as descriptive words.

*Example*:  I like the *red* hat.

I like *his* hat.

Descriptive pronouns are never a problem in the above context. However, errors tend to be made in sentences such as the following:

INCORRECT:  I do not like *him* smoking.

CORRECT:  I do not like *his* smoking.

INCORRECT:  Of course I approve of *you* jogging.

CORRECT:  Of course I approve of *your* jogging.

PRACTICE
VII

*Directions:*  Underline the pronoun that correctly completes each sentence.

1. Tom is very proud of (him, his) swimming.
2. I don't like (you, your) calling me at the office.
3. The professor was glad to hear about (me, my) writing a story.
4. We wondered (who's, whose) contribution to medicine was greatest.
5. I don't like (them, their) refusing to take BHA and BHT out of foods.

# Pronoun Clue 7:

Words such as *to, from, between, except, among* are followed by pronouns that receive action. Here are some examples.

1. Between you and *me*, I don't enjoy cooking.
2. The package is for *her*.
3. Please divide the workload among *them*.
4. Everyone, except *us*, is attending the meeting.

_Directions:_ Underline the pronoun that correctly completes each sentence.

1. From (who, whom) did you learn that myth about not eating before swimming?
2. Many secrets have passed between you and (he, him).
3. The personnel director gave notices to John and (they, them).
4. Everyone, except (she, her), plans to take the test.
5. The host and his friends divided the four bottles of beer among (they, them).

# Pronoun Clue 8:

A pronoun must agree in number with the word to which it refers. Here are some examples.

1. One of the men in the back of the room could not project _his_ voice.

   _His_ refers to one. Both words are singular.

2. All of those women left _their_ coats after the rally.
   _Their_ refers to _all_. Both words are plural.

_Directions:_ Select the word that correctly completes each sentence.

1. Everyone must decide for (himself, themselves).
2. Each of the painters worked (his, their) best.
3. They each performed to the best of (his, their) ability.
4. All of the members brought (his, their) wives.

## REVIEW EXERCISES

PRACTICE
X

*Directions:*    Blacken the circle that corresponds to the number of the incorrect word in each sentence. If there is no error, blacken number 5.

1. *He* and *his* brother strenuously object to *me*    ① ② ③ ④ ⑤
   1          2                                                      3
   *smoking*. *No error*
   4             5

2. Although *she* is interesting and *she's* witty, I    ① ② ③ ④ ⑤
                 1                                        2
   don't think that *she* is the right girl for *my*
                        3                              4
   friend. *No error*
            5

3. Sam finds *my* singing offensive, but *he* enjoys    ① ② ③ ④ ⑤
                 1                              2
   *me* playing *the* piano. *No error*
    3          4           5

4. The man *who* you called is out and *his* assistant    ① ② ③ ④ ⑤
              1                              2
   insists *that* *he* will not return again today.
             3      4
   *No error*
    5

5. If you are wondering *who* it was *who* called *you*    ① ② ③ ④ ⑤
                            1           2          3
   earlier in the week, it was *him*. *No error*
                                  4        5

6. Although *he* plays tennis better than *I* do, *I*    ① ② ③ ④ ⑤
                1                             2      3
   bowl better than *him*. *No error*
                       4        5

7. Would *you* please buy tickets for the basketball    ① ② ③ ④ ⑤
             1
   game *for* *him* and *I*? *No error*
          2      3        4        5

8. _He_ invited Jim and _she_ to join _his_ car pool _that_    ① ② ③ ④ ⑤
     1                 2        3         4

   day. _No error_
       5

9. Don wanted _us_, John and _I_, to help _him_ build    ① ② ③ ④ ⑤
             1         2        3

   _his_ new garage. _No error_
     4           5

10. Jane and _me_ invited _our_ husbands and _them_ to    ① ② ③ ④ ⑤
            1       2          3

    join _our_ physical fitness class. _No error_
       4                 5

**PRACTICE XI**

_Directions:_   Blacken the circle that corresponds to the number of the incorrect sentence in each group. If there is no error, blacken number 5.

1. (1)  Them and us play gin rummy each Wednesday.    ① ② ③ ④ ⑤
   (2)  Please write to the folks and me while you're away.
   (3)  The friendliest person on the street is he.
   (4)  I did not give the information about the adverse effects of food additives to him.
   (5)  No error

2. (1)  Who told you that oil drilling equipment does not cause pollution?    ① ② ③ ④ ⑤
   (2)  Rita is a more knowledgeable gardener than me.
   (3)  For whom did you buy that impractical gift?
   (4)  The person responsible for creating the Equal Rights Amendment is she.
   (5)  No error

3. (1) In the bright light, Theresa and I could see their faces clearly.  ① ② ③ ④ ⑤
   (2) Either she or I am working late.
   (3) A package just arrived, and it is marked for either him or her.
   (4) The person who gave the lecture did not speak well.
   (5) No error

4. (1) Since they went for marriage counseling, Simon fights more fairly than she.  ① ② ③ ④ ⑤
   (2) In 1954, Roberto and me saw Stan Musial hit five home runs in one game.
   (3) Arthur and he claim to have seen several UFO's.
   (4) At whose request do I announce the slate?
   (5) No error

5. (1) Who's going to pay for education if all funding legislation is defeated?  ① ② ③ ④ ⑤
   (2) Please call Henry and I as soon as you know the election returns.
   (3) Do you really approve of his playing football?
   (4) Arlene will always be younger than I.
   (5) No error

6. (1) Who called?  ① ② ③ ④ ⑤
   (2) After you've repaired the sink, give the tools to John and him.
   (3) Mike and me will carry the steel beam.
   (4) In case you didn't know, the new mayor is he.
   (5) No error

7. (1) We hope the new police commissioner will be as friendly as him.    ① ② ③ ④ ⑤

(2) The Jensens and they organize a block party each year to raise money for the Fresh Air Fund.

(3) Who do you think will run his campaign?

(4) Give responsible jobs to Kate and her because they have had the most experience.

(5) No error

8. (1) Daniel and I exchange information with them about the Bermuda Triangle.    ① ② ③ ④ ⑤

(2) I have always worked harder than he.

(3) If you don't do the job, who will?

(4) He really shouldn't have objected to me leaving since my work had been finished.

(5) No error

9. (1) I was very pleased with them for thinking of me when they decided to expand their company.    ① ② ③ ④ ⑤

(2) If it is his turn, then allow him to take it.

(3) Davis has always been more punctual than us.

(4) The Boss is one of those musicians who are full of surprises.

(5) No error

10. (1) Give me your word that you and he will comply with our terms.    ① ② ③ ④ ⑤

(2) Jean and I completed  the forms and left them at the main desk.

(3) If I can find you and her, I will give you his instructions.

(4) According to a survey among writers, one of the finest authors of the century is Saul Bellow.

(5) No error

# Chapter 10    Pronouns

**Practice I** *Page 93.*

Answers will vary.

   *Sample* answers:

1. I, You, He, She, We, They
2. 1, You, He, She, We, They
3. him, her, you, them
4. him, me, you, her, us, them
5. Who
6. whom

**Practice II** *Page 94.*

For explanations of these answers, see *Pronoun Clue 1.*

1. *Whom* did you call?
2. *Who* answered?
3. *Who* will help?
4. from *whom*
5. *whom* Tony likes

**Practice III** *Page 94.*

For explanations of these answers, see *Pronoun Clue 2.*

1. *he* ran
2. *They* went
3. My friend and *I* are
4. *She, he* were
5. *we* go
6. *Who* will work

**Practice IV** *Page 95.*

For explanations of these answers, see *Pronoun Clue 3.*

1. call *me*
2. gave to *her*
3. Tell *them*

4. speaking to *him*
5. sent to *us*

**Practice V** *Page 96.*

For explanations of these answers, see *Pronoun Clue 4.*

1. than *I* (am)
2. than *she* (sews)
3. as *he* (feels)
4. than *we* (are)
5. as *they* (argue)

**Practice VI** *Page 96.*

For explanations of these answers, see *Pronoun Clue 5.*

1. *she* (is my secretary)
2. *he* (was the winner)
3. *who* (seems)
4. *they* (were the culprits)
5. *I* (was the person)
6. *we* (are it)

**Practice VII** *Page 97.*

For explanations of these answers, see *Pronoun Clue 6.*

1. *his* swimming
2. *your* calling
3. *my* writing
4. *whose* contribution
5. *their* refusing

**Practice VIII**  *Page 98.*

For explanations of these answers, see *Pronoun Clue 7.*

1. from *whom*
2. between you and *him*
3. to John and *them*
4. except *her*
5. among *them*

**Practice IX**  *Page 98.*

For explanations of these answers, see *Pronoun Clue 8.*

1. *himself* refers to everyone (singular).
2. *his* refers to each (singular).
3. *their* refers to they (plural).
4. *their* refers to all (plural).

**Practice X**  *Page 99.*

1. **(3)** *my* smoking
   See Pronoun Clue 6.
2. **(5)** No error
3. **(3)** *my* playing
   See Pronoun Clue 6.
4. **(1)** *whom*
   See Pronoun Clues 3 and 7.
5. **(4)** *he* was it
   See Pronoun Clue 5.
6. **(4)** he (bowls)
   See Pronoun Clue 8.
7. **(4)** for *me*
   See Pronoun Clues 3 and 7.
8. **(2)** he invited *her*
   See Pronoun Clue 3.
9. **(2)** Don wanted *me*
   See Pronoun Clue 3.
10. **(1)** *I* invited
    See Pronoun Clue 2.

**Practice XI**  *Page 100.*

1. **(1)** *They* and *we* play gin rummy each Wednesday.
2. **(2)** Rita is a more knowledgeable gardener than *I* (am).
3. **(5)** No error
4. **(2)** In 1954, Roberto and *I* saw Stan Musial hit five home runs in one game.
5. **(2)** Please call Henry and *me* as soon as you know the election returns.
6. **(3)** Mike and *I* will carry the steel beam.
7. **(1)** We hope the new police commissioner will be as friendly as *he* (is).
8. **(4)** He really shouldn't have objected to *my* leaving since my work had been finished.
9. **(3)** Davis has always been more punctual than *we* (have been).
10. **(5)** No error

# CHAPTER 11

# CUMULATIVE REVIEW

This review covers:

- Agreement in Time and Number
- Correct Use of Descriptive Words and Phrases
- Recognizing Complete and Incomplete Thoughts
- Special Problems in Agreement
- Special Problems in Time
- Correct Use of Pronouns

After completing the Cumulative Review exercises, evaluate your ability using the SUMMARY OF RESULTS chart on page 112. Acceptable scores for each practice are given.

To learn your areas for skill improvement, find the question numbers you answered incorrectly on the SKILLS ANALYSIS table. The table will show which of your skills need improvement and the necessary chapters to review.

## Practice Exercises

PRACTICE
I

_Directions:_ Blacken the circle that corresponds to the number of the incorrect word in each sentence. If there is no error, blacken number 5.

1. The _angry_ man _ran_ _hurriedly_ into the crowded ① ② ③ ④ ⑤
        1       2    3
   room and shouted _loud_ at the guest. _No error_
                4            5

2. Airman Donald G. Farrell _grimaced_ as _he_ ① ② ③ ④ ⑤
                          1       2
   _squeezed_ into the simulated space cabin _that was_
      3                           4
   to be his home for seven days. _No error_
                  5

3. _What_ _is_ the _social_ implications of the _small_ car?  ① ② ③ ④ ⑤
    1  2       3                      4

   _No error_
    5

4. Although Jan _worked_ all day, she _did_ not _feel_  ① ② ③ ④ ⑤
                  1              2    3

   _good._ _No error_
    4      5

5. There again, I must _insist_ that I _do_ not like _you_  ① ② ③ ④ ⑤
                    1       2       3

   smoking in _my_ home. _No error_
          4        5

6. Just between _we_ two, I _believe_ Jim did not _write_  ① ② ③ ④ ⑤
             1        2              3

   the contract _properly._ _No error_
            4     5

7. Without _fail,_ Carlo and _she_ _attend_ _monthly_ board  ① ② ③ ④ ⑤
         1           2   3    4

   of education meetings. _No error_
               5

8. Neither the congressman _nor_ the people _whom_  ① ② ③ ④ ⑤
                      1              2

   he _represents_ _approves_ of this bill. _No error_
      3      4          5

9. _Somehow_ a misunderstanding about _this_ situation  ① ② ③ ④ ⑤
   1                             2

   _has developed_ between you and _me._ _No error_
      3              4    5

**PRACTICE II**

_Directions:_ Blacken the circle that corresponds to the number of the incorrect sentence in each group. If there is no error, blacken number 5.

1. (1) Mark and Eloise gave gifts to Bill and her.  ① ② ③ ④ ⑤
   (2) A waiting room crowded with impatient patients were common at Dr. Rizzo's.
   (3) George Sampson is one man whom I trust.
   (4) Every one of those boxes represents a large investment.
   (5) No error

2.  (1) Is this the man who you gave the informa-   ① ② ③ ④ ⑤
        tion to?
    (2) Mrs. Stover is one of those teachers who rel-
        ish new ideas.
    (3) If anyone can be unfailingly stubborn, it is she.
    (4) The L.A. Dodgers and their manager are in
        the dugout.
    (5) No error

3.  (1) All of our energy should be directed toward   ① ② ③ ④ ⑤
        maintaining a clean environment.
    (2) Please remind all of the members of your
        organization to vote for Alex and him.
    (3) There was several short stories in the maga-
        zine, but the last was by far the best one.
    (4) Whoever calls the radio station within three
        minutes with the name of the third vice presi-
        dent of the United States will win the contest.
    (5) No error

4.  (1) There goes Chester Kallow and his wife,   ① ② ③ ④ ⑤
        Olga, to their weekly bowling game.
    (2) Mrs. Jana, along with her teacher's aide, ini-
        tiates a new science project each week.
    (3) There are no correct or incorrect answers
        when speaking of the interpretations of
        dreams.
    (4) If the inflation continues and the political
        scandal goes on, we are headed for hard
        times.
    (5) No error

5.  (1) When you can't find the solution to a prob-   ① ② ③ ④ ⑤
        lem and help is not forthcoming and you
        don't know where to turn.
    (2) Of all the recipes for quiche, this is the
        quickest.
    (3) The musician who lives in the downstairs
        apartment plays ragtime piano loudly.
    (4) The cold, icy wind cut through the cabin
        walls and made sleeping uncomfortable.
    (5) No error

6.  (1) The young boy and his companion spent the ① ② ③ ④ ⑤
        afternoon pretending that the pond was a
        lake and that they were explorers.
    (2) Neither the merchants nor their customers
        approve of the town ordinance to close at 6
        P.M.
    (3) Kicking and splashing, the dog finished his
        bath.
    (4) Before signing the order, on the telephone
        the salesman finished his conversation.
    (5) No error

7.  (1) Of all the women in the race, Amelia runs ① ② ③ ④ ⑤
        quickest.
    (2) Everyone in our group believes that the or-
        ganization must collect dues in order to sus-
        tain itself.
    (3) Please hire whomever you think is best
        suited for this exacting job.
    (4) Do you agree that whoever speaks last will
        make the most lasting impression upon the
        audience?
    (5) No error

8.  (1) The rising price of food, coupled with a re- ① ② ③ ④ ⑤
        cession, would make it impossible for an av-
        erage family to obtain even the slightest
        luxury.
    (2) Although she enjoys fishing, Theresa be-
        coming dizzy because of the motion of the
        sea and increasingly nauseated by the smell
        of the fish.
    (3) Any of the three dresses is suitable for this
        occasion.
    (4) Here is the file that you requested.
    (5) No error

PRACTICE
III

*Directions:* Blacken the circle that corresponds to the correct rewriting of the underlined portion of the sentence. Choice 1 is always the same as the underlined portion and is sometimes the right answer.

1. The shy girl <u>stood hesitantly</u> in the doorway before she entered the crowded bar.     ① ② ③ ④ ⑤
   (1) stood hesitantly
   (2) standed hesitantly
   (3) has stood hesitantly
   (4) had stood hesitantly
   (5) stands hesitantly

2. <u>Either the grass or the shrubs need</u> cutting weekly.     ① ② ③ ④ ⑤
   (1) Either the grass or the shrubs need
   (2) Either the grass or the shrubs needs
   (3) Either the shrubs or the grass need
   (4) Either the grass or the shrubs needing
   (5) Either the shrubs or the grass needing

3. <u>Here's</u> my mother and father.     ① ② ③ ④ ⑤
   (1) Here's
   (2) Here is
   (3) Here are
   (4) Here was
   (5) Here were

4. Last week I <u>went to the boringest party.</u>     ① ② ③ ④ ⑤
   (1) went to the boringest party.
   (2) went to the most boringest party.
   (3) went to the more boring party.
   (4) had gone to the most boring party.
   (5) went to the most boring party.

5. David performed the difficult experiment <u>more precisely than any student</u> in the class.     ① ② ③ ④ ⑤
   (1) more precisely than any student
   (2) most precisely than any student
   (3) more precise than any student
   (4) more precisely than any other student
   (5) more precise than any other student

PRACTICE
IV

*Directions:* Blacken the circle that corresponds to the number of the incorrect sentence in each group. If all sentences are correct, blacken number 5.

1. (1) Neither Mrs. Jones nor any of her children were at the school play.
   (2) Each of the three entries in the 4-H contest has merit.
   (3) Any one of those sandwich meats is an excellent choice for lunch.
   (4) That painting hangs in my mother's hallway of which I am proud.
   (5) No error

   ① ② ③ ④ ⑤

2. (1) That lecturer, about whom I've told you, has agreed to speak at our meeting.
   (2) Any of the four candidates would serve well.
   (3) Neither the child nor his father want to take the responsibility for walking the dog.
   (4) The cheese in the refrigerator is no longer fresh.
   (5) No error

   ① ② ③ ④ ⑤

3. (1) This excellent thesis surpasses all others and presented the facts most coherently.
   (2) He is a terrible golfer, but the most tenacious would-be sportsman I know.
   (3) If you are wondering who left the book in your mailbox, it was I.
   (4) When you visit Yosemite Park, please take a deep breath for Marty and me.
   (5) No error

   ① ② ③ ④ ⑤

4. (1) Isaac Asimov, Frank Herbert, and Robert Heinlein write good science fiction.
   (2) All of the twelve contestants are talented.
   (3) The tall, handsome man, wearing a plaid jacket and striped pants, stepping snappily off the curb.
   (4) An English garden, filled with a variety of colors and strains, is an enchanting sight.
   (5) No error

   ① ② ③ ④ ⑤

5. (1) Tom and she frequently read the same books.   ① ② ③ ④ ⑤
   (2) If you don't see us, leave.
   (3) In addition to being rude, he is the most stubborn man I know.
   (4) How can you expect everyone to do his best when you place them under constant pressure?
   (5) No error

6. (1) This is the worst project I've ever been involved in.   ① ② ③ ④ ⑤
   (2) According to a spokesman for the members, they each gave their own opinions at the meeting.
   (3) The stapler belongs to that woman on the table.
   (4) Of the two methods of bidding, I like this one better.
   (5) No error

7. (1) None of our group is ready for the meet.   ① ② ③ ④ ⑤
   (2) There's several avenues of approach open to us.
   (3) The gymnast performed the difficult exercise so well that he received a near-perfect score.
   (4) I do not.
   (5) No error

8. (1) Of the two airplanes, the DC 10 ascends quicker.   ① ② ③ ④ ⑤
   (2) No one understands the situation better than he.
   (3) Maria and I climbed a street that wound around like a spiral staircase.
   (4) Neither Sheila nor I was particularly pleased with the color of the paint.
   (5) No error

9. (1) I, myself, completed the difficult job.　　　①②③④⑤
   (2) Before they completed the building, the contractors discovered that the heating system was insufficient.
   (3) The Jacksons and the Walters take day trips together each summer and visit each other frequently in the winter.
   (4) This is the liveliest color combination of all.
   (5) No error

10. (1) Henry and Will have been living in their　　　①②③④⑤
    parents' house for eight years.
    (2) When I was a child, my family went to the beach every summer.
    (3) Please check the calendar to see if you are available on the 20th.
    (4) If you arrive at the theater earlier than me, please buy my ticket.
    (5) No error

---

After reviewing the Answer Key on page 114, chart your scores below for each practice exercise.

**SUMMARY OF RESULTS**

| Practice Number | Number Correct | Number Incorrect *(Including Omissions)* | Acceptable Score |
|---|---|---|---|
| I | | | 7 Correct |
| II | | | 6 Correct |
| III | | | 4 Correct |
| IV | | | 8 Correct |

To identify your areas for skill improvement, locate the questions you answered incorrectly and circle the numbers on this Skills Analysis chart. Wherever you have circled errors, review the chapters listed in the last column.

**SKILLS ANALYSIS**

| Skill | Question Number | Review Chapter |
|---|---|---|
| **Practice I** | | |
| Correct Use of Descriptive Words | 1, 4 | 3 |
| Agreement of Subject and Action or Linking Word in Number | 2, 7 | 2 and 7 |
| Correct Use of Pronouns | 5, 6 | 10 |
| Agreement: Special Problems | 3, 8 | 8 |
| **Practice II** | | |
| Agreement: Special Problems | 3, 4 | 8 |
| Correct Use of Pronouns | 2 | 10 |
| Complete and Incomplete Thoughts | 5, 8 | 1 |
| Agreement of Subject and Linking Word | 1 | 7 |
| Correct Use of Descriptive Phrases | 6 | 5 |
| Correct Use of Descriptive Words | 7 | 3 |
| **Practice III** | | |
| Time: Special Problems | 1 | 9 |
| Agreement: Special Problems | 2, 3 | 8 |
| Correct Use of Descriptive Words | 4, 5 | 4 |
| **Practice IV** | | |
| Correct Use of Descriptive Phrases | 1, 6 | 5 |
| Agreement: Special Problems | 2, 7 | 8 |
| Action Words: Agreement in Time | 3 | 2 |
| Complete and Incomplete Thoughts | 4 | 1 |
| Correct Use of Descriptive Words | 8 | 4 |
| Time: Special Problems | 9 | 9 |
| Correct Use of Pronouns | 5, 10 | 10 |

# Chapter 11   Cumulative Review

**Practice I** *Page 105.*

1. **(1)** *Loudly* describes shouted.

2. **(5)** No error

3. **(2)** *Are* agrees with the plural subject, *implications.*

4. **(4)** *Well* describes a state of health.

5. **(3)** *Your* describes smoking.

6. **(1)** Use *us* after between.

7. **(5)** No error

8. **(4)** *Approve* agrees with the plural performer, *people.*

9. **(5)** No error

**Practice II** *Page 106.*

1. **(2)** A waiting room (crowded with impatient patients) *was.* Was agrees with the singular subject, *room.*

2. **(1)** *whom* you gave the information to (to whom). Use whom after *to.*

3. **(3)** Several short stories *were* there. *Were* agrees with the plural performer, *stories.*

4. **(1)** Chester Kallow and his wife, Olga, *go. Go* agrees with the plural performer, *Chester Kallow and his wife.*

5. **(1)** Incomplete thought. Possible thought completion: When you can't find the solution to a problem, and help is not forthcoming, and you don't know where to turn, *call me.*

6. **(4)** Before signing the order, the salesman finished his conversation on the telephone. *On the telephone* describes conversation and should be placed after it.

7. **(1)** runs most *quickly.* Descriptive words ending in *-ly* describe actions; therefore, the correct form is *most quickly.*

8. **(2)** Incomplete thought. Possible thought completion: Although she enjoys fishing, Theresa, becoming dizzy because of the motion of the sea and the smell of the fish, *asked to return to shore.*

**Practice III** *Page 109.*

1. **(4)** *Stood* occurred *before* entered, so you must use the helping word *had* with *stood.*

2. **(1)** *Need* agrees with the closest performer, *shrubs,* which is plural.

3. **(3)** *Are* agrees with the plural subject, mother and father.

4. **(5)** *Most boring.* Do not add *-er* or *-est* to a descriptive word ending in *-ing;* use *more* or *most.*

5. **(4)** *Any other* (He did not perform more precisely than himself.)

**Practice IV** *Page 110.*

1. **(4)** That painting, of which I am proud, hangs in my mother's hallway. *Of which I am proud* describes painting, not hallway.

2. **(3)** Neither the child nor his father *wants* to take the responsibility for walking the dog. In an either/or neither/nor construction, the action or linking word agrees in number with the closest performer or subject.

3. **(1)** This excellent thesis surpasses all others and *presents* the facts most coherently. *Presents* should have the same form as *surpasses*.

4. **(3)** Incomplete thought. Possible thought completion: The tall, handsome man, wearing a plaid jacket and striped pants, and stepping snappily off the curb, *tripped.*

5. **(4)** How can you expect everyone to do his best when you place *him* under constant pressure? Because *everyone* is singular and *his* is singular, use *him* rather than *them* to balance the sentence.

6. **(3)** The stapler on the table belongs to that woman. *On the table* describes stapler and should be next to it.

7. **(2)** There are several avenues of approach open to us. *Are* must agree with the plural subject, *avenues.*

8. **(1)** Of the two airplanes, the DC 10 ascends *more quickly.* Descriptive words ending in *-ly* describe actions; therefore the correct form is *more quickly.*

9. **(2)** Before they *completed* the building, the contractors *had discovered* that the heating system was insufficient. *Discovered* occurred *before completed,* so you must use the helping word *had* with *discovered.*

10. **(4)** If you arrive at the theater earlier than *I* (do), please buy my ticket. Since you would not say, If you arrive earlier than *me do,* you do not say, If you arrive earlier than *me.*

# BALANCED SENTENCES

One of the things that used to irritate me in my junior high English classes was the corrections some teachers made in the margins of my compositions. I didn't mind when they wrote "sp." and circled the misspelled word on the line, or "cap." to indicate that I had written "french" with a small "f."

What got me all riled up, however, were the mysterious jottings such as "awk." and "frag." And one term I had a former C.I.A. agent as a teacher, and he used secret codes, it seemed to me. His favorite was a couple of parallel lines in the margin—and his cryptic explanation to my query was "lack of parallelism." I never got to know what he meant, and, at the time, couldn't see that anything was wrong with "I like swimming, hunting, and to fish."

—**Paul Allen**
*Trouble Deaf Heaven*

## *A Word With You . . .*

Paul Allen's teacher did a good job in spotting the error in "I like swimming, hunting, and to fish" but he failed to show his students why it was incorrect. The parallel slash marks in the margins were no substitute for a lesson explaining the need for balance in sentence structure.

You will find that the mystery is removed from that topic in the following pages and why in Paul Allen's latest book we can find a sentence such as, *"Listening* to Beverly Sills, *looking* at a Rembrandt, and *sipping* Chivas Regal all give me goose pimples."

## Understanding Correct Sentence Structure

Correctly and effectively written sentences are balanced sentences. *A balanced sentence is one in which related actions, descriptions, or ideas are presented in the same form.* The following sentences are not balanced. Why not?

1. He liked swimming and *to dive.*
2. Mrs. Thompson is pleasant and *has intelligence.*
3. Tennis is both stimulating and *makes me exhausted.*
4. Gary is not only a good carpenter *but a fine electrician also.*

In sentence 1 the related actions are not expressed in the same form. One action word ends with *ing;* the other action takes an entirely different form, using *to.* Now, you must choose the form you prefer. Either one would be correct, but the same form must be used for both action words.

He liked swimming and diving.

or

He liked to swim and to dive.

In sentence 2, what are the two terms that describe Mrs. Thompson? _____ and _____. You've probably chosen *pleasant* and *has intelligence.* The sentence would be balanced if *has intelligence* were replaced by one word. *Pleasant* is a descriptive word, describing Mrs. Thompson. What descriptive word means *has intelligence?* In other words, how do you change the form of *has intelligence* to balance with *pleasant?*

*Example:*    Mrs. Thompson is pleasant and *intelligent.*

In sentence 3, what are the two terms that describe tennis? _____ and _____. You've probably chosen *stimulating* and *makes me exhausted.* The sentence would be balanced if *makes me exhausted* were replaced by one word. *Stimulating* is a descriptive word, describing tennis. What descriptive word means *makes me exhausted?* In other words, how do you change the form of *makes me exhausted* to balance with *stimulating?*

*Example:*    Tennis is both stimulating and *exhausting.*

In sentence 4, Gary is two things. He is a *good carpenter* and a *fine electrician.* What two phrases relate carpenter to electrician? _____ and _____. You've probably chosen *not only* and *but.* The relationship is shown, however, by *not only* and *but also.* Just as *not only* comes immediately before *a good carpenter,* so must *but also* come immediately before *a fine electrician.*

*Example:*   Gary is not only a good carpenter *but also a fine electrician.*

Look at a few more examples:

INCORRECT: I like to walk in the rain, to sing in the shower, and stamping in puddles.

CORRECT: I like to walk in the rain, to sing in the shower, and to stamp in puddles.

INCORRECT: The eagle has majesty, strength, and is graceful.

CORRECT: The eagle has majesty, strength, and grace.

PRACTICE
I

_Directions:_   Blacken the circle that corresponds to the number of the word or phrase that correctly completes each sentence.

1. The long-time servant was faithful and          ① ② ③ ④
   (1) honestly.
   (2) with honesty.
   (3) honest.
   (4) honesty.

2. Please write your evaluation carefully, truthfully, and          ① ② ③ ④
   (1) concise.
   (2) concisely.
   (3) with concision.
   (4) be concise.

3. The advertisement said that at the "Y" Camps our chil-          ① ② ③ ④
   dren would learn to swim, play tennis, row boats, and
   (1) how to get along with others.
   (2) getting along with others.
   (3) friendship.
   (4) get along with others.

4. Henry is not only a good doctor          ① ② ③ ④
   (1) but also an excellent friend.
   (2) but he is also an excellent friend.
   (3) but he is an excellent friend also.
   (4) but is also an excellent friend.

5. If you want this job,          ① ② ③ ④
   (1) you must be prompt.
   (2) one must be prompt.
   (3) they must be prompt.
   (4) you must have been prompt.

6. This book is a monument to its author and  ① ② ③ ④
   (1) it pays tribute to its subject.
   (2) a tribute to its subject.
   (3) it tributes its subject.
   (4) pays tribute to its subject.

7. This weekend Arthur will fence in the backyard,  ① ② ③ ④
   mow the lawn, and
   (1) paints the house.
   (2) he plans to paint the house.
   (3) paint the house.
   (4) will be painting the house.

8. The teenage boy's mother insisted that he hang up  ① ② ③ ④
   his clothes and
   (1) make his bed.
   (2) he should make his bed.
   (3) why doesn't he make his bed.
   (4) to make his bed.

9. The tennis game was invigorating and  ① ② ③ ④
   (1) excitement.
   (2) had excitement.
   (3) excited.
   (4) exciting.

PRACTICE
II  _Directions:_  Blacken the circle that corresponds to the number of the
incorrect word or group of words in each paragraph. If there is no
error, blacken number 5.

1. Soft drinks _satisfy_ the appetite, _offer_ absolutely  ① ② ③ ④ ⑤
              1            2

   nothing toward building health, _taking_ up valuable
              3

   space, and particularly _crowd_ out milk needed
             4

   for growth and normal bone and teeth structure.

   _No error_
     5

2. Personal health educators would be people who   ① ② ③ ④ ⑤

know the basic facts of <u>nutrition</u>, <u>food buying</u>,
                        1          2

<u>cooking</u>, physical fitness, <u>how to motivate people</u>,
  3                          4

and interviewing. <u>No error</u>
              5

3. <u>Doctors are doing</u> very little health education.   ① ② ③ ④ ⑤
    1

They <u>are not oriented or trained</u> to be health
           2

educators, <u>cannot make money</u> dispensing
           3

health education, and <u>there is no interest</u> in
                    4

being health educators. <u>No error</u>
             5

## PRACTICE III

*Directions:*   Balance each of the following sentences by rewriting them in the spaces provided.

1. The winner's attitude toward the loser was conciliatory yet not with condescension.

_____

_____

2. Mrs. Smith is conservative not only in business but also politically.

_____

_____

3. The judge asked the defendant to swear to tell the truth and if he would cite the evidence.

_____

_____

4. I cannot abide congested subways or elevators with crowds in them.

_____

_____

5. This project is to be a benefit to the neighborhood and it will credit the sponsors.

_____

_____

6. Math, reading, and to write are my favorite subjects.

_____

_____

7. The professor lectured on anthropology, and he was outlining the child-rearing habits of the Polynesians.

_____

_____

8. I splashed cold water on my face and looking into the mirror.

_____

_____

9. The rain splashes onto the walk and soaked into the ground.

_____

_____

10. Outside the wind rustled the leaves in the trees, while inside the children sleep quietly.

_____

_____

PRACTICE IV

_Directions:_   In each of the following groups of sentences, one sentence contains an error in either agreement, placement of a descriptive phrase, or balance. Blacken the circle that corresponds to the number of the incorrect sentence in each group.

1. (1) After killing his victim, the assassin out of the window jumped.
   (2) Harry S. Truman enjoyed reading not only fiction but also nonfiction.
   (3) The labor negotiations were deadlocked.
   ① ② ③

2. (1) Many people believe in stronger consumer protection and better consumer information.
   (2) Walking quickly down the street, I lost my balance.
   (3) I enjoy knitting and to crochet.
   ① ② ③

3. (1) Don't automation deprive many of jobs?      ① ② ③
   (2) Neither the supervisor nor the assemblymen report directly to the president.
   (3) While reading a dull book, I was interrupted.

4. (1) A true guru must have discipline and concentration.      ① ② ③
   (2) The attainment of freedom and achieving national security were their goals.
   (3) None of the representatives is lying.

5. (1) Although the system has defects, it still functions well.      ① ② ③
   (2) I not only endorse his candidacy, but also urge it.
   (3) The mayor divided among his largest contributors the best municipal positions.

6. (1) The reasons for shortening the working day is logical.      ① ② ③
   (2) Dashing home from work, the busy woman prepared a menu in her mind.
   (3) Clouds hang heavily in the sky, signaling rain.

7. (1) While talking on the telephone, the painting on the kitchen wall caught my eye.      ① ② ③
   (2) In the summer, the rosebushes climb along the side of the house.
   (3) My feelings were hurt, so I cried a little.

8. (1) Spring is enjoyable, pretty, and fragrant.      ① ② ③
   (2) A duck swam across the lake and dived under the water.
   (3) Many people in the wealthiest nation in the world are destitute, malnourished, and don't have jobs.

9. (1) Before ending their dispute, the doorbell interrupted the two women.      ① ② ③
   (2) They each pass the dish to their right.
   (3) Several ladies in the class play tennis.

10. (1) Bacon and eggs is my favorite breakfast.      ① ② ③
    (2) Each of the topics on the agenda sound interesting.
    (3) Tea and toast is a common cure-all.

# Chapter 12   Balanced Sentences

**Practice I** *Page 118.*

1. **(3)** *honest* agrees with faithful.
2. **(2)** *concisely* agrees with carefully and truthfully.
3. **(4)** *get (along with others)* agrees with swim, play, and row.
4. **(1)** Henry is two things: *a good doctor, an excellent friend. Not only* precedes *a good doctor,* and *but also* precedes *an excellent friend.*
5. **(1)** *you* agrees with you.
6. **(2)** *a tribute* agrees with a monument.
7. **(3)** *paint* agrees with fence and mow.
8. **(1)** *make* agrees with hang.
9. **(4)** *exciting* agrees with *invigorating.*

**Practice II** *Page 119.*

1. **(3)** *take* agrees with satisfy, offer, and crowd.
2. **(4)** *motivation* agrees with nutrition, buying, cooking, and interviewing.
3. **(4)** *are not interested* agrees with are doing, are not oriented or trained, and cannot make.

**Practice III** *Page 120.*

(Note: Although there is more than one way of rewriting these sentences to make them balanced, the following answers indicate and explain one possible way.)

1. The winner's attitude toward the loser was conciliatory yet not condescending. *Yet not condescending* agrees with conciliatory.

2. Mrs. Smith is conservative not only in business but also in politics. *In politics* agrees with in business.
3. The judge asked the defendant to swear to tell the truth and to cite the evidence. *To cite the evidence* agrees with to swear to tell the truth.
4. I cannot abide congested subways or crowded elevators. *Crowded elevators* agrees with congested subways.
5. This project is to be a benefit to the neighborhood and a credit to the sponsors. *A credit to the sponsors* agrees with a benefit to the neighborhood.
6. Math, reading, and writing are my favorite subjects. *Writing* agrees with math and reading.
7. The professor lectured on anthropology, and he outlined the child-rearing habits of the Polynesians. *Outlined* agrees with lectured.
8. I splashed cold water on my face and looked into the mirror. *Looked* agrees with splashed.
9. The rain splashes onto the walk and soaks into the ground. *Soaks* agrees with splashes.
10. Outside, the wind rustled the leaves in the trees, while inside the children slept quietly. *Slept* agrees with rustled.

**Practice IV** *Page 121.*

1. **(1)** After killing his victim, the assassin *jumped out of the window.*
2. **(3)** I enjoy *knitting* and *crocheting.*

3. **(1)** *Doesn't automation* deprive many of jobs?

4. **(2)** The attainment of freedom and *achievement* of national security were their goals.

5. **(3)** The mayor divided the *best municipal positions among his largest contributors.*

6. **(1)** The *reasons* for shortening the working day *are* logical.

7. **(1)** While talking on the telephone, *I noticed* the painting on the kitchen wall.

8. **(3)** Many people in the wealthiest nation in the world are destitute, malnourished, and *jobless.*

9. **(1)** Before ending their dispute, *the two women were interrupted* by the doorbell.

10. **(2)** *Each* of the topics on the agenda *sounds* interesting.

# PUNCTUATION

> To punctuate or not to punctuate that is the question
> is it better in the long run to omit the periods and
> question marks of English sentences or to include them
> against a large number of misunderstandings by using
> them we end all misinterpretation all the problems and
> confusion that the reader faces this is a result to be
> greatly valued
>
> > Adaptation of a monologue in
> > William Shakespeare's
> > *Hamlet*, Act III, Scene 1

## *A Word With You . . .*

Hamlet pondered the question, "To be or not to be." To punctuate or not to punctuate is not open to question. In order to write clearly and meaningfully, we must punctuate. Standard rules of punctuation help all of us gain the same meaning from written material. In this chapter, we review with you some of the more common rules of punctuation.

## End Marks

Punctuation is simply a way of keeping ideas straight. The most commonly used forms of punctuation are end marks, which are used at the ends of sentences. These include the period (.), the question mark (?), and the exclamation mark (!). Read the following paragraph to see the confusion that results from not using end marks.

### *Paragraph I:*
Preheat oven to 375° in a medium saucepan, melt 3 tablespoons butter stir in flour, salt, and pepper add milk and cook, stirring constantly, until thickened add mushrooms and parsley cook noodles as package directs.

Now place end marks where necessary in order to clarify the recipe.

Consider the following paragraph and place the proper end mark above each number.

***Paragraph 2:***

We have always considered heartbeat and breathing the basic signs of

life__Legally and medically, their absence indicates death__But heart-
   1                                                                                                            2

beat and breathing are controlled by the brain__Is a patient still alive
                                                       3

when these functions occur only through the use of a machine__A clin-
                                                            4

ical decision to turn off the machines is either a recognition that life is

over or a form of murder__Many will agree with the former, but an
                     5

equal number will cry, "Murder__"
                                 6

Turn to the answer key on page 135 to see if you've punctuated correctly.

# Commas

The comma is the most difficult form of punctuation because of its varied uses. After studying the comma style sheet, do Practice I to determine where your comma strengths and areas for improvement lie.

---
### COMMA STYLE SHEET
---

1. Commas are used to separate items in a series to ensure clarity.

   *Example:*    Check the tires, the oil, and the battery.

2. Commas separate more than one descriptive word describing the same word.

   *Example:*    Racing car drivers like long, low, streamlined cars.

3. Commas separate words or groups of words that interrupt the flow of the sentence.

   *Examples:*    Jimmy Doolittle, Air Force squadron leader during WW II, was admired by those who flew with him.

                    Chow mein, if you must know, is my favorite food.

---
## COMMA STYLE SHEET
---

4. The words *therefore, however, nevertheless, inasmuch as,* are set off by commas when they interrupt a complete thought.

   *Examples:*     Unfortunately for Herbert Hoover, however, he became president a year before the crash of 1929.

   Can we, therefore, call environmentalists overcautious?

5. A comma separates an introductory word or group of words from the complete thought.

   *Examples:*     Before the New Deal, laissez-faire economics was practiced.

   Before Roosevelt introduced the New Deal, laissez-faire economics was practiced.

6. Commas separate two complete thoughts that are joined by a connecting word such as *and, or, but, or for.*

   *Example:*     The office building will be torn down, and a parking lot will replace it.

7. A comma always separates the day from the year, and a comma separates the year from the rest of the sentence.

   *Example:*     His son graduated on June 14, 1972, from New York University.

8. Separate a direct quotation from the rest of the sentence by using commas.

   *Examples:*     "I cannot attend," he said.

   The master of ceremonies shouted, "Attention, ladies and gentlemen!"

   "I can understand how you feel," he said, "but please try to see it my way."

9. A comma separates the name of a city from the name of a state or country.

   *Examples:*     Madeline Manning Jackson is from Cleveland, Ohio.

   Paul Martin will be stationed in Paris, France.

---
**COMMA STYLE SHEET**

---

10. A comma follows the salutation in a friendly letter.
A comma follows the closing in a friendly letter, as well as in a business letter.

   *Examples:*     Dear Tom,

   Sincerely,
   Harvey

---

## COMMON COMMA ERRORS

Frequently, commas are included where they should not be. Following are two common examples.

1. A comma is *not* used to separate two actions if the sentence has one performer.

INCORRECT: *I returned* to the library, and *left* the unread book.

CORRECT:   *I returned* to the library and *left* the unread book.

2. When a sentence begins with a complete thought followed by an incomplete thought, a comma is not used.

INCORRECT: The party became lively, when John arrived.

CORRECT:   The party became lively when John arrived.

---

PRACTICE

I

*Directions:*   Insert the missing commas in the sentences below. Use the Comma Style Sheet.

1. The "Day in the City" tour included visits to the Metropolitan Museum the Museum of Natural History the Planetarium and Central Park Zoo.

2. The local theater group presented *Death of a Salesman* on June 14 1996.

3. The company transferred my brother from Cleveland Ohio to New York City.

4. After escaping from his pursuers the innocent victim ran breathlessly into the room and he collapsed into a chair.

5. Dear Joe

   We arrived in Phoenix Arizona on July 10 and we were fortunate to find pleasant accommodations. We will come home in January. Feed the cat.

   Love

   Mother

6. Michael Jordan the basketball player left baseball.

7. After reading the newspaper Terence Morgan decided to write to his congressman.

8. Will stood up when Mrs. Sullivan the mayor's wife entered the room.

9. "Please bring your camera to the game" said Juan.

10. "I would like to" Mitchell replied "but I can't afford the film."

PRACTICE
II

---

*Directions:*    Blacken the circle that corresponds to the number of the incorrectly punctuated sentence in each group. If there is no error, blacken number 5.

1. (1) Before eating breakfast, Tom ran two miles.    ① ② ③ ④ ⑤
   (2) Tom ran two miles before eating breakfast.
   (3) Tom's brother jogs, before eating breakfast.
   (4) Before any physical activity, John eats breakfast.
   (5) No error

2. (1) Because he was late John missed most of the    ① ② ③ ④ ⑤
       lecture.
   (2) Professor Simmons always begins on time.
   (3) John often misses the opening remarks because he is late.
   (4) Whenever he is late, he copies my notes.
   (5) No error

3. (1) Hubert Humphrey, as well as Adlai Stevenson accepted the Democratic nomination but lost the election.    ① ② ③ ④ ⑤
   (2) Jimmy Carter ran for a second term as president of the U. S. in 1980 but did not win.
   (3) When I attend the lectures, I bring a notebook, a pencil, my eyeglasses, and a *People* magazine.
   (4) Each morning the sun rises, and each evening it sets.
   (5) No error

4. (1) Teddy, along with his friends, enjoys stripping cars.    ① ② ③ ④ ⑤
   (2) The local Memorial Day Committee plans many exciting events for this summer and the Committee will continue to function each summer.
   (3) I cannot drive when the roads are icy.
   (4) Ricky was elated because he won the car.
   (5) No error

5. (1) Because she had overslept, Rosa was late for work.    ① ② ③ ④ ⑤
   (2) *Fit or Fat* by Covert Bailey helps you lose weight and put new vitality in your life.
   (3) The thief stole a bracelet, a diamond ring, a wallet containing $100 and a fur coat.
   (4) I cannot smile when I am angry.
   (5) No error

PRACTICE
III

_Directions:_   Blacken the circle that corresponds to the number of each error in the passage below.

For example,␣ another story that appeared in the    ① ② ③ ④
    1

*Herald* on April 20␣ 1995␣states,␣ "Many home econ-
        2       3      4

omists report that mothers overfeed their children

and allow improper foods."

The story says serious future effects_can result from          ⑤ ⑥ ⑦ ⑧
                              5
such habits. Many children are fed_more than neces-
                              6
sary__and they have many unnecessary sweets on
        7
their  menus.  These  children  may  develop  future

_incurable diseases.
8
    These    same    parents    will    donate    generous          ⑨ ⑩ ⑪ ⑫

sums,_ of money for research for cures for these dis-
        9
eases. But on the other hand,__ they don't realize
                              10
that their overindulgence,_ spoiling, and doting are
                        11
not in their children's best_interests.
                        12

# Semicolons

The semicolon is a strong mark of punctuation. It signals the end of a thought. Unlike a period, it is used in the middle of a sentence because it connects two complete thoughts that are closely related.

*Examples:*    The world acclaimed the Great Houdini's
        feats of escape. He earned the world's praise.
        The world acclaimed the Great Houdini's
        feats of escape; he earned the world's praise.

The semicolon can also be used to separate two complete and related thoughts that would otherwise be separated by *and, but, or, nor, for, so.*

*Examples:*    The world acclaimed the Great Houdini's
        feats of escape, and he earned the world's praise.
        The world acclaimed the Great Houdini's
        feats of escape; he earned the world's praise.

*Directions:* Each of the following sentences is missing either a comma or a semicolon. If the sentence is missing a comma, blacken circle 1. If there is a missing semicolon, blacken circle 2.

1. In 1871, Kate O'Leary's cow kicked over a lamp the City of Chicago burned to the ground. ① ②

2. We accepted the invitation but we canceled because of illness. ① ②

3. Our backs were weak but our spirit was strong. ① ②

4. The Louisiana Purchase enlarged America by about 140 percent in area fifteen states were later carved from it. ① ②

5. Lemmings travel toward the sea and they eat everything that is available on the way. ① ②

6. Dr. Toselli, our physician, was delayed at the hospital my husband left. ① ②

7. An ancient temple in Mexico was cut out of a mountain and water was the natural stonecutting tool used by its builders. ① ②

8. Please walk in don't run. ① ②

9. Julius Caesar knew that it would be dangerous to transport an army across rough waters but it was the only way he could learn more about Britain. ① ②

10. I am working late tonight don't expect me for dinner. ① ②

Occasionally, one or both of two complete and related thoughts will contain commas.

*Example:*   John, my older brother, is not a very good pool player; but even though he never wins, he enjoys the game.

Notice that in this type of sentence, in order to avoid the confusion that too many commas can cause, a semicolon is used to separate the two complete thoughts even though a connecting word is present. Study these examples:

Although Jane is five years old, she has never been swimming; and, personally, I think that is a shame.
When you are ready, please call me; and I, although occupied, will meet you at once.

The following large connecting words are always preceded by a semicolon and followed by a comma when connecting two complete thoughts:

therefore
nevertheless
however
inasmuch as

For example:

I don't like the terms of the contract; therefore, I will not sign it.

PRACTICE
V

_Directions:_    Blacken the circle that corresponds to the number of the incorrect sentence in each group. If there is no error, blacken number 5.

1. (1) We, therefore, cannot accept your terms.                    ① ② ③ ④ ⑤
   (2) The first universities began as scholastic guilds, and arose gradually and with great difficulty.
   (3) The contract is unfair; therefore, we cannot sign it.
   (4) The day was very hot; we cooled ourselves in the park.
   (5) No error

2. (1) I had wanted to attend, nevertheless, other                 ① ② ③ ④ ⑤
       commitments prevented my doing so.
   (2) You look, however, as though you like this bargain.
   (3) The aristocratic Watusi are towering African men with fine features, and they are also remarkable athletes.
   (4) My friend, Jane Smith, whom you met last week, arrived today; and, in spite of her long trip, she was eager to see the town.
   (5) No error

3. (1) I went home after work; John went to the game.       ① ② ③ ④ ⑤

   (2) The town plans to demolish the old buildings, and to replace them with new structures.

   (3) The painters plan to remove all of the old paint, and they are going to repaint the entire house.

   (4) Our neighbors, the Wilsons, went on their first camping trip; they loved it.

   (5) No error

4. (1) The ancient people adapted their construction methods to the quality of their stone, and they used the forces of nature that were available.       ① ② ③ ④ ⑤

   (2) The Watusi is a gentleman farmer, and his specialty is cattle.

   (3) I worked on the project all day; however, I was not successful.

   (4) My checkbook balance, however, will not support that purchase.

   (5) No error

5. (1) Joe was late; therefore, he missed the essence of the lecture.       ① ② ③ ④ ⑤

   (2) I cannot smile when I'm angry, and I'm not smiling today.

   (3) James Beckwourth was the son of an African-American soldier, nevertheless, James was known to the Crow Indians as the brave Medicine Calf.

   (4) When the science demonstration began, the children became quiet; when the demonstration became exciting, the children became noisy.

   (5) No error

# Chapter 13    Punctuation

## END MARKS

**Introductory Paragraph 1** *Page 125.*

Preheat oven to 375°. In a medium saucepan, melt 3 tablespoons butter. Stir in flour, salt, and pepper. Add milk and cook, stirring constantly, until thickened. Add mushrooms and parsley. Cook noodles as package directs.

**Introductory Paragraph 2** *Page 126.*

We have always considered heartbeat and breathing the basic signs of life. Legally and medically, their absence indicates death. But heartbeat and breathing are controlled by the brain. Is a patient still alive when these functions occur only through the use of a machine? A clinical decision to turn off the machines is either a recognition that life is over or a form of murder. Many will agree with the former, but an equal number will cry, "Murder!"

## COMMAS

**Practice I** *Page 128.*

1. The "Day in the City" tour included visits to the Metropolitan Museum, the Museum of Natural History, the Planetarium, and the Central Park Zoo.
2. The local theater group presented *Death of A Salesman* on June 14, 1996.
3. The company transferred my brother from Cleveland, Ohio to New York City.
4. After escaping from his pursuers, the innocent victim ran breathlessly into the room, and he collapsed into a chair.

5. Dear Joe,

   We arrived in Phoenix, Arizona on July 10, and we were fortunate to find pleasant accommodations. We will come home in January. Feed the cat.

   Love,

   Mother

6. Michael Jordan, the basketball player, left baseball.
7. After reading the newspaper, Terence Morgan decided to write to his congressman.
8. Will stood up when Mrs. Sullivan, the mayor's wife, entered the room.
9. "Please bring your camera to the game," said Juan.
10. "I would like to," Mitchell replied, "but I can't afford the film."

**Practice II** *Page 129.*

1. **(3)** Tom's brother jogs before eating breakfast.

   When a sentence begins with a complete thought followed by an incomplete thought, a comma is not used.
2. **(1)** Because he was late, John missed most of the lecture.

   An introductory word or group of words is separated from the complete thought by a comma
3. **(1)** Hubert Humphrey, as well as Adlai Stevenson, accepted the Democratic nomination but lost the election.

   *As well as Adlai Stevenson* interrupts the flow of the sentence. Hubert Humphrey accepted the Democratic nomination but lost the election is the main idea of the sentence; therefore, *as well as Adlai Stevenson* must be set off by commas.

4. **(2)** The local Memorial Day Committee plans many exciting events for this summer, and the Committee will continue to function each summer.

When two complete thoughts are connected by *and, and* must be preceded by a comma.

5. **(3)** The thief stole a bracelet, a diamond ring, a wallet containing $100, and a fur coat.

A comma precedes the *and* in a list of three or more items to ensure clarity.

**Practice III**  *Page 130.*

**(3)** For example, another story that appeared in the *Herald* on April 20, 1995,
                                                             3
states, "Many home economists report that mothers overfeed their children and allow improper foods."

**(7)** The story says serious future effects can result from such habits. Many children are fed more than necessary, and
                                                     7
they have many unnecessary sweets on their menus. These children may develop future, incurable diseases.

**(9)** These same parents donate generous sums__of money for research for
                                 9
cures for these diseases. But on the other hand, they don't realize that their overindulgence, spoiling, and doting are not in their children's best interests.

**COMMAS AND SEMICOLONS**

**Practice IV**  *Page 132.*

1. **(2)** Use a semicolon to connect two complete, related thoughts when there is no connecting word such as *and, but, or.*

2. **(1)** Use a comma when connecting two complete thoughts joined by *and, but, or.*

3. **(1)** See answer 2 above.

4. **(2)** See answer 1 above.

5. **(1)** See answer 2 above.

6. **(2)** See answer 1 above.

7. **(1)** See answer 2 above.

8. **(2)** See answer 1 above.

9. **(1)** See answer 2 above.

10. **(2)** See answer 1 above.

**Practice V**  *Page 133.*

1. **(2)** *guilds and* No comma; *and arose gradually and with great difficulty* is not a complete thought.

2. **(1)** *attend; nevertheless,* When connecting two complete thoughts by *nevertheless, however,* etc., precede the connecting word with a semicolon and follow it with a comma.

3. **(2)** *buildings and* See answer 1 above.

4. **(5)** No error

5. **(3)** *soldier; nevertheless,* See answer 2 above.

# CUMULATIVE REVIEW

This review covers:

- Balanced Sentences
- Correct Sentence Structure
- Punctuation That Affects Sentence Structure

After completing the Cumulative Review exercises, evaluate your ability using the SUMMARY OF RESULTS chart on page 146. Acceptable scores for each practice are given.

To learn your areas for skill improvement, find the question numbers you answered incorrectly on the SKILLS ANALYSIS table. The table will show which of your skills need improvement and the necessary chapters to review.

## Practice Exercises

PRACTICE
I

_Directions:_  Blacken the circle that corresponds to the correct rewriting of the underlined portion of the sentence. Choice 1 is always the same as the underlined portion and is sometimes the right answer.

1. In the autumn of 2001 we prepared for the colonization of Venus. We encountered _difficulties although_ our technology was advanced.    ① ② ③ ④ ⑤
   (1) difficulties although
   (2) difficulties, although
   (3) difficulties! Although
   (4) difficulties. Although
   (5) difficulties; although

2. My Aunt Bell, the woman in the _green dress speaks five languages._    ① ② ③ ④ ⑤
   (1) green dress speaks five languages.
   (2) green dress, speaks five languages.
   (3) green dress; speaks five languages.
   (4) green dress. speaks five languages.
   (5) green dress? She speaks five languages.

3. *After the baseball game we* bought lettuce, toma-    ① ② ③ ④ ⑤
toes, onions, luncheon meats, and Italian bread
and made hero sandwiches.
   (1) After the baseball game we
   (2) After the baseball game. We
   (3) After the baseball game, we
   (4) After the baseball game ended we
   (5) After the baseball game; we

4. She was an attractive woman, an excellent    ① ② ③ ④ ⑤
*speaker and a charming hostess; but* she dressed
outlandishly.
   (1) speaker and a charming hostess; but
   (2) speaker and a charming hostess, but
   (3) speaker, and a charming hostess; but
   (4) speaker, and a charming hostess, but
   (5) speaker, and a charming hostess but

PRACTICE
II°
*Directions:*   Blacken the circle that corresponds to the correct rewriting of the underlined portion of the sentence. Choice 1 is always the
same as the underlined portion and is sometimes the right answer.

1. The bicycle is a fairly pleasant machine for lim-    ① ② ③ ④ ⑤
ited use by a few *people, but claims* that it can
substitute for the automobile as a device for moving people around town are grossly overstated.
   (1) people, but claims
   (2) people, But claims
   (3) people but claims
   (4) people; but claims
   (5) people, but, claims

---
°Practice II is adapted from Russell Baker's "Backwards Wheels the Mind," *The New York Times,* July 1, 1973. © 1973 by
The New York Times Company. Reprinted by permission.

2. Most old people will not be happy aboard _it, and mothers who must take along small children during a shopping trip to the supermarket won't be either._  ① ② ③ ④ ⑤

    (1) it, and mothers who must take along small children during a shopping trip to the supermarket won't be either.

    (2) it, and mothers who must take along small children during a shopping trip to the supermarket won't be.

    (3) it, nor will mothers who must take along small children during a shopping trip to the supermarket.

    (4) it, or will mothers who must take along small children during a shopping trip to the supermarket.

    (5) it, for mothers who take along small children during a shopping trip to the supermarket.

3. It is an exhausting and brutal machine in cities built on _hills, and being_ the most unattractive way to travel wherever and whenever the temperature is over 90° and under 30°.  ① ② ③ ④ ⑤

    (1) hills, and being

    (2) hills, and is said to be

    (3) hills, and it is

    (4) hills, and has been

    (5) hills, but being

4. If parked, even chained, out of eyesight for more than 10 _minutes; it is_ a cinch to be stolen.  ① ② ③ ④ ⑤

    (1) minutes; it is

    (2) minutes it, is

    (3) minutes it is

    (4) minutes, it is

    (5) minutes. It is

5. And *then, of course,* there is the awkward ques-   ① ② ③ ④ ⑤
   tion of courage.
   (1) then, of course,
   (2) then, of course
   (3) then of course,
   (4) then; of course
   (5) then; of course;

PRACTICE
III
Directions:   Blacken the circle that corresponds to the correct rewriting of the underlined portion of the sentence. Choice 1 is always the
same as the underlined portion and is sometimes the right answer.

1. Because he did not enjoy last week's *lecture,*   ① ② ③ ④ ⑤
   *Tom* decided to skip this week's.
   (1) lecture, Tom
   (2) lecture! Tom
   (3) lecture Tom
   (4) lecture; Tom
   (5) lecture. Tom

2. The carnival was exciting, the games were *fun*   ① ② ③ ④ ⑤
   *but* the children became very tired.
   (1) fun but
   (2) fun; but
   (3) fun, but
   (4) fun. But
   (5) fun, the

3. We decided to play tennis, have lunch, *and then*   ① ② ③ ④ ⑤
   *we played bridge.*
   (1) , and then we played bridge.
   (2) , and played bridge.
   (3) ; and then we played bridge.
   (4) , and play bridge.
   (5) ; we played bridge

4. Their living room lights were *shining we* de-   ① ② ③ ④ ⑤
   cided to stop to say hello.
   (1) shining we
   (2) shining, we
   (3) shining. And we
   (4) shining; and we
   (5) shining; we

5. We should first measure the room, then order   ① ② ③ ④ ⑤
   the carpeting, and, finally, *we will paint the*
   *walls.*
   (1) we will paint the walls.
   (2) we would paint the walls.
   (3) paint the walls.
   (4) we will be painting the walls.
   (5) to paint the walls.

6. Among all the causes of sedition and basic   ① ② ③ ④ ⑤
   changes of *the state; none* is more important
   than excessive wealth of the few and extreme
   poverty of the many.
   (1) the state; none
   (2) the state none
   (3) the state? None
   (4) the state, none
   (5) the state, so none

7. From a thousand feet, flapping his wings as hard   ① ② ③ ④ ⑤
   as he could, he pushed over into a blazing steep
   dive toward the *waves, and* learned why seagulls
   don't make blazing steep power-dives.*
   (1) waves, and
   (2) waves and
   (3) waves; and
   (4) waves. And
   (5) waves and,

---

*Quote from Richard Bach's *Jonathan Livingston Seagull.* © 1975, Macmillan Publishing Co., Inc. Reprinted by permission.

8. The beach was extremely *crowded, nevertheless,*  ① ② ③ ④ ⑤
   we found Joan.
   (1) crowded, nevertheless,
   (2) crowded; nevertheless,
   (3) crowded; nevertheless
   (4) crowded nevertheless
   (5) crowded, nevertheless

9. Because the landlord has refused *to testify our*  ① ② ③ ④ ⑤
   *attorney* will have to subpoena him.
   (1) to testify our attorney
   (2) to testify. Our attorney
   (3) to testify; our attorney
   (4) to testify our attorney,
   (5) to testify, our attorney

10. Della Mason is a competent accountant *and she*  ① ② ③ ④ ⑤
    *cooks well.*
    (1) and she cooks well.
    (2) , and she cooks well.
    (3) and a good cook.
    (4) and she cooks competently.
    (5) ; and she cooks well.

PRACTICE
IV

*Directions:*   Blacken the circle that corresponds to the number of
the incorrect sentence in each group. If there is no error, blacken number 5.

1. (1) Increasing unemployment, in my opinion, is  ① ② ③ ④ ⑤
      a major problem of the decade.
   (2) Our baby-sitter never cleans the kitchen and
      leaves the den in a mess.
   (3) I, however, spoke to John and alerted him to
      expect the shipment.
   (4) I like the painting, but not enough to buy it.
   (5) No error

2. (1) The aphids have eaten the roses, the mealworms have destroyed the cucumbers, and the cinchbugs have ruined the lawn.

   (2) After we had paid the painter, we called the mason for an estimate on rebuilding the front stairs.

   (3) When the carpenter ants invade your kitchen, and the termites swarm under your porch, you know that spring is here.

   (4) Owning a home is a pleasurable experience; however, there is a great deal of work involved.

   (5) No error

   ① ② ③ ④ ⑤

3. (1) Having considered the backgrounds of the prospective candidates, the members of the Republican National Committee began to consider its options.

   (2) Although history records the names of many famous women, many women remain anonymous.

   (3) According to Tom Seaver, confidence, self-discipline, and experience are prerequisites for a successful pitcher.

   (4) After a massive stroke, President Woodrow Wilson was partially paralyzed; nevertheless, the White House functioned under the leadership of Edith Bolling Wilson, the president's wife.

   (5) No error

   ① ② ③ ④ ⑤

4. (1) Television should instruct, inform, and entertain.

   (2) Arthur rushed out of the barber shop, his face buried in lather; however, the meter maid already had written out his parking ticket.

   (3) Although the city council's meeting was lengthy, it proved beneficial.

   (4) Coughing, sneezing, and wheezing, the speaker descended from the stage.

   (5) No error

   ① ② ③ ④ ⑤

5. (1) I enjoy sad movies, but I dislike books that ① ② ③ ④ ⑤
depress me.
(2) The young author had a compulsion to do the
research, assemble his notes, and write the
paper in one evening.
(3) If you believe that I am correct, then why
won't you support me publicly?
(4) The community pool is not only crowded, but
also shadeless.
(5) No error

6. (1) If you don't like the heat, get out of the ① ② ③ ④ ⑤
kitchen.
(2) Don't jump!
(3) During our trip to London, we visited Westminster Abbey, we also viewed the Crown
Jewels in the Tower of London and saw the
Changing of the Guard.
(4) Because they were planning a picnic lunch,
the children asked for pretzels, potato chips,
cookies, and marshmallows for dessert.
(5) No error

7. (1) Although, in recent years, many efforts have ① ② ③ ④ ⑤
been made; we can never compensate for the
injustice inflicted upon the American Indian.
(2) I could wait no longer because I had
promised to begin the meeting promptly at
eight o'clock.
(3) Once one attains freedom of purpose, any
task is possible.
(4) The current hearings are interesting, but last
year's scandal bored me.
(5) No error

PRACTICE
V

*Directions:*   Blacken the circle that corresponds to the number of the incorrect word in each group. If there is no error, blacken number 5.

1. Men are bent intently over *chessboards. They* are         ① ② ③ ④ ⑤
                                        1

   men of all *ages, but* most are closer to life's
                    2

   twilight than its *dawn. They* are in battle with one
                           3

   *another, the* chessboard is their battlefield.
        4

   *No error*
        5

2. The sun is *hot. Never* mind. Sometimes a drizzle         ① ② ③ ④ ⑤
                 1

   *begins. Never* mind. This is not some silly
        2

   pastime to idle time *away, this* is *chess! This*
                              3              4

   outdoor chess congregation is the only one of

   its kind in the borough. *No error*
                                 5

3. *Yet, it* boasts not a single authentic chess master.      ① ② ③ ④ ⑤
        1

   Is this *sad? No,* it's irrelevant. *For, if* a man is
                2                          3

   seeking out excellence in *chess he* would do well
                                  4

   to stay away from St. James Park. *No error*
                                         5

4. What he would find here is *grimness, determi-*            ① ② ③ ④ ⑤
                                      1

   *nation, anguish, wisdom after the fact,* bitter-
        2            3

   ness under the breath, and *there are a number*
                                      4

   *of accidental brilliances. No error*
                                5

5. Good chess is not being played in St. James *Park,*    ① ② ③ ④ ⑤
                                                    1
   *but* life is being played. Here sits *Liebowitz,* he
                                                    2
   has escaped again from his wife. She will be along

   about 7 o'clock to remind him loudly that he is

   a married man with children. "Your supper is cold

   again, Liebowitz!" She has never called him

   Liebowitz anywhere in the *world but* in St.
                                          3
   James Park. It is the circumstances, the men

   there, the *lateness* of the hour. *No error*
                    4                      5

---

After reviewing the Answer Key on page 148, chart your scores below
for each practice exercise.

**SUMMARY OF RESULTS**

| Practice Number | Number Correct | Number Incorrect *(Including Ommissions)* | Acceptable Score |
|---|---|---|---|
| I | | | 3 Correct |
| II | | | 4 Correct |
| III | | | 7 Correct |
| IV | | | 5 Correct |
| V | | | 4 Correct |

To identify your areas for skill improvement, locate the questions you answered incorrectly and circle the numbers on this Skills Analysis chart. Wherever you have circled errors, review the chapters listed in the last column.

**SKILLS ANALYSIS**

| Skill | Question Number | Review Chapter |
|---|---|---|
| **Practice I** | | |
| Balanced Sentences | 3, 4 | 12 |
| Punctuation That Affects Sentence Structure | 2 | 13 |
| **Practice II** | | |
| Punctuation That Affects Sentence Structure | 1, 4, 5 | 13 |
| Balanced Sentences | 2, 3 | 12 |
| **Practice III** | | |
| Punctuation That Affects Sentence Structure | 1, 4, 6, 7, 8, 9 | 13 |
| Balanced Sentences | 2, 3, 5, 10 | 13 |
| **Practice IV** | | |
| Balanced Sentences | 1, 5, 7 | 12 |
| Punctuation That Affects Sentence Structure | 6 | 13 |
| **Practice V** | | |
| Balanced Sentences | 4 | 12 |
| Punctuation That Affects Sentence Structure | 1, 2, 3, 5 | 13 |

# Chapter 14    Cumulative Review

**Practice I** *Page 137.*

1. (**1**) No error

2. (**2**) My Aunt Bell, the woman in the green dress, speaks five languages.

3. (**3**) After the baseball game, we bought lettuce, tomatoes, onions, luncheon meats, and Italian bread and made hero sandwiches.

4. (**3**) She was an attractive woman, an excellent speaker, and a charming hostess; but she dressed outlandishly.

**Practice II** *Page 138.*

1. (**1**) The bicycle is a fairly pleasant machine for limited uses by a few *people, but claims* that it can substitute for the automobile as a device for moving people around town are grossly overstated.

   Use a comma between two complete thoughts connected by *and, but, or.*

2. (**3**) Most old people will not be very happy aboard *it, nor will mothers who must take along small children during a shopping trip to the supermarket.* This choice states the idea most clearly.

3. (**3**) It is an exhausting and brutal machine in cities built on *hills, and it is* a most unattractive way to travel wherever and whenever the temperature is over 90° or under 30°.

   *And it is* agrees with *It is* at the beginning of the sentence.

4. (**4**) If parked, even chained, out of eyesight for more than 10 *minutes, it is* a cinch to be stolen.

   When a sentence begins with an incomplete thought followed by a complete thought, the two are separated by a comma.

5. (**1**) And *then, of course,* there is the awkward question of courage.

   Set off an interrupting group of words with commas.

**Practice III** *Page 140.*

1. (**1**) Because he did not enjoy last week's *lecture, Tom* decided to skip this week's.

2. (**3**) The carnival was exciting, the games were *fun, but* the children became very tired.

3. (**4**) We decided to play tennis, have lunch, *and play bridge.*

4. (**5**) Their living room lights were *shining; we* decided to stop to say hello.

5. (**3**) We should first measure the room, then order the carpeting, and, finally, *paint the walls.*

6. (**4**) Among all the causes of sedition and basic changes of *the state, none* is more important than excessive wealth of the few and extreme poverty of the many.

7. (**2**) From a thousand feet, flapping wings as hard as he could, he pushed over into a blazing steep dive toward the *waves and* learned why seagulls don't make blazing steep power-dives.

8. **(2)** The beach was extremely _crowded;_ _nevertheless,_ we found Joan.

9. **(5)** Because the landlord has refused _to_ _testify, our attorney_ will have to subpoena him.

10. **(3)** Della Mason is a competent accountant _and a good cook._

## Practice IV _Page 142._

1. **(2)** Our babysitter never cleans the kitchen or the den.

2. **(5)** No error

3. **(5)** No error

4. **(5)** No error

5. **(1)** I enjoy sad movies, but I dislike depressing books.

6. **(3)** During our trip to London, we visited Westminster Abbey; we also viewed the Crown Jewels in the Tower of London, and saw the Changing of the Guard.

7. **(4)** The current hearings are interesting, but last year's scandal was boring.

## Practice V _Page 145._

1. **(4)** another; the _or_ another, _and_ the _or_ another. _T_he

2. **(3)** away; _this or_ away. _T_his

3. **(4)** chess, _h_e

4. **(4)** _a number of accidental brilliances_

5. **(2)** Liebowitz; _h_e _or_ Liebowitz. _H_e

# EFFECTIVE EXPRESSION

I never say, "The trip it was a lovely cruise,"
Nor make a boorish error of that type.
"The reason is because" I hesitate to use
And regard "he hardly never" as sheer tripe.
When it comes to proper style, I've paid my dues.

—Lorraine Lockwood
from "Paying One's Dues" in
*A Housewife and Her Poems*

## *A Word With You . . .*

The common errors pointed out by the poet are all treated in Chapter 15. She "paid her dues" by learning how to avoid such repetitive expressions and how to write in a clear, concise, uncluttered fashion.

Care to pay your dues?

## Style and Clarity

Many sentences that seem correctly written are, in fact, incorrect because of:

- the misuse of words or phrases.
- the addition of unnecessary words or phrases.

See if you can locate the errors in style and clarity in the following paragraphs. Mark your corrections directly in the paragraph.

### *Paragraph A*

My reason for sending the children to Happy Days Camp was that I thought they might learn to swim. Much of the time, the weather was cloudy, but they didn't go swimming. At the end of the season, the campers gave a party for their parents, but they didn't enjoy it. Since our expectations were not fulfilled, we signed the children up for the next year.

Did you find these errors?

1. INCORRECT: My reason for sending the children to Happy Days Camp was that I thought they might learn to swim.

   PROBLEM: The incorrect sentence uses too many words to make the point. "My reason . . . was that" can be condensed simply to "I sent the children to Happy Days Camp because . . ."

   CORRECT: I sent the children to Happy Days Camp *because* I thought they might learn to swim.

2. INCORRECT: Much of the time, the weather was cloudy, but they didn't go swimming.

   PROBLEM: The sentence states that they didn't go swimming *in spite of* the cloudy weather. In fact, they didn't go swimming *because of* the cloudy weather.

   CORRECT: a. Much of the time, the weather was cloudy, so they didn't go swimming.
   b. Much of the time, the weather was cloudy; therefore, they didn't go swimming.
   c. Much of the time, they didn't go swimming because the weather was cloudy.

3. INCORRECT: At the end of the season, the campers gave a party for their parents, but they didn't enjoy it.

   PROBLEM: It is unclear whether *they* refers to the campers or their parents. The sentence must be changed in order to convey the true meaning.

   CORRECT: a. At the end of the season, the campers gave a party for their parents, but the campers didn't enjoy it.
   b. At the end of the season, the campers gave a party for their parents, but their parents didn't enjoy it.
   c. Although they didn't enjoy it, at the end of the season, the campers gave a party for their parents.
   d. At the end of the season, the campers gave a party for their parents, who didn't enjoy it.

4. INCORRECT: Since our expectations were not fulfilled, we signed the children up for next year.

PROBLEM: The sentence states that we enrolled the children for next year *since* our expectations were not fulfilled. In fact, we enrolled the children for next year *although* our expectations were not fulfilled.

CORRECT: Although our expectations were not fulfilled, we enrolled the children for next year.

The corrected paragraph would look like this:

I sent the children to Happy Days Camp because I thought they might learn to swim. Much of the time, the weather was cloudy, so they didn't go swimming. At the end of the season, the campers gave a party for their parents, but the campers didn't enjoy it. Although our expectations were not fulfilled, we enrolled the children for next year.

### Paragraph B

The bus tour of Philadelphia on the bus was interesting. I don't never remember a livelier group. The highlight of the trip was when we saw the Liberty Bell. The reason I enjoyed that sight was because I love history. The bus driver, he gave an informative speech.

Did you find these errors?

1. INCORRECT: The bus tour of Philadelphia on the bus was interesting.

PROBLEM: The phrase *on the bus* is a repetition. Bus *tour* means that the tour was on the bus.

CORRECT: The bus tour of Philadelphia was interesting.

2. INCORRECT: I don't never remember a livelier group.

PROBLEM: The incorrect sentence uses a double negative, *don't never.* These two negative words, in effect, cancel each other. Other negative words that should not be used in combination are: hardly, scarcely, neither, only, never, no one, nobody, no, none, nothing, not.

CORRECT: I don't ever remember a livelier group.

3. INCORRECT:   The highlight of the trip was when we saw the Liberty Bell.

   PROBLEM:   The use of *was when* is poor style. A more concise form of expression should be chosen.

   CORRECT:   The highlight of the trip was seeing the Liberty Bell.

4. INCORRECT:   The reason I enjoyed that sight was because I love history.

   PROBLEM:   *The reason . . . was because* creates an awkward sentence. Simplify the sentence by stating *A* because *B* without the unnecessary words.

   CORRECT:   I enjoyed that sight because I love history.

5. INCORRECT:   The bus driver, he gave an informative speech.

   PROBLEM:   Wordiness results from the repetition in the phrase *the bus driver, he.* Use one or the other, but not both terms. In this sentence you need to use *bus driver,* since there has been no prior reference to him.

   CORRECT:   The bus driver gave an informative speech.

The corrected paragraph would look like this:

The bus tour of Philadelphia was interesting. I don't ever remember a livelier group. The highlight of the trip was seeing the Liberty Bell. I enjoyed that sight because I love history. The bus driver gave an informative speech.

PRACTICE

I

*Directions:*   Blacken the circle that corresponds to the number of the incorrect sentence in each group. If there is no error, blacken number 5.

1. (1) He hardly never writes home.          ① ② ③ ④ ⑤
   (2) Charlie accepted the job because the pay was good.
   (3) I hardly ever visit my childhood friend, Eddie.
   (4) Manuel doesn't like fishing.
   (5) No error

2. (1) My reasons for leaving the firm are personal. ① ② ③ ④ ⑤

   (2) Leonardo da Vinci, he painted *The Last Supper.*

   (3) I had scarcely opened the book when I fell asleep.

   (4) Albert Einstein was one man whom many people admired.

   (5) No error

3. (1) Money was very tight during the early 1980s, so major automobile manufacturers offered customer rebates. ① ② ③ ④ ⑤

   (2) Britons and Americans have never spoken the same language.

   (3) Since I enjoy music, I never attend concerts.

   (4) Although the hour was late, Congress voted to remain in session.

   (5) No error

4. (1) Since the weather has been unusually dry, forests are in danger of burning. ① ② ③ ④ ⑤

   (2) Dolores visited her former employer, Martha Cummins, and she gave her a lovely gift.

   (3) Although I like to play chess, I cannot play now.

   (4) I have never known anyone else who has so consistently disregarded the rules.

   (5) No error

5. (1) There isn't no easy way of solving the problem. ① ② ③ ④ ⑤

   (2) Since Martin Luther King had been an advocate of non-violence, his violent death was particularly shocking.

   (3) An impasse occurs when either party refuses to listen.

   (4) If you regulate your sleeping habits, you will feel better.

   (5) No error

6.  (1) Good sense told the ambassador not to continue in that area of conversation.     ① ② ③ ④ ⑤
    (2) When my young neighbor asked for permission to use my car, I denied it.
    (3) My brother, he refused to admit that he'd broken the stereo.
    (4) After he had signed the bill, the president gave the Boy Scout leader the pen.
    (5) No error

7.  (1) The librarian had given no one permission to use the reference books.     ① ② ③ ④ ⑤
    (2) Susan B. Anthony was a pioneer for women's suffrage during a period in history when it was hardly popular for a woman to be an activist.
    (3) The babysitter gave the child her lunch and she continued to play.
    (4) Since the crew had heard the twelve o'clock whistle, they knew it was lunchtime.
    (5) No error

8.  (1) If the play is not a success, the reason is because the actors never learned their lines well.     ① ② ③ ④ ⑤
    (2) A green-eyed, black cat darted in front of us.
    (3) A high school graduate is neither too young nor too inexperienced for that job.
    (4) As the bus rounded the corner, the tourists could see the traffic jam.
    (5) No error

9.  (1) Rupert cannot understand your unclear notes.     ① ② ③ ④ ⑤
    (2) Maria washed her car this morning, so she is tired.
    (3) Don't say that you haven't been warned.
    (4) The reason I called this meeting is because there have been some misunderstandings.
    (5) No error

10. (1) Didn't Mattie say that she would complete the job?   ① ② ③ ④ ⑤
    (2) Why don't you ask her if she would?
    (3) The ancient, old castle stood on the hill.
    (4) We visited an old, well-kept inn.
    (5) No error

PRACTICE
II

*Directions:*   Blacken the circle that corresponds to the correct rewriting of the underlined portion of the sentence. Choice 1 is always the same as the underlined portion and is sometimes the right answer. These sentences are presenting a story.

1. Our *family, we* went to the craft show.   ① ② ③ ④ ⑤
   (1) family, we
   (2) we
   (3) whole family, we
   (4) family
   (5) family, when we

2. The *craft show* included displays of pottery, needlepoint, jewelry, leaded-glass, and other crafts.   ① ② ③ ④ ⑤
   (1) craft show
   (2) crafts show
   (3) show of crafts
   (4) show
   (5) craft's show

3. My favorite part of the afternoon *was when I tried* the potter's wheel.   ① ② ③ ④ ⑤
   (1) was when I tried
   (2) was trying
   (3) was the time I tried
   (4) was when trying
   (5) is when I tried

4. I *didn't never do anything* that creative before.   ① ② ③ ④ ⑤
   (1) didn't never do anything
   (2) never did nothing
   (3) didn't ever do nothing
   (4) never did anything
   (5) did not never do anything

5. I had difficulty trying the spinning wheel, _and_ I    ① ② ③ ④ ⑤
   had never done it before.
   (1) and
   (2) therefore
   (3) but
   (4) however
   (5) since

6. The artists permitted the children to try their    ① ② ③ ④ ⑤
   media, _and they enjoyed_ sharing this creative experience.
   (1) and they enjoyed
   (2) and the artists enjoyed
   (3) and then they enjoyed
   (4) and they also enjoyed
   (5) and, despite this, they enjoyed

7. When I was a child, _nobody never_ took me to    ① ② ③ ④ ⑤
   such an exciting event.
   (1) nobody never
   (2) anybody never
   (3) anybody ever
   (4) no one never
   (5) nobody ever

PRACTICE
III    _Directions:_    Blacken the circle that corresponds to the correct rewriting of the underlined portion of the sentence. Choice 1 is always the
   same as the underlined portion and is sometimes the correct answer.

1. The graduates and their teachers gathered in the    ① ② ③ ④ ⑤
   auditorium _where they received diplomas._
   (1) where they received diplomas.
   (2) in which they received diplomas.
   (3) where the graduates received their diplomas.
   (4) to receive diplomas.
   (5) where diplomas were received.

2. The mailman *he comes promptly* at noon.      ① ② ③ ④ ⑤
   (1) he comes promptly
   (2) who comes promptly
   (3) comes promptly
   (4) coming promptly
   (5) he come promptly

3. *The reason I bought the outfit was because it was*      ① ② ③ ④ ⑤
   *on sale.*
   (1) The reason I bought the outfit was because it
       was on sale.
   (2) The reason I bought the outfit was it was on
       sale.
   (3) I bought the outfit for the reason that it was
       on sale.
   (4) I bought the outfit because it was on sale.
   (5) The reason it was on sale was because I
       bought the outfit.

4. The polite time to comment *was when he fin-*      ① ② ③ ④ ⑤
   *ished his entire speech.*
   (1) was when he finished his entire speech.
   (2) was when he had finished his entire speech.
   (3) was when he was finishing his speech.
   (4) was while he was finishing his speech.
   (5) came after he had finished his speech.

5. *Don't you never* have to work on weekends?      ① ② ③ ④ ⑤
   (1) Don't you never
   (2) Don't you ever
   (3) Didn't you never
   (4) Haven't you never
   (5) Do you not never

6. All of the graduates *who graduated in the class of*      ① ② ③ ④ ⑤
   *'94* met at the school for a party.
   (1) who graduated in the class of '94
   (2) whom graduated in the class of '94
   (3) graduated in the class of '94
   (4) who graduate in the class of '94
   (5) of the class of '94

7. _Since I had cooked dinner, we did not go out to_   ① ② ③ ④ ⑤
   _eat._
   (1) Since I had cooked dinner, we did not go out
       to eat.
   (2) Since I had cooked dinner, we went out to
       eat.
   (3) We went out to eat since I had cooked dinner.
   (4) We went out to eat because I cooked dinner.
   (5) Since I cooked dinner, we did not go out to
       eat.

PRACTICE
IV

_Directions:_   Blacken the circle that corresponds to the number of the
proper completion for each sentence below.

1. Paula entered the room laughing,   ① ② ③ ④
   (1) because she tripped at the doorway.
   (2) when she saw that her father was angry.
   (3) but stopped when she saw that her father was
       angry.
   (4) but stopped when she saw her father who was
       not laughing because he was angry.

2. Lyndon Johnson chose not to run for reelection in   ① ② ③ ④
   1968
   (2) since the growing antiwar sentiment did not in-
       fluence him.
   (2) because the growing antiwar sentiment did not
       influence him.
   (3) because the growing antiwar sentiment influ-
       enced him.
   (4) because his reason was that the growing anti-
       war sentiment influenced him.

3. The roads were flooded   ① ② ③ ④
   (1) , so we went for a drive.
   (2) since we went for a drive.
   (3) although we turned back.
   (4) , so we turned back.

4. Because the building was old and irreparable,  ① ② ③ ④
   (1) the city planners decided to use it for student housing.
   (2) the city planners decided that the thing to do was that they should tear it down.
   (3) the city planners decided to tear it down.
   (4) the city planners asked the students if they would tear it down.

5. After climbing thirty flights of stairs,  ① ② ③ ④
   (1) the package was still in the delivery boy's hands.
   (2) the feet of the delivery boy were sore he said.
   (3) the delivery boy he refused to walk home.
   (4) the delivery boy's feet were sore.

6. The combined meeting of the bus drivers and taxi drivers  ① ② ③ ④
   (1) resulted from the passenger boycott.
   (2) was for the men who drove buses and taxis.
   (3) was because of the passenger boycott.
   (4) met for the bus drivers and taxi drivers.

7. I'm very sorry for leaving early,  ① ② ③ ④
   (1) but I couldn't never understand the speaker.
   (2) so I couldn't understand the speaker.
   (3) but I couldn't hardly understand the speaker.
   (4) but I couldn't understand the speaker.

8. Although we celebrated the occasion,  ① ② ③ ④
   (1) we were very happy about it.
   (2) was because we were happy about it.
   (3) we were not very happy about it.
   (4) was that we were happy about it.

9. Thomas Jefferson, the President of the United States,  ① ② ③ ④
   (1) he was a creative thinker.
   (2) who was a creative thinker.
   (3) who thought creatively.
   (4) was a creative thinker.

10. If you did not enjoy that movie,                    ① ② ③ ④
    (1) the reason is because you have no sense of
        humor.
    (2) the reason is because that you have no sense of
        humor.
    (3) you have no sense of humor.
    (4) it could also be the reason is because you have
        no sense of humor.

---

# Problems With Logic*

When you use a descriptive word or phrase in a sentence, be sure your sentence also includes the word being described. Look at what happens to logic when the word being described is left out of the sentence.

| | |
|---|---|
| 1. INCORRECT: | Tired from the long climb, a rest seemed in order. |
| PROBLEM: | As it is written, the sentence means that a *rest was tired*. The people being described as *tired* are missing from the sentence. |
| CORRECT: | Tired from the long climb, *we* thought a rest seemed in order. |
| ANOTHER SOLUTION: | Move the person or thing being described to the beginning of the sentence. |
| CORRECT: | Because *we* were *tired* from the long climb, a rest seemed in order. |
| 2. INCORRECT: | After signing the bill, the pen was given to the Boy Scout leader. |
| PROBLEM: | As it is written, the sentence means that the pen—with no help from a person—signed the bill. The person who used the pen to sign the bill is missing from the sentence. |
| CORRECT: | After signing the bill, the president gave the pen to the Boy Scout leader. |
| ANOTHER SOLUTION: | After the president signed the bill, he gave the pen to the Boy Scout leader. |

*From P. Dutwin and H. Diamond's *Grammar In Plain English*. © 1989, Barron's Educational Series, Inc.

*Directions:*    The following items are based on a paragraph containing numbered sentences. Some of the sentences may contain errors in logic. Other sentences are correct as they appear in the paragraph. Read the paragraph and then answer the questions based on it. Choose the one best answer for each item.

(1) A computer collects the information, or data, as input. (2) Using a typewriter-like keyboard, information passes from the keyboard to the computer's storage area. (3) Stored, the computer will need to work with the information later. (4) After the computer processes the data in some way, the information is passed to an output machine called a visual display unit.

1. Sentence 1: A computer collects the information, or data, as input.    ① ② ③ ④ ⑤
   What correction should be made to this sentence?
   (1) Insert *it* after computer.
   (2) Change *collects* to *collect.*
   (3) Remove the comma after *information.*
   (4) Remove the comma after *data.*
   (5) No correction is necessary.

2. Sentence 2: Using a typewriter-like keyboard, information passes from the keyboard to the computer's storage area.    ① ② ③ ④ ⑤
   If you rewrote sentence 2 beginning with <u>Using a typewriter-like keyboard, the operator</u> the next words should be
   (1) passes from the keyboard
   (2) passes information from the keyboard
   (3) computes the information from the keyboard
   (4) keyboards to the computer's storage area
   (5) passes to the computer's storage area

3. Sentence 3: Stored, the computer will need to work with the information later.    ① ② ③ ④ ⑤
   If you rewrote sentence 3 beginning with <u>The computer will need to</u> the next words should be
   (1) store the work with
   (2) store the information
   (3) compute the work
   (4) work with the stored
   (5) work the information

Reminder: In Chapter 5 you learned to place descriptive phrases close to the words they describe. Follow that rule to ensure that your sentences are clear and logical.

| | | |
|---|---|---|
| 1. INCORRECT: | | Problems are solved by computer scientists that are very complicated. |
| | PROBLEM: | Written this way, the sentence states that scientists are very complicated. The descriptive words, *that are very complicated* are placed incorrectly. |
| | CORRECT: | Problems that are very complicated are solved by computer scientists. |
| | ANOTHER SOLUTION: | Computer scientists solve problems that are very complicated. |
| 2. INCORRECT: | | The scientists types questions and the computer answers on the keyboard. |
| | PROBLEM: | According to this sentence, answers appear on the keyboard. The descriptive words *on the keyboard* are placed incorrectly. |
| | CORRECT: | The scientist types questions on the keyboard and the computer answers. |

PRACTICE
VI

*Directions:*   The sentences that follow are illogical because they contain incorrectly placed descriptive phrases. Correct the errors using the spaces provided.

1. We noticed a small dog in the back of the kennel that was a perfect choice for us.

   _____

2. We had seen a dog also in the window of a local store that we liked. (CAUTION: Find *two* placement errors here.)

   _____

3. The cafeteria serves lunch to everyone from noon to two o'clock in my office.

   _____

4. Students blocked the hall who were strolling to the final class of the day.

   _____

5. He said he had seen a man in the cab wearing a cowboy hat.

   _____

# Chapter 15   Effective Expression

**Practice I** *Page 153.*

1. **(1)** Do not use a negative word such as never with *hardly* or *scarcely*. The sentence should read: He hardly *ever* writes home.

2. **(2)** *He* is repetitious. The sentence should read: *Leonardo da Vinci painted The Last Supper.*

3. **(3)** The second part of the sentence is contradictory to the first. The sentence should read: Since I enjoy music, *I frequently attend* concerts.

4. **(2)** The use of *she* and *her* makes the sentence unclear. Who gave the gift to whom? The sentence should read: Dolores *visited* her former employer, Martha Cummins, and *gave her* a lovely gift.

5. **(1)** Don't use *not* and *no* together. The sentence should read: There *is no* easy way of solving the problem. or There *isn't any* easy way of solving the problem.

6. **(3)** *He* is repetitious. The sentence should read: *My brother refused* to admit that he'd broken the stereo.

7. **(3)** The use of *her* and *she* make the sentence unclear. The sentence should read: The baby-sitter gave the child lunch, *and the child* continued to play.

8. **(1)** *The reason is because* makes the sentence unwieldy. The sentence should read: If the play is not a success, *it is because* the actors never learned their lines well.

9. **(4)** See #8. The sentence should read: *I called this meeting because* there have been some misunderstandings.

10. **(3)** *Old* is repetitious. The sentence should read: The *ancient castle* stood on a hill.

**Practice II** *Page 156.*

1. **(4)** *We* is repetitious. The sentence should read: Our <u>*family*</u> went to the craft show.

2. **(4)** *Craft* is repetitious. The sentence should read: The <u>*show*</u> included displays of pottery, needlepoint, jewelry, beaded glass objects, and other crafts.

3. **(2)** *Was when* is an awkward construction. The sentence should read: My favorite part of the afternoon <u>*was trying*</u> the potter's wheel.

4. **(4)** Don't use *didn't* and *never* together. The sentence should read: I <u>*never did anything*</u> that creative before.

5. **(5)** *Since* coordinates the two thoughts; *and* does not. The sentence should read: I had difficulty trying the spinning wheel, <u>*since*</u> I had never done it before.

6. **(2)** The word to which *they* refers is unclear. The sentence should read: The artists permitted the children to try their media, <u>*and the artists*</u> enjoyed sharing this creative experience.

7. **(5)** Don't use *nobody* and *never* together. The sentence should read: When I was a child, <u>*nobody ever*</u> took me to such an exciting event.

**Practice III** *Page 157.*

1. **(3)** The graduates and their teachers gathered in the auditorium *where the graduates received their diplomas.*

2. **(3)** The mailman *comes promptly* at noon.

3. **(4)** *I bought the outfit because it was on sale.*

4. **(5)** The polite time to comment *came after he had finished his speech.*

5. **(2)** *Don't you ever* have to work on weekends?

6. **(5)** All of the graduates *of the class of '94* met at the school for a party.

7. **(1)** *Since I had cooked dinner, we did not go out to eat.*

**Practice IV** *Page 159.*

1. **(3)** Paula entered the room laughing, but stopped when she saw that her father was angry.

2. **(3)** Lyndon Johnson chose not to run for reelection in 1968 because the growing antiwar sentiment influenced him.

3. **(4)** The roads were flooded, so we turned back.

4. **(3)** Because the building was old and irreparable, the city planners decided to tear it down.

5. **(4)** After climbing thirty flights of stairs, the delivery boy's feet were sore.

6. **(1)** The combined meeting of the bus drivers and taxi drivers resulted from the passenger boycott.

7. **(4)** I'm very sorry for leaving early, but I couldn't understand the speaker.

8. **(3)** Although we celebrated the occasion, we were not very happy about it.

9. **(4)** Thomas Jefferson, the president of the United States, was a creative thinker.

10. **(3)** If you did not enjoy that movie, you have no sense of humor.

**Practice V** *Page 162.*

1. **(5)** No correction is necessary.

2. **(2)** Using a typewriter-like keyboard, the operator passes information from the keyboard to the computer's storage area.

   The person using the keyboard is missing from the original sentence. Use the word *operator* to tell who is using the keyboard.

3. **(4)** The computer will need to work with the stored information later.

   In the original sentence, the computer is stored. The correction places the performer—the computer—where it belongs, that is, at the beginning of the sentence.

**Practice VI** *Page 162.*

1. We noticed a small dog *that was a perfect choice for us* in the back of the kennel.

2. We *also* had seen a dog *that we liked* in the window of a local store.

3. The cafeteria serves lunch to everyone *in my office* from noon to two o'clock.

4. Students *who were strolling to the final class of the day* blocked the hall.

5. He said he had seen a man *wearing a cowboy hat* in the cab.

# CHAPTER 16

# MORE PUNCTUATION

## *A Word With You . . .*

Charlie Brown knows that strong writers don't just "sprinkle in the little curvy marks" or any other mark of punctuation. Punctuation, used correctly, guides your reader through your writing. This chapter introduces marks of punctuation that many people avoid. Learn to use them correctly, and your writing will stand out.

## Quotation Marks

Quotation marks are used to set off the *exact* words said by somebody or taken from a source.

DIRECT QUOTATION: The young mother remarked, "Thank Heavens for our community's parks and recreation program!"

INDIRECT QUOTATION: The young mother remarked that she was grateful for her community's parks and recreation program.

In the first sentence, the woman's exact words are quoted. In the second sentence, the word *that* signals the fact that the sentence is a report of what was said, not a direct quotation.

## QUOTATION MARK
## STYLE SHEET

1. Use quotation marks to set off the exact words of a speaker. Note the comma between the speaker and the words spoken in each example. Note the period *inside* the quotation marks at the end of the first sentence.

    *Examples:*    The teacher instructed, "Complete the vocabulary list at home."

    "Review the vocabulary list for our last class," the teacher instructed.

2. Use quotation marks to set off both parts of a broken quotation. Do not capitalize the first word of the second part of the quotation unless it is the beginning of a new sentence.

    *Examples:*    "Well," exclaimed Anita, "what did you expect?"

    "Stop complaining, Billy," said his brother. "It won't help."

3. Place a semicolon after the closing quotation marks.

    *Example:*    You said, "Wait until you see me"; so I waited.

4. Never use two forms of punctuation at the end of a quotation. When the entire sentence is a question but the quoted portion is not, place a question mark *after* the closing quotation marks.

    *Example:*    Did Jane say, "Meet at our house"?

5. Never use two forms of punctuation at the end of a quotation. When the entire sentence is an exclamation but the quoted portion is not, place the exclamation point *after* the closing quotation marks.

    When the quoted portion is an exclamation, place the exclamation mark *inside* the quotes.

    *Examples:*    I could scream each time you call and say, "I'll be late for dinner tonight, dear"!

    The guard shouted, "Stop him! Stop him!"

---
**QUOTATION MARK
STYLE SHEET**
---

6. Use single quotation marks for a quotation within a quotation.

> *Example:*    The history student asked, "Is it true that Patrick Henry said, 'Give me liberty or give me death' when America's freedom was in question?"

7. Use quotation marks to enclose titles of poems, articles, chapters, or any part of a book or magazine. If the quoted title is followed by a comma, the comma should be placed inside the quotation marks.

> *Example:*    The third chapter of *Our World,* entitled, "Views of the Middle East," is the most interesting.

---

## COMMON ERRORS WITH QUOTATION MARKS

Quotations require marks of punctuation in addition to quotation marks. The most common errors in quotations involve the omission or misuse of commas, periods, and capital letters. Following are common examples.

1.  Place a comma between what is quoted and the person quoted.

> INCORRECT:   "When you finish packing the last box, start loading all of them onto the truck" the shipping manager instructed.

> CORRECT:   "When you finish packing the last box, start loading all of them onto the truck," the shipping manager instructed.

2.  In a broken quotation, do not capitalize the first word of the second part of the quotation unless it is the beginning of a new sentence.

> INCORRECT:   "When you finish packing the last box," the shipping manager instructed. "Start loading all of them onto the truck."

> CORRECT:   "When you finish packing the last box," the shipping manager instructed, "start loading all of them onto the truck."

> CORRECT:   "You have finished packing the last box," the foreman said. "Start loading all of them onto the truck."

3. Place the period inside the quotation marks at the end of a sentence.

    INCORRECT:  Dr. D'Amato said, "Before you leave the office, please give your Medicare number to the nurse".

    CORRECT:  Dr. D'Amato said, "Before you leave the office, please give your Medicare number to the nurse."

4. Place a question mark *after* the closing quotation marks when the entire sentence is a question, but the quoted portion is not.

    INCORRECT:  Did Dr. D'Amato say, "Please leave your Medicare number with the nurse?"

    CORRECT:  Did Dr. D'Amato say, "Please leave your Medicare number with the nurse"?

5. Place a question mark *inside* the closing quotation marks when the quoted portion is a question, but the entire sentence is not.

    INCORRECT:  Dr. D'Amato asked, "Is this your correct Medicare number"?

    CORRECT:  Dr. D'Amato asked, "Is this your correct Medicare number?"

PRACTICE
I   _Directions:_   Punctuate the following sentences.

1. The manager said three men must work overtime
2. The manager said that three men must work overtime
3. Three men said the manager must work overtime
4. The manager asked who will work overtime
5. Why didn't the manager say everyone must work
6. Imagine if the manager had said everyone must work overtime
7. Imagine if the manager had said that everyone must work overtime
8. The manager shouted everyone must work overtime

**PRACTICE**
**II**    *Directions:*    Blacken the circle that corresponds to the number of the error in each sentence. If there is no error, blacken number 5.

1. Mrs. Romano *e*xclaimed,_ *F*rankie,_ the parakeet    ① ② ③ ④ ⑤
                 1          2      3
   has disappeared*!*_" *No error*
              4    5

2. Frankie answered,___"Mom,_ I don't know why*;*_    ① ② ③ ④ ⑤
                   1    2                 3
   it was there when I tried to clean it with the

   vacuum cleaner._ *No error*
            4    5

3. _"*Y*ou will never catch me*!*_" shouted Batman._    ① ② ③ ④ ⑤
   1                   2              3
   The pursuers vowed to catch him._ *No error*
                         4    5

4. The student sai*d t*hat he now understands the    ① ② ③ ④ ⑤
              1
   theory behind these problems._ He said,_ "Sud-
                       2          3
   denly, everything falls into place."_ *No error*
                         4    5

5. The author said,_ "You can learn to write only    ① ② ③ ④ ⑤
                 1
   through writing."_ He said that one can never
               2
   learn to write by reading *how-to* book*s*._ *No error*
                        3      4    5

6. Alice told Marion sh*e w*as to stay at home    ① ② ③ ④ ⑤
                       1
   and be a babysitter._ Marion exclaimed,_ "*w*hat a
                 2                  3
   shame*!*_" *No error*
         4     5

7. "Clean your room; take the laundry to the    ① ② ③ ④ ⑤
    1              2

    basement; and wash the car," instructed
           3                4

    Mother. *No error*
            5

8. After you turn over the earth, add some plant    ① ② ③ ④ ⑤
    1                    2

    food and water. Then you'll be ready to plant

    the flower," concluded the gardener. *No error*
            3               4     5

9. Was it Elsa who said, "Our sales meeting    ① ② ③ ④ ⑤
    1                2 3

    begins at 9:30 A.M. sharp?" *No error*
                 4     5

10. "When will you ever," asked the foreman,    ① ② ③ ④ ⑤
      1             2

    "Arrive at work on time?" *No error*
    3            4    5

11. "I know when I will arrive on time," answered    ① ② ③ ④ ⑤
    1                      2

    Marie. "it will be when my alarm clock is
          3

    finished being repaired." *No error*
                4    5

12. The show is called "Day After Day;" it starts    ① ② ③ ④ ⑤
               1         2

    at 2:30 P.M. *No error*
      3    4    5

13. He replied encouragingly, "Remember that    ① ② ③ ④ ⑤
                      1

    Ted said, "Let Irene wait. I'll interview her
         2  3

    as soon as I return.'" *No error*
                4    5

14. After having read the third chapter, entitled ① ② ③ ④ ⑤
                                   1
"Spring-time Planting", I felt that I was ready
2                    3
to tackle the gardening job. *No error*
                   4     5

15. After the vicious dog had attacked the tres- ① ② ③ ④ ⑤

passer, the dog's owner said, "Didn't you see the
                           1
sign that reads 'Beware of Dog' before you
            2                  3
entered my property?" *No error*
            4     5

# Other Marks of Punctuation: Colon, Hyphen, Apostrophe, Dash, Parentheses, Brackets

You have already studied the major punctuation marks. There are several marks of punctuation that we encounter less frequently. These are the colon, the hyphen, the apostrophe, the dash, parentheses, and brackets.

---
**OTHER MARKS OF PUNCTUATION
STYLE SHEET**
---

1. **Colon** Use a colon to introduce a list. Don't use a colon when the list is preceded by an action or linking word.

   *Example:* Bring the following equipment: a tent, a cot or sleeping bag, basic cooking utensils, and matches. Necessary equipment for such a trip includes a tent, a cot or sleeping bag, basic cooking utensils, and matches.

2. Use a colon after the salutation in a business letter.

   *Examples:* Dear Mr. Williams:
   Dear Sir:

**OTHER MARKS OF PUNCTUATION**
**STYLE SHEET**

3. Use a colon between numbers to show time.

*Example:*    4:15 P.M.

4. **<u>Hyphen</u>** Use a hyphen to divide a word at the end of a line. Divide between syllables with a hyphen.

*Example:*    The new, downtown building is enormous, yet un-
ornamented.

5. Use a hyphen to divide compound numbers from twenty-one to ninety-nine.

*Example:*    twenty-two, eighty-seven

6. Hyphenate descriptive words that are brought together to form a new word.

*Example:*    well-to-do, fly-by-night, half-yearly, self-supporting

7. Hyphenate certain prefixes and the words to which they are added. For example, ex-husband.

*Example:*    My favorite art form is pre-Columbian sculpture.

8. **<u>Apostrophe</u>** Use an apostrophe to show the omission of a letter from a word.

*Example:*    We aren't (are not) responsible for breakage.

9. Use an apostrophe to show possession. Note that apostrophes are placed differently according to whether the word is singular or plural and according to the way the word forms its plural. Exceptions: *Its* is the possessive form of *it. It's* means *it is. His* and *hers* are the possessive forms of *he* and *she.*

*Example:*    the lamb's wool, the dogs' kennels, the men's department, the ladies' club

## OTHER MARKS OF PUNCTUATION
## STYLE SHEET

10. Use an apostrophe to show the plural of letters when necessary to avoid confusion. Use the apostrophe with all lower case letters and with those upper case/lower case combinations that create words.

   *Examples:*   A's, Bs, I's, r's, v's, U's, T's

11. **Dash** Use dashes to emphasize an interruption within a sentence.

   *Example:*   Be home on time—no later than midnight—or I shall be very worried.

12. **Parentheses** Use parentheses for words not strictly related to the main thought of the sentence. Do not use a capital letter or final punctuation (except the question mark) within the parentheses.

   *Examples:*   I managed (somehow or other) to drag three heavy suitcases to the terminal.

   I called you last night (or was it Friday?) to give you the message.

13. **Brackets** Use brackets within parentheses and within a quotation.

   *Examples:*   They tried some French wines (Bordeaux [Medoc], Burgundy, and Chablis).

   We were asked to read a poem and Tom said, "The one I've chosen [by Wilde] is called 'The Ballad of Reading Gaol.'"

**PRACTICE III**

*Directions:*   Blacken the circle that corresponds to the number of the error in each sentence. If there is no error, blacken number 5.

1. The presiden*t's* desk was covered with all sorts   ① ② ③ ④ ⑤
   1

   of business paper*s:* invoices, receipts, minutes
   2

   of his last meeting*,* and projected plans for
   3

   the new building   *No error*
   4          5

2. We expect to arrive at Kennedy Airport at     ① ② ③ ④ ⑤

    <u>8 15 P.M.</u> on Thursda<u>y,</u> June <u>8, 199</u>6. <u>No error</u>
    ⠀⠀1⠀⠀⠀⠀⠀⠀⠀⠀⠀⠀⠀2⠀⠀⠀3⠀⠀4⠀⠀⠀5

3. Although we had met only onc<u>e,</u> he recognized     ① ② ③ ④ ⑤
    ⠀⠀⠀⠀⠀⠀⠀⠀⠀⠀⠀⠀⠀⠀⠀⠀⠀1

    me immediately and began to regale me with

    the followin<u>g:</u> he had just arrived in tow<u>n;</u> he
    ⠀⠀⠀⠀⠀⠀⠀⠀⠀2⠀⠀⠀⠀⠀⠀⠀⠀⠀⠀⠀⠀⠀3

    had bought a hous<u>e;</u> and he had just been
    ⠀⠀⠀⠀⠀⠀⠀⠀⠀⠀⠀4

    promoted within his company. <u>No error</u>
    ⠀⠀⠀⠀⠀⠀⠀⠀⠀⠀⠀⠀⠀⠀⠀⠀⠀⠀⠀5

4. Do you really <u>*believe*</u> that you were a different     ① ② ③ ④ ⑤
    ⠀⠀⠀⠀⠀⠀⠀⠀1

    person at <u>*twenty nine*</u> from the one you are at
    ⠀⠀⠀⠀⠀⠀⠀⠀⠀2

    <u>*thirty*</u> <u>?</u>  <u>No error</u>
    ⠀3⠀⠀4⠀⠀⠀5

5. If you are planning to send a present to Lauri<u>e,</u>     ① ② ③ ④ ⑤
    ⠀⠀⠀⠀⠀⠀⠀⠀⠀⠀⠀⠀⠀⠀⠀⠀⠀⠀⠀⠀⠀⠀⠀⠀⠀1

    go to the <u>*half-yearly*</u> sale in the children<u>s'</u>
    ⠀⠀⠀⠀⠀⠀⠀2⠀⠀⠀⠀⠀⠀⠀⠀⠀⠀⠀⠀3

    departmen<u>t.</u>  <u>No error</u>
    ⠀⠀⠀⠀4⠀⠀⠀⠀5

6. <u>*Dont*</u> forget to write two <u>*r's*</u> in <u>*"de*</u>ferre<u>d."</u>     ① ② ③ ④ ⑤
    ⠀1⠀⠀⠀⠀⠀⠀⠀⠀⠀⠀⠀⠀⠀⠀⠀⠀2⠀⠀⠀3⠀⠀⠀⠀4
    <u>No error</u>
    ⠀5

7. When I arrived (<u>*after a four-hour drive*</u>),     ① ② ③ ④ ⑤
    ⠀⠀⠀⠀⠀⠀⠀⠀⠀⠀⠀⠀⠀1

    I found that my <u>*cousin's*</u> <u>*weren't*</u> at hom<u>e.</u>
    ⠀⠀⠀⠀⠀⠀⠀⠀⠀⠀2⠀⠀⠀⠀⠀⠀3⠀⠀⠀⠀⠀⠀⠀4
    <u>No error</u>
    ⠀5

8. The _ex Senator_ hoped that his _protege's_ bill    ① ② ③ ④ ⑤
       1            2

 would pass the _two-thirds_ mar_k_. _No error_
            3      4    5

9. Although September_,_ June_,_ and April have    ① ② ③ ④ ⑤
            1    2

 thirty day_s,_ December and January have
        3

 _thirty-one_ days. _No error_
       4          5

10. At _11:45_ A.M. the _commuter's_ _train_ pulled them    ① ② ③ ④ ⑤
       1           2      3

 into the _jam-packed_ station. _No error_
          4         5

**PRACTICE IV**

_Directions:_ Blacken the circle that corresponds to the number of the incorrect sentence in each group. If there is no error, blacken number 5.

1. (1) Let's talk about Mozart's music first.    ① ② ③ ④ ⑤
 (2) If you leave after I do, do this: put the cat out, close the windows, and lock the front door.
 (3) Henrys new car seems to be a poor sample of this year's cars.
 (4) Mr. Jones is a good example of a self-satisfied person.
 (5) No error

2. (1) In November, 1994, unusually high temperatures reached the 50s and even the 60s.    ① ② ③ ④ ⑤
 (2) Dot your i's and cross your t's.
 (3) Who's going to Ellen's party?
 (4) It's wheel is no longer round.
 (5) No error

3. (1) Many experts skills have been brought to      ① ② ③ ④ ⑤
       bear upon our energy needs.
   (2) Mr. Evans hadn't stepped out of the room
       before the whispering began.
   (3) After her work's finished, she'll be home.
   (4) My mother-in-law's house was the scene of
       our recent reunion.
   (5) No error

4. (1) The United Nations' subcommittees meet      ① ② ③ ④ ⑤
       regularly.
   (2) Have you ever bought tickets to the Fire-
       mens' Ball?
   (3) My friends' letters demand that I be a good
       correspondent.
   (4) The children's club meets at 3:45 P.M. on
       Tuesdays.
   (5) No error

5. (1) Yesterday I had lunch with Mr. Templeton.      ① ② ③ ④ ⑤
   (2) Learn the meanings of the following
       words—"petition," "council," and "elec-
       torate."
   (3) The children—in the midst of our frantic
       activity—asked for chocolate ice cream sun-
       daes.
   (4) Take the bicycle (John's), and don't forget
       my fishing rod.
   (5) No error

6. (1) If you consult James Beard's newest cook-      ① ② ③ ④ ⑤
       book, you will find some excellent shellfish
       recipes.
   (2) I'd rather you didn't do that.
   (3) When I heard (last night) that you were ill, I
       drove all night to get here.
   (4) Is that pen his or her's?
   (5) No error

7. (1) Take my shirts to the laundry tomorrow!　　① ② ③ ④ ⑤
   (2) We listed the stolen items a ring, a bracelet, and a TV set.
   (3) All of this pre-Christmas rush has ruined Terry's disposition.
   (4) Jan's sister-in-law agreed to join us for bridge.
   (5) No error

8. (1) When it is 10:30 A.M. in New York, what time is it in Chicago?　　① ② ③ ④ ⑤
   (2) A famous critic (Lionel Trilling) said that a nation's literature reflects its deepest philosophies.
   (3) Listening to everyone's ideas sometimes confuses me.
   (4) I've decided to take a year's subscription to *Your Health*.
   (5) No error

9. (1) We've discovered that students' absences have decreased this month.　　① ② ③ ④ ⑤
   (2) The seashore is only an hour's ride from here.
   (3) Have you read *The Record*'s lead article?
   (4) This book's most important theme is the development of the Puritan ethic.
   (5) No error

10. (1) A person's health depends somewhat upon his mental attitude.　　① ② ③ ④ ⑤
    (2) Don't call him un American because he disagrees with your opinions.
    (3) While you're at the store, buy wire, nails, and a hammer.
    (4) Almost three-fourths of our organization voted against the admission of new members.
    (5) No error

# Chapter 16   More Punctuation

## QUOTATION MARKS

**Practice I** *Page 169.*

1. The manager said, "Three men must work overtime."

2. The manager said that three men must work overtime.

3. "Three men," said the manager, "must work overtime."

4. The manager asked, "Who will work overtime?"

5. Why didn't the manager say, "Everyone must work"?

6. Imagine if the manager had said, "Everyone must work overtime"!

7. Imagine if the manager had said that everyone must work overtime!

8. The manager shouted, "Everyone must work overtime!"

**Practice II** *Page 170.*

For explanations of answers, refer to the punctuation rules on pages 172–174.

1. **(2)** Mrs. Romano exclaimed, *"F*rankie, the parakeet has disappeared!"
   See Rule 1.

2. **(4)** Frankie answered, "Mom, I don't know why, since it was there when I tried to clean it with the vacuum cleaner*."*
   See Rule 1.

3. **(5)** No error

4. **(5)** No error

5. **(5)** No error

6. **(3)** Alice told Marion she was to stay at home and be a babysitter. Marion exclaimed*, "W*hat a shame!"

See Rule 1.

7. **(5)** No error

8. **(1)** *"After* you turn over the earth, add some plant food and water. Then you'll be ready to plant the flower," concluded the gardener.
   See Rule 1.

9. **(4)** Was it Elsa who said, "Our sales meeting begins at 9:30 A.M. shar*p"?*
   See Rule 4.

10. **(3)** "When will you ever," asked the foreman, *"arrive* at work on time?"
    See Rule 2.

11. **(3)** "I know when I will arrive on time," answered Marie. *"It* will be when my alarm clock is finished being repaired."
    See Rule 2.

12. **(2)** The show is called "Day After Da*y";* it starts at 2:30 P.M.
    See Rule 3.

13. **(3)** He replied encouragingly, "Remember that Ted said, *'L*et Irene wait. I'll interview her as soon as I return.'"
    See Rule 6.

14. **(3)** After having read the third chapter, entitled "Spring-time Planting*," I* felt that I was ready to tackle the gardening job.
    See Rule 7.

15. **(4)** After the vicious dog had attacked the trespasser, the dog's owner said, "Didn't you see the sign that reads 'Beware of Dog' before you entered my propert*y?"*
    See Rule 4.

## OTHER MARKS OF PUNCTUATION
**Practice III** *Page 174.*

For explanations of answers, refer to the punctuation rules on pages 172–174.

1. **(2)** The president's desk was covered with all sorts of business papers<u>: in</u>voices, receipts, minutes of his last meeting, and projected plans for the new building.
See Rule 1.

2. **(1)** We expect to arrive at Kennedy Airport at <u>8:15</u> on Thursday, June 8, 1983.
See Rule 3.

3. **(1)** Although we had met only once, he <u>r</u>ecognized me immediately.
See Rule 4.

4. **(2)** Do you really believe that you were a different person at <u>twenty-nine</u> from the one you are at thirty?
See Rule 5.

5. **(3)** If you are planning to send a present to Laurie, go to the half-yearly sale in the <u>children's</u> department.
See Rule 8.

6. **(1)** <u>Don't</u> forget to write two r's in "deferred".
See Rule 8.

7. **(2)** When I arrived (after a four-hour drive), I found that my <u>cousins</u> weren't at home.
See Rule 8.

8. **(1)** The <u>ex-Senator</u> hoped that his protege's bill would pass the two-thirds mark.
See Rule 7.

9. **(5)** No error

10. **(2)** At 11:45 A.M., the <u>commuters'</u> train pulled them into the jam-packed station.
See Rule 9.

**Practice IV** *Page 176.*

For explanations of answers, refer to the punctuation rules on pages 172–174.

1. **(3)** <u>Henry's</u> new car seems to be a poor sample of this year's cars.
See Rule 9.

2. **(4)** <u>Its</u> wheel is no longer round.
See Rule 9.

3. **(1)** Many <u>experts'</u> skills have been brought to bear upon our energy needs.
See Rule 8.

4. **(2)** Have you ever bought tickets to the <u>Firemen's Ball?</u>
See Rule 9.

5. **(2)** Learn the meanings of the following <u>words:</u> petition, council, and electorate.
See Rule 1.

6. **(4)** Is that pin his or <u>hers?</u>
See Rule 9.

7. **(2)** We listed the stolen <u>items:</u> a ring, a bracelet, and a TV set.
See Rule 1.

8. **(5)** No error

9. **(4)** This book's theme is the <u>development</u> of the Puritan ethic.
See Rule 4.

10. **(2)** Don't call him <u>un-American</u> because he disagrees with your opinions.
See Rule 7.

# CHAPTER 17

# CAPITALIZATION

When I was a young writer, submitting poems and thought pieces to arty little magazines, I refused to capitalize anything—not my own name, not kentucky, not broadway, not belgium, not even e. e. cummings or don marquis' cockroach, archy.

It was a period I was going through when I explained to my courtiers that only God was deserving of capitalization. You can't imagine how that nonsensical pose won approbation with my admirers, but, come to think of it, it never made much of an impression on the editors of *Partisan Review*. When they sent me my usual rejection slip, they always used CAPITAL LETTERS.

—Tim Wolfe
*The Child That's Got His Own*

## *A Word With You . . .*

Some writers, for purposes best known to themselves, use lowercase letters at all times, refusing to capitalize anything. Instead of "Dear Sir" in the salutation of a letter, they prefer "dear sir," that is, when they take the trouble to write a formal letter.

When one is a professional writer with a philosophical point of view about capitalization, one can afford to use lowercase letters. The rest of us had better learn where and when to capitalize. Chapter 17 will help.

Capitalization, like punctuation, is applied according to rules. Study the style sheet and then take the survey test that follows.

---

### CAPITALIZATION STYLE SHEET

---

1. Capitalize the first letter of the first word in a sentence, unless it is a sentence within parentheses.

    *Example:*   Language changes continually (note all the once-slang words in your current dictionary) but slowly.

2. Capitalize the first word of a direct quotation.

    *Example:*   He cautioned, "If you buy a ticket beforehand, you will secure a seat for the performance."

3. Capitalize the word *I*.

    *Example:*   In case you are late, *I* will cover for you.

4. Capitalize the deity, place names, street names, persons' names, organization names, languages, and specific course names.

    *Example:*   God and His universe, Blue Ridge Mountains, Delaware River, Forty-second Street, John Masters, Knights of Columbus, Spanish, History II (not sociology, math, etc.)

5. Capitalize names of important historical events, documents, and ages.

    *Example:*   World War I, Magna Carta, Declaration of Independence, Victorian Era

6. Capitalize days of the week, months, and special holidays.

    *Example:*   Monday, January, Memorial Day

---
**CAPITALIZATION STYLE SHEET**
---

7. Capitalize east, west, north, and south only when they are used as sections of the country, not as directions.

   *Examples:* Rod Lewis lived in the East for three years, then moved to the Midwest.

   Turn east at the next corner.

8. In a title (of a play, book, poem, magazine, etc.) capitalize the first word and each important word.

   *Example:* *Death of a Salesman, The Odyssey, The Wasteland, The Last of the Mohicans*

9. Capitalize the initials of a person's name.

   *Example:* T. J. Phillips

10. Capitalize a title when it is used as a form of address.
    *Do not* capitalize a title when it is not used as a form of address.

    *Examples:* Captain T. J. Phillips

    T. J. Phillips, captain of *Star Lady,* . . .

    The captain of *Star Lady,* T. J. Phillips. . . .

11. Capitalize the first word in each line of poetry.

    *Example:* "A thing of beauty is a joy forever:
    Its loveliness increases . . ."

# Survey Test

---
*Directions:* Place capital letters where they are needed in the following sentences.
---

1. after considering all the facts, i have chosen an appropriate action.

2. don't you think that fred might enjoy owning a french-english dictionary?

3. he said, "leave new jersey at noon, and you will reach new york city by 1 p.m. at the latest."

4. john is planning to take german, geography, history, and economics this year at city college.

5. we're expecting guests for dinner on friday night. i hope you can join us.

6. mary stark bought a chevrolet last tuesday, although she hadn't planned on buying a car this year.

7. in history II we will study the industrial revolution, world war I, world war II, and the atomic age.

8. this course will be offered to adults on mondays, wednesdays, and fridays in the spring only.

9. his original home, in california, was his favorite; and he plans on returning to the west in november.

10. captain and mrs. ryan made reservations at island beach motel on the cape's north shore for labor day.

---

Before beginning Practice 1, check your answers on the Survey Test and review the rules pertaining to the errors you made.

PRACTICE
I

*Directions:* Blacken the circle that corresponds to the number of the capitalization error in each group. If there is no error, blacken number 5.

1. *Our* *History* course this semester highlights ① ② ③ ④ ⑤
     1     2
   *civilizations* of the *East.* *No error*
     3        4    5

2. *My* family plans to move to *Cypress street* in ① ② ③ ④ ⑤
    1                         2
   *Millville,* *Ohio.* *No error*
     3    4    5

3. *"If* you plan see the entire *art* exhibit," *Joan* ① ② ③ ④ ⑤
     1                    2         3
   *said,* *"Be* sure to arrive at 10 A.M." *No error*
     4                        5

4. The *Thompkins'* plans for *Labor day* include ① ② ③ ④ ⑤
         1                  2
   a *visit* to the *beach.* *No error*
      3      4    5

5. *Proceed* two blocks *north* to the traffic light,　①②③④⑤
   　　1　　　　　　　　　　2

   and turn right onto *Rumson Lane. No error*
   　　　　　　　　　　3　　　4　　　5

6. I asked *father* to lend me the *Chevrolet* so that　①②③④⑤
   　　　　1　　　　　　　　　　2

   we can drive to the *Rosemont Club,* which is on
   　　　　　　　　　　　3

   the *east* side of town. *No error*
   　　4　　　　　　　　5

7. Speaking to the *town's Community Action*　①②③④⑤
   　　　　　　　　1　　　　2

   *Council, Dr. j. l. Raio* suggested revamping
   　　2　　　　3

   mental health *services. No error*
   　　　　　　4　　　5

8. This *September,* both of my children, Bob and　①②③④⑤
   　　　1

   Ronny, will be attending *Cedar High school.*
   　　　　　　　　　　　　2　　3　　4

   *No error*
   5

9. Waiting for the *Twenty-second Street* bus, we　①②③④⑤
   　　　　　　　　1

   had time to admire the *arrow shirts* displayed
   　　　　　　　　　　　　2

   in *Stone's Haberdashery. No error*
   　3　　　4　　　　　5

10. *"Why* don't you read the *Winston Item,"* said　①②③④⑤
    　1　　　　　　　　　　2

    *Mother, "and* check for sales on air condition-
    　3　　4

    ers?" *No error*
    　　　5

11. *Uncle* John and my *father* are going to *Crystal*　①②③④⑤
    　1　　　　　　　2　　　　　　　　3

    *Lake* on *saturday* to try out their new fishing
    　　　　4

    gear. *No error*
    　　　5

12. I've already crossed the _Atlantic_ _ocean_ by air;    ① ② ③ ④ ⑤
                             1      2
   but this summer, in _July,_ I hope to make the
                     3
   crossing on an _Italian_ freighter. _No error_
                 4             5

13. _More_ and more elementary _schools_ are teaching    ① ② ③ ④ ⑤
    1                       2
   in _spanish_ in order to meet the needs of the
       3
   _community._ _No error_
     4      5

14. You recall _Reverend_ _Hempstead_ saying that he    ① ② ③ ④ ⑤
               1       2
   will study _religious_ philosophies of the _east._
             3                   4
   _No error_
     5

15. The Ridgedale _Garden_ _club_ developed a    ① ② ③ ④ ⑤
               1     2
   hybrid _rose_ and named it _Everlasting_
         3               4
   _Beauty._ _No error_
       5

16. Including _caucasians,_ _African-Americans,_ and    ① ② ③ ④ ⑤
         1          2
   _Asians,_ the population of _Winfield,_ Pennsylvania
    3                4
   has grown to one and a half million. _No error_
                         5

**PRACTICE**
**II**

*Directions:*    Blacken the circle that corresponds to the number of the incorrect sentence in each group. If there is no error, blacken number 5.

1. (1) Each year our community celebrates the Fourth Of July with races, entertainment, and fireworks.
   (2) Because of its beauty and natural resources, the state of Colorado now boasts many new residents.
   (3) John works for the Ford Motor Company in Cleveland.
   (4) I asked Gerry, "Do you think we'll get to the game in time for the first quarter?"
   (5) No error

   ① ② ③ ④ ⑤

2. (1) Last year we celebrated that Holiday on a Monday.
   (2) This year the holiday falls in the third week of September.
   (3) Shall we cross the bridge or take the tunnel?
   (4) Archaeologists found evidence that the pagan gods were worshipped on that spot.
   (5) No error

   ① ② ③ ④ ⑤

3. (1) Dean Jones just became an administrator this September.
   (2) Andy joined the travel-American Club and enjoyed a six week tour with the group.
   (3) We have a subscription to the *Reader's Digest.*
   (4) *The Bridges of Madison County* was a very popular book.
   (5) No error

   ① ② ③ ④ ⑤

4. (1) "Don't forget your umbrella," Aunt Jean said, "for you know the forecast indicates rain for today."

   (2) At Ohio State university, students take courses year-round.

   (3) Our curriculum needs to stress reading skills in the areas of science, social studies, and American literature.

   (4) Evan Greene, who lives in Syracuse, New York, joined the Professional Photographers Club.

   (5) No error

   ① ② ③ ④ ⑤

5. (1) The train trip was most scenic since the route wound through the White Mountains and ended at Pleasant Lake.

   (2) when did you say that Bud had called me?

   (3) Last summer, in July, we camped in Colorado.

   (4) That company, Ferro Metals, has increased its volume of business through advanced advertising and promotion techniques.

   (5) No error

   ① ② ③ ④ ⑤

6. (1) In the West, we plan to visit the Grand Canyon as well as the southern half of California.

   (2) The course, interestingly enough, was entitled, "God and His Relationship to Man."

   (3) Let's make a date to meet on Sunday, June 2nd.

   (4) The poem reads: Up the airy mountain,
                         down the rushy glen . . .

   (5) No error

   ① ② ③ ④ ⑤

7. (1) We're leaving Kennedy International Airport at 8 P.M., and we arrive in Lisbon seven hours later.

   (2) My friend, Fred, was elected President of the Rescue Squad.

   (3) "This new wing contains our intensive care unit," explained the director.

   ① ② ③ ④ ⑤

(4) France and Belgium are both French-speaking countries.

(5) No error

8. (1) The group turned its attention to a tall, drawling Texan in its midst.

(2) A well-known senator was accused of un-American activities.

(3) "Don't do that!" said Jack. "you'll ruin the machine!"

(4) Each time I see the Tappan Zee Bridge, I am impressed by its size and beauty.

(5) No error

① ② ③ ④ ⑤

9. (1) A river in Wisconsin is called the Fox River.

(2) The Indian language is composed of many dialects.

(3) The Empire State Building is still an impressive sight although it is no longer the tallest building in the world.

(4) While you are in London, be sure to shop at Simpson's, Ltd.

(5) No error

① ② ③ ④ ⑤

10. (1) It was two years ago that judge Billings was appointed to the bench.

(2) I remember seeing Uncle John at the family gathering; but, as I recall, my aunt was not there.

(3) Our study group discussed a few books of the Bible.

(4) An essay question regarding the French Revolution might involve the major causes leading up to the disquiet of the times.

(5) No error

① ② ③ ④ ⑤

# Chapter 17  Capitalization

**Survey Test** *Page 183.*

1. After considering all the facts, I have chosen an appropriate action.

2. Don't you think that Fred might enjoy owning a French-English dictionary?

3. He said, "Leave New Jersey at noon, and you will reach New York City by 1 P.M. at the latest."

4. John is planning to take German, geography, history, and economics this year at City College.

5. We're expecting guests for dinner on Friday night. I hope you can join us.

6. Mary Stark bought a Chevrolet last Tuesday, although she hadn't planned on buying a car this year.

7. In History II we will study the Industrial Revolution, World War I, World War II, and the Atomic Age.

8. This course will be offered to adults on Mondays, Wednesdays, and Fridays in the spring only.

9. His original home, in California, was his favorite; and he plans on returning to the West in November.

10. Captain and Mrs. Ryan made reservations at Island Beach Motel on the Cape's north shore for Labor Day.

**Practice I** *Page 184.*

1. **(2)** Our *history* course this semester highlights civilizations of the East.
    Capitalize only *specific* course names, ie., History IA.

2. **(2)** My family plans to move to *Cypress Street* in Millville, Ohio.
    Capitalize entire street names.

3. **(4)** "If you plan to see the entire art exhibit," Joan said, *"be* sure to arrive at 10 A.M."
    Do not capitalize the first word in a broken quotation unless it is the beginning of a complete thought.

4. **(2)** The Thompkins' plans for *Labor Day* include a visit to the beach.
    Capitalize the name of a holiday.

5. **(5)** No error

6. **(1)** I asked *Father* to lend me the Chevrolet so that we can drive to the Rosemont Club, which is on the east side of town.
    Capitalize Father or Mother when they are used as names.

7. **(3)** Speaking to the town's Community Action Council, Dr. *J. L.* Raio suggested revamping mental health services.
    Capitalize initials in a name.

8. **(4)** This September both of my children, Bob and Ronny, will be attending Cedar High *School.*
    Capitalize the entire name of a school.

9. **(2)** Waiting for the Twenty-second Street bus, we had time to admire the *Arrow* shirts displayed in Stone's Haberdashery.
    Capitalize the name of a company.

10. **(5)** No error

11. **(4)** Uncle John and my father are going to Crystal Lake on *Saturday* to try out their new fishing gear.

Capitalize the names of the days of the week.

12. **(2)** I've already crossed the Atlantic *Ocean* by air; but this summer, in July, I hope to make the crossing on an Italian freighter.

Capitalize the entire name of an ocean.

13. **(3)** More and more elementary schools are teaching in *Spanish* in order to meet the needs of the community.

Capitalize the name of a language.

14. **(4)** You recall Reverend Hempstead saying that he will study religious philosophies of the *East*.

Capitalize North, South, East, and West when they designate an area.

15. **(2)** The Ridgedale Garden *Club* developed a hybrid rose and named it Everlasting Beauty.

Capitalize the entire name of a club.

16. **(1)** Including *Caucasians,* African-Americans and Asians, the population of Winfield, Pennsylvania, has grown to one and a half million.

Capitalize the name of a race.

**Practice II**

*Page 186.*

1. **(1)** Each year our community celebrates the Fourth *of* July with races, entertainment, and fireworks.

2. **(1)** Last year we celebrated that *holiday* on a Monday.

3. **(2)** Andy joined the *Travel-American Club* and enjoyed a six-week tour with the group.

4. **(2)** At Ohio State *University,* students take courses year-round.

5. **(2)** *When* did you say that Bud had called me?

6. **(4)** The poem reads:
Up the airy mountain
*Down* the rushy glen . . .

7. **(2)** My friend, Fred, was elected *president* of the Rescue Squad.

8. **(3)** "Don't do that!" said Jack. *"You'll* ruin the machine!"

9. **(5)** No error

10. **(1)** It was two years ago that *Judge* Billings was appointed to the bench.

# CHAPTER 18

# SPELLING

"The other people that was involved in the Lincoln assination later exexuded or killed themselves. Mary Tood Lincoln locked herself up in a closet and went crazy. She was declared mentally insane and put in a insane silome.

One day a long time later a man walked into Lincoln's office and found his son, Robert Tood, burning some of his daddy's old pappers. The man asked him why he was burning the pappers and Robert Tood said, 'Maybe they will criminate one of the members of the goverment,' which his daddy was in."

—Bill Lawrence, Editor
*Then Some Other Stuff Happened*

## A Word With You . . .

It isn't easy to become a good speller; in fact, many people never master the art. The high school student whose work is quoted above proves our point.

One famous English writer, George Bernard Shaw, was critical of our many spelling rules and the strange appearance of many of our words. He invested a goodly sum of money in a campaign to reform certain spelling practices. Shaw, however, was an excellent speller, regardless of his complaints.

There is no magic formula for learning how to spell. The ability to spell correctly results from persistent study. Here are some useful suggestions for studying spelling:

1. Use a small notebook exclusively for recording your personal spelling problem words.
2. Each time that you discover a problem word, enter it in your notebook. Check a dictionary for the correct syllabification and pronunciation.
3. Look at the word and say it in syllables.
4. Try to apply a rule that will help you to understand *why* the word is spelled as it is.

5. Close your eyes and picture the way the word looks.
6. Write the word. Check it. Rewrite it if necessary.
7. Review words you have already studied until you are absolutely sure that you know how to spell them.

Some words are correctly spelled in more than one way. For example, the word *catalogue* appears in one dictionary in the following way:

**cat-a-logue,** n. Also **catalog** . . .

In another dictionary, the entry says:

**catalogue** or **catalog,** n. . . .

In the examples above, the use of the words *also* and *or* is important. For example, while *or* means that both spellings are equally common, *also* means that the first spelling is more common. How do you know for sure what policy a dictionary follows? Look at the front of the dictionary where all the rules and standards for that dictionary are explained. When in doubt, choose the first spelling unless the dictionary entry explains that there is a special reason for choosing the second.

There are many commonly misspelled words. Careful study of the list beginning on page 216 of this chapter will improve your spelling. There are also a number of hints and rules that are helpful in learning to spell.

# Building Blocks of Words: Consonants, Vowels, Syllables

Of the twenty-six letters in the alphabet, twenty-one letters are consonants: b, c, d, f, g, h, j, k, l, m, n, p, q, r, s, t, v, w, x, y, z. The other five letters of the alphabet are vowels: a, e, i, o, u. Sometimes the consonant y is used as a vowel. When a consonant or consonants are combined with at least one vowel, a word or syllable results.

*Example:*                                        let

A syllable is a word or part of a word pronounced with a single uninterrupted sound.

Nonsense syllable:  ki
Meaningful syllable:  sat

Learning to spell a long word is a much easier task if you divide the word into syllables.

*Example:*          complacency = com • pla • cen • cy

You can learn to spell each syllable and, finally, put the word together.

## ADDING TO WORDS

Many words are formed by adding to the root (basic part) of the word. Prefixes are added to the beginning of a word, whereas suffixes are added to the end of a word.

| prefix | root | suffix |
|:---:|:---:|:---:|
| *dis*quiet | quiet | quiet*ly* |

# Rules Concerning Spelling

### RULE 1:

In most cases, a prefix can be added to a word without changing the spelling of that word.

| Prefix | (Meaning) | Word Combination |
|---|---|---|
| il | (not) | literate = illiterate |
| ir | (not) | regular = irregular |

PRACTICE
I

*Directions:*   Add the correct prefix from the list below to each of the following words.

| ac- | il- | in- | mis- | over- | mal- |
|---|---|---|---|---|---|
| dis- | ir- | un- | re- | im- | co- |

1. _____instate

2. _____illusion

3. _____necessary

4. _____operate

5. _____mortal

6. _____spell

7. _____reverent

8. _____legal

9. _____climate

10. _____rate

11. _____content

12. _____accurate

## RULE 2:

When adding a suffix that begins with a consonant, the spelling of most words does not change.

|             | Word    | Suffix |   |              |
| ----------- | ------- | ------ | - | ------------ |
|             | careless | ness  | = | carelessness |
|             | active  | ly     | = | actively     |
| *Exceptions:* | true  | ly     | = | truly        |
|             | due     | ly     | = | duly         |

## RULE 3:

Suffixes do change the spelling of words that end in *y*.

| Word   | Suffix |   |           |
| ------ | ------ | - | --------- |
| happy  | ness   | = | happiness |
| hearty | ly     | = | heartily  |

## RULE 4:

When adding a suffix that begins with a vowel to a word that ends in *e*, drop the final *e*.

| Word     | Suffix |   |            |
| -------- | ------ | - | ---------- |
| fame     | ous    | = | famous     |
| continue | ous    | = | continuous |

*Exceptions:*  Words that end in *-ge* or *-ce* must retain the final *e* to maintain the soft sound of the *g* or *c*.

|                       | Word    | Suffix |   |            |
| --------------------- | ------- | ------ | - | ---------- |
|                       | courage | ous    | = | courageous |
|                       | notice  | able   | = | noticeable |
| *Another exception:*  | is the word *dye*. |  |  |    |
|                       | dye     | ing    | = | dyeing     |

PRACTICE
II

*Directions:* Opposite each word below is a suffix that, when combined with the word, forms a new word. In the space provided, write the new word, making sure to spell it correctly.

| Word | Suffix | | |
|------|--------|---|---|
| 1. announce | ment | = | _____ |
| 2. dye | ing | = | _____ |
| 3. snappy | ness | = | _____ |
| 4. associate | ion | = | _____ |
| 5. dispense | able | = | _____ |
| 6. definite | ly | = | _____ |
| 7. economic | al | = | _____ |
| 8. courage | ous | = | _____ |
| 9. move | able | = | _____ |
| 10. necessary | ly | = | _____ |
| 11. practical | ly | = | _____ |
| 12. port | able | = | _____ |
| 13. rude | ness | = | _____ |
| 14. guide | ance | = | _____ |
| 15. true | ly | = | _____ |

PRACTICE
III

*Directions:* Blacken the circle that corresponds to the number of the incorrectly spelled word in each group. If there is no error, blacken number 5.

1. (1) unimportant   (4) irational      ① ② ③ ④ ⑤
   (2) revelation    (5) no error
   (3) cumulative

2. (1) brighter      (4) berate        ① ② ③ ④ ⑤
   (2) happyness     (5) no error
   (3) unaccustomed

3. (1) impossible    (4) mispell       ① ② ③ ④ ⑤
   (2) cooperation   (5) no error
   (3) inactive

4. (1) commencment   (4) extraction    ① ② ③ ④ ⑤
   (2) coverage      (5) no error
   (3) practically

5. (1) safty      (4) amusement      ① ② ③ ④ ⑤
   (2) forgiveness      (5) no error
   (3) shining

6. (1) becoming      (4) actually      ① ② ③ ④ ⑤
   (2) truly      (5) no error
   (3) plainness

7. (1) adorable      (4) supervise      ① ② ③ ④ ⑤
   (2) contagious      (5) no error
   (3) acumulate

8. (1) loneliness      (4) noticable      ① ② ③ ④ ⑤
   (2) personal      (5) no error
   (3) barely

9. (1) continuation      (4) usage      ① ② ③ ④ ⑤
   (2) arguement      (5) no error
   (3) ridiculous

10. (1) surprised      (4) virtuous      ① ② ③ ④ ⑤
    (2) acquisitiveness      (5) no error
    (3) carefully

---

# The Role of Accent Marks

A word that contains more than one syllable has an accent on one of those syllables. Say this word in syllables: punc • tu • ate. Which syllable is stressed? Yes, the first syllable is stressed or accented, and its accent is marked in this way:

punc´ • tu • ate

*Directions:* The following words have been divided into syllables. In each word, place an accent mark to show which syllable is stressed. The first word is done for you.

1. paint´ • er
2. pri • vate
3. of • fice
4. e • con • o • my
5. ad • vise
6. bal • ance
7. dis • sat • is • fy
8. de • vel • op • ment

9. in • di • vid • u • al
10. pre • fer
11. pref • er • ence
12. psy • chol • o • gy
13. vac • il • late
14. u • nan • i • mous
15. wretch • ed

## RULE 5:

When changing the form of a one-syllable action word that ends in a consonant preceded by a vowel, double the final consonant.

| | |
|---|---|
| plan | planned |
| sun | sunning |
| run | runner |

## RULE 6:

Double the final consonant when changing the form of a two-syllable word that ends in a consonant preceded by a vowel *and* that is accented on the second syllable.

| | |
|---|---|
| re<u>fer</u> | re<u>fer</u>red |
| oc<u>cur</u> | oc<u>cur</u>red |
| oc<u>cur</u> | oc<u>cur</u>rence |

## RULE 7:

In a two- or three-syllable word, if the accent changes from the final syllable to a preceding one when a suffix is added (prefer, preference), do not double the final consonant.

| | |
|---|---|
| re<u>fer</u> | <u>re</u>ference |
| con<u>fer</u> | <u>con</u>ference |

PRACTICE
V

*Directions:* Blacken the circle that corresponds to the number of the incorrectly spelled word in each group. If there is no error, blacken number 5.

1. (1) referred     (4) winding     ① ② ③ ④ ⑤
   (2) preferrence     (5) no error
   (3) stunning

2. (1) thinner     (4) detered     ① ② ③ ④ ⑤
   (2) conferred     (5) no error
   (3) reference

3. (1) binder     (4) reared     ① ② ③ ④ ⑤
   (2) funnier     (5) no error
   (3) pictured

4. (1) cunning     (4) banning     ① ② ③ ④ ⑤
   (2) preferable     (5) no error
   (3) deterent

5. (1) preferred     (4) occurence     ① ② ③ ④ ⑤
   (2) canning     (5) no error
   (3) fanned

## RULE 8:

Use *i* before *e* except after *c*. *Examples:* relief, receipt. *Exception:* Use *e* before *i* in words that sound like ā. *Examples:* neighbor, weigh.

*Other exceptions:* weird, seize, either, leisure, neither.

PRACTICE
VI

*Directions:* Complete the following words with *ei* or *ie*.

1. n_____ce     6. rec_____ve
2. dec_____ve     7. conc_____ve
3. th_____f     8. bel_____f
4. rel_____ve     9. n_____ther
5. n_____gh     10. s_____ze

**RULE 9:**

There are rules for forming the plurals of words. Following are the rules and a few examples of each.

A. Most words form plurals by adding *s*.

| | |
|---|---|
| radio | radios |
| towel | towels |
| chair | chairs |
| tray | trays |

B. Words ending in *y* preceded by a consonant form plurals by changing *y* to *i* and adding *es*.

| | |
|---|---|
| sky | skies |
| story | stories |

C. Words ending in *o* preceded by a consonant form plurals by adding *es*.

| | |
|---|---|
| tomato | tomatoes |
| hero | heroes |

*Exception:*  words ending in o, preceded by a consonant, but referring to music, form their plurals by adding only *s*.

| | |
|---|---|
| alto | altos |
| piano | pianos |

D. Words ending in *s*, *sh*, *ch*, and *x* form plurals by adding *es*.

| | |
|---|---|
| bunch | bunches |
| sex | sexes |
| boss | bosses |
| crush | crushes |

E. A compound word forms its plural by adding *s* to the principal word.

*fathers*-in-law
baby*sitters*

F. Words ending in *-ful* form their plurals by adding *s*.

mouthfuls
cupfuls

G. Some words have one spelling for singular and plural.

> deer
> trout
> Chinese
> sheep

H. Numbers and letters form plurals by adding 's.

> 5's                     h's

I. Some words form their plurals by irregular changes.

| | |
|---|---|
| thief | thieves |
| knife | knives |
| leaf | leaves |
| woman | women |
| child | children |
| tooth | teeth |
| louse | lice |
| crisis | crises |
| alumnus | alumni |
| datum | data |
| appendix | appendices |

PRACTICE
VII

_Directions:_   Blacken the circle that corresponds to the number of the incorrectly spelled word in each group. If there is no error, blacken number 5.

1. (1) geese
   (2) mouthsful
   (3) commanders-in-chief
   (4) firemen
   (5) no error
   ① ② ③ ④ ⑤

2. (1) Chinese's
   (2) bases
   (3) workmen
   (4) ?'s
   (5) no error
   ① ② ③ ④ ⑤

3. (1) bacilli
   (2) son-in-laws
   (3) series
   (4) handkerchiefs
   (5) no error
   ① ② ③ ④ ⑤

4. (1) women
   (2) alumni
   (3) passersby
   (4) mice
   (5) no error
   ① ② ③ ④ ⑤

5. (1) 8s    (4) men-of-war    ① ② ③ ④ ⑤
   (2) Frenchmen    (5) no error
   (3) alumni

---

## RULE 10:

Following are rules regarding *sede, ceed,* and *cede.*

A. Only one word is spelled with a *sede* ending:

supersede

B. Only three words are spelled with a *ceed* ending:

succeed    exceed    proceed

C. All other words of this type are spelled with a *cede* ending:

precede    recede    concede

# Spelling Review

PRACTICE
VIII    *Directions:*    Blacken the circle that corresponds to the number of the incorrectly spelled word in each group. If there is no error, blacken number 5.

1. (1) acknowledge    (4) commodity    ① ② ③ ④ ⑤
   (2) fireman    (5) no error
   (3) conclusivly

2. (1) incurred    (4) herald    ① ② ③ ④ ⑤
   (2) coranation    (5) no error
   (3) voluntary

3. (1) simular    (4) quizzes    ① ② ③ ④ ⑤
   (2) bulletin    (5) no error
   (3) bored

4. (1) duchess    (4) fertile    ① ② ③ ④ ⑤
   (2) achevement    (5) no error
   (3) monarchial

5. (1) distribute    (4) tonnage    ① ② ③ ④ ⑤
   (2) sieze    (5) no error
   (3) premises

6. (1) monthly     (4) dupped     ① ② ③ ④ ⑤
   (2) primarily     (5) no error
   (3) condemned

7. (1) cancellation     (4) utilize     ① ② ③ ④ ⑤
   (2) derrick     (5) no error
   (3) pertinant

8. (1) nowadays     (4) guardian     ① ② ③ ④ ⑤
   (2) courtesies     (5) no error
   (3) negotiate

9. (1) loot     (4) axle     ① ② ③ ④ ⑤
   (2) faculties     (5) no error
   (3) loveable

10. (1) fragrance     (4) athletic     ① ② ③ ④ ⑤
    (2) accompanied     (5) no error
    (3) preference

## PRACTICE IX

_Directions:_   Blacken the circle that corresponds to the number of the incorrectly spelled word in each group. If there is no error, blacken number 5.

1. (1) liquify     (4) dissolve     ① ② ③ ④ ⑤
   (2) disappear     (5) no error
   (3) swirling

2. (1) inexorable     (4) arboreal
   (2) mercyful     (5) no error
   (3) potable

3. (1) disolution     (4) diseases     ① ② ③ ④ ⑤
   (2) agreeable     (5) no error
   (3) planned

4. (1) minimize     (4) candidacy     ① ② ③ ④ ⑤
   (2) sophomore     (5) no error
   (3) attorneys

5. (1) unnecessary     (4) judgment     ① ② ③ ④ ⑤
   (2) carnage     (5) no error
   (3) wierd

6. (1) roses            (4) churches      ① ② ③ ④ ⑤
   (2) goverment        (5) no error
   (3) absence

7. (1) emergency        (4) citizen       ① ② ③ ④ ⑤
   (2) eager            (5) no error
   (3) cordialy

8. (1) benefit          (4) peice         ① ② ③ ④ ⑤
   (2) boxes            (5) no error
   (3) consequence

9. (1) journey          (4) relief        ① ② ③ ④ ⑤
   (2) majority         (5) no error
   (3) necessarily

10. (1) yacht           (4) principle     ① ② ③ ④ ⑤
    (2) traveler        (5) no error
    (3) profession

PRACTICE
X    _Directions:_    Blacken the circle that corresponds to the number of the incorrectly spelled word in each group. If there is no error, blacken number 5.

1. (1) overrate         (4) greenness     ① ② ③ ④ ⑤
   (2) misapprehend     (5) no error
   (3) habitualy

2. (1) deferred         (4) defference    ① ② ③ ④ ⑤
   (2) hoping           (5) no error
   (3) approval

3. (1) candys           (4) files         ① ② ③ ④ ⑤
   (2) valleys          (5) no error
   (3) torches

4. (1) immaterial       (4) unabated      ① ② ③ ④ ⑤
   (2) dissapoint       (5) no error
   (3) practically

5. (1) potatos          (4) sopranos      ① ② ③ ④ ⑤
   (2) teeth            (5) no error
   (3) radios

6. (1) preparing  (4) controlled  ① ② ③ ④ ⑤
   (2) writing  (5) no error
   (3) propeling

7. (1) crises  (4) trucksful  ① ② ③ ④ ⑤
   (2) geese  (5) no error
   (3) concertos

8. (1) truely  (4) famous  ① ② ③ ④ ⑤
   (2) moving  (5) no error
   (3) running

9. (1) shelves  (4) churches  ① ② ③ ④ ⑤
   (2) benches  (5) no error
   (3) knives

10. (1) salarys  (4) nameless  ① ② ③ ④ ⑤
    (2) basketfuls  (5) no error
    (3) reddest

11. (1) disagree  (4) casually  ① ② ③ ④ ⑤
    (2) benefited  (5) no error
    (3) gases

12. (1) oxen  (4) solves  ① ② ③ ④ ⑤
    (2) desirable  (5) no error
    (3) data

PRACTICE
XI

_Directions:_  Blacken the circle that corresponds to the number of the incorrectly spelled word in each group. If there is no error, blacken number 5.

1. (1) belief  (4) weigh  ① ② ③ ④ ⑤
   (2) achieve  (5) no error
   (3) neice

2. (1) yield  (4) releif  ① ② ③ ④ ⑤
   (2) neighbor  (5) no error
   (3) deceive

3. (1) benefited  (4) equipped  ① ② ③ ④ ⑤
   (2) appealed  (5) no error
   (3) refered

4. (1) preference     (4) colonel     ① ② ③ ④ ⑤
    (2) reference     (5) no error
    (3) asessment

5. (1) stationery     (4) similar     ① ② ③ ④ ⑤
    (2) stationary     (5) no error
    (3) sophomore

6. (1) primarily     (4) receit     ① ② ③ ④ ⑤
    (2) principal     (5) no error
    (3) principle

7. (1) aquired     (4) height     ① ② ③ ④ ⑤
    (2) brief     (5) no error
    (3) contemptible

8. (1) erred     (4) lieutenent     ① ② ③ ④ ⑤
    (2) millionaire     (5) no error
    (3) misanthrope

9. (1) adjournament     (4) digestible     ① ② ③ ④ ⑤
    (2) caucus     (5) no error
    (3) contagious

10. (1) cheff     (4) preceding     ① ② ③ ④ ⑤
    (2) calendar     (5) no error
    (3) macaroni

## PRACTICE XII

_Directions:_ Blacken the circle that corresponds to the number of the incorrectly spelled word in each group. If there is no error, blacken number 5.

1. (1) changeable     (4) fortissimo
    (2) atheletic     (5) no error
    (3) grammar

2. (1) filial     (4) treachery     ① ② ③ ④ ⑤
    (2) leisure     (5) no error
    (3) temperture

3. (1) bulletin     (4) kindergarten     ① ② ③ ④ ⑤
    (2) amendment     (5) no error
    (3) incessent

4. (1) legitiment      (4) courtesies      ① ② ③ ④ ⑤
   (2) vivisection      (5) no error
   (3) pervade

5. (1) prefer      (4) patrolled      ① ② ③ ④ ⑤
   (2) preferred      (5) no error
   (3) preference

6. (1) ninth      (4) hideous      ① ② ③ ④ ⑤
   (2) correspondent      (5) no error
   (3) canon

7. (1) apparently      (4) forfeit      ① ② ③ ④ ⑤
   (2) foreign      (5) no error
   (3) carriage

8. (1) aggregate      (4) tetnus      ① ② ③ ④ ⑤
   (2) massacre      (5) no error
   (3) omissions

9. (1) exceed      (4) procedure      ① ② ③ ④ ⑤
   (2) intercede      (5) no error
   (3) proceed

10. (1) fundimental      (4) penitentiary      ① ② ③ ④ ⑤
    (2) misspell      (5) no error
    (3) odyssey

**PRACTICE XIII**

*Directions:*   Blacken the circle that corresponds to the number of the incorrectly spelled word in each group. If there is no error, blacken number 5.

1. (1) torches      (4) shelves      ① ② ③ ④ ⑤
   (2) salaries      (5) no error
   (3) valleys

2. (1) absense      (4) citizen      ① ② ③ ④ ⑤
   (2) gases      (5) no error
   (3) accident

3. (1) executive      (4) eager      ① ② ③ ④ ⑤
   (2) divide      (5) no error
   (3) discusion

4. (1) contrary   (4) banquet   ① ② ③ ④ ⑤
 (2) atheletic   (5) no error
 (3) critical

5. (1) association   (4) decide   ① ② ③ ④ ⑤
 (2) character   (5) no error
 (3) earliest

6. (1) Wenesday   (4) executive   ① ② ③ ④ ⑤
 (2) knives   (5) no error
 (3) concerning

7. (1) appreciate   (4) numerous   ① ② ③ ④ ⑤
 (2) except   (5) no error
 (3) scene

8. (1) national   (4) volume   ① ② ③ ④ ⑤
 (2) posession   (5) no error
 (3) industrious

9. (1) patient   (4) probably   ① ② ③ ④ ⑤
 (2) quantity   (5) no error
 (3) boundary

10. (1) warrant   (4) libary   ① ② ③ ④ ⑤
 (2) laboratory   (5) no error
 (3) interesting

PRACTICE
XIV   *Directions:*   Blacken the circle that corresponds to the number of the incorrectly spelled word in each group. If there is no error, blacken number 5.

1. (1) biased   (4) vacuum   ① ② ③ ④ ⑤
 (2) aberation   (5) no error
 (3) wholly

2. (1) capitol   (4) essential   ① ② ③ ④ ⑤
 (2) ecstasy   (5) no error
 (3) embarrass

3. (1) asertain   (4) diocese   ① ② ③ ④ ⑤
 (2) correlation   (5) no error
 (3) abeyance

4. (1) ninth     (4) official     ① ② ③ ④ ⑤
   (2) resileince     (5) no error
   (3) nickel

5. (1) salable     (4) policy     ① ② ③ ④ ⑤
   (2) ordinance     (5) no error
   (3) illegitimate

6. (1) subversive     (4) prairie     ① ② ③ ④ ⑤
   (2) predatory     (5) no error
   (3) lucritive

7. (1) pacifist     (4) surfiet     ① ② ③ ④ ⑤
   (2) senior     (5) no error
   (3) source

8. (1) weild     (4) transaction     ① ② ③ ④ ⑤
   (2) vacillate     (5) no error
   (3) vengeance

9. (1) queue     (4) marital     ① ② ③ ④ ⑤
   (2) masquerade     (5) no error
   (3) loose

10. (1) psicology     (4) impeccable     ① ② ③ ④ ⑤
    (2) possession     (5) no error
    (3) imminent

**PRACTICE XV**

*Directions:* Blacken the circle that corresponds to the number of the incorrectly spelled word in each group. If there is no error, blacken number 5.

1. (1) derogatory     (4) yacht     ① ② ③ ④ ⑤
   (2) neglagible     (5) no error
   (3) rehearsal

2. (1) queue     (4) gelatin     ① ② ③ ④ ⑤
   (2) jeopardy     (5) no error
   (3) forfiet

3. (1) bureau     (4) harass     ① ② ③ ④ ⑤
   (2) blamable     (5) no error
   (3) desecration

4. (1) falibility     (4) remnant     ① ② ③ ④ ⑤
  (2) heinous     (5) no error
  (3) myriad

5. (1) hygienic     (4) prommisory     ① ② ③ ④ ⑤
  (2) medallion     (5) no error
  (3) midget

6. (1) complacency     (4) realize     ① ② ③ ④ ⑤
  (2) efemeral     (5) no error
  (3) exaggerate

7. (1) lacquer     (4) emolument     ① ② ③ ④ ⑤
  (2) currency     (5) no error
  (3) exortation

8. (1) apologetic     (4) exzema     ① ② ③ ④ ⑤
  (2) coroner     (5) no error
  (3) clique

9. (1) disatisfied     (4) surgeon     ① ② ③ ④ ⑤
  (2) moribund     (5) no error
  (3) warrant

10. (1) defered     (4) intercede     ① ② ③ ④ ⑤
  (2) extraordinary     (5) no error
  (3) journal

## PRACTICE XVI

_Directions:_ Blacken the circle that corresponds to the number of the incorrectly spelled word in each group. If there is no error, blacken number 5.

1. (1) responsibility     (4) rhetoric     ① ② ③ ④ ⑤
  (2) resonence     (5) no error
  (3) rheostat

2. (1) salient     (4) parliament     ① ② ③ ④ ⑤
  (2) patronize     (5) no error
  (3) pateint

3. (1) secretery     (4) innocuous     ① ② ③ ④ ⑤
  (2) piquancy     (5) no error
  (3) integrity

4. (1) diphtheria    (4) cemetery    ① ② ③ ④ ⑤
   (2) distinguised    (5) no error
   (3) category

5. (1) abscess    (4) ingenuous    ① ② ③ ④ ⑤
   (2) chamois    (5) no error
   (3) effects

6. (1) accessible    (4) inimitable    ① ② ③ ④ ⑤
   (2) chauffur    (5) no error
   (3) elaborate

7. (1) impromptu    (4) precede    ① ② ③ ④ ⑤
   (2) incongruity    (5) no error
   (3) permissable

8. (1) tremendous    (4) tariff    ① ② ③ ④ ⑤
   (2) punctilious    (5) no error
   (3) recognizible

9. (1) reasonable    (4) repetitious    ① ② ③ ④ ⑤
   (2) mischivous    (5) no error
   (3) picnicking

10. (1) sobriquet    (4) stretch    ① ② ③ ④ ⑤
   (2) soveriegn    (5) no error
   (3) staunch

**PRACTICE XVII**

_Directions:_ Blacken the circle that corresponds to the number of the incorrectly spelled word in each group. If there is no error, blacken number 5.

1. (1) addressee    (4) murmuring    ① ② ③ ④ ⑤
   (2) carburator    (5) no error
   (3) intercede

2. (1) biscut    (4) preceding    ① ② ③ ④ ⑤
   (2) financier    (5) no error
   (3) previous

3. (1) hearth    (4) heritage    ① ② ③ ④ ⑤
   (2) bounteous    (5) no error
   (3) judgment

4. (1) aversion    (4) bookkeeping    ① ② ③ ④ ⑤
   (2) aquatic    (5) no error
   (3) facilitation

5. (1) dilapidated    (4) regrettable    ① ② ③ ④ ⑤
   (2) function    (5) no error
   (3) relevent

6. (1) dearth    (4) wethar    ① ② ③ ④ ⑤
   (2) deceive    (5) no error
   (3) proceed

7. (1) excede    (4) vacuum    ① ② ③ ④ ⑤
   (2) feudal    (5) no error
   (3) grandeur

8. (1) realize    (4) matinee    ① ② ③ ④ ⑤
   (2) foriegn    (5) no error
   (3) nevertheless

9. (1) criticism    (4) preferably    ① ② ③ ④ ⑤
   (2) plagiarism    (5) no error
   (3) equiped

10. (1) beatitude    (4) succeed    ① ② ③ ④ ⑤
   (2) corruggated    (5) no error
   (3) existence

## PRACTICE XVIII

*Directions:* Blacken the circle that corresponds to the number of the incorrectly spelled word in each group. If there is no error, blacken number 5.

1. (1) angle    (4) compel    ① ② ③ ④ ⑤
   (2) conciliatory    (5) no error
   (3) exersise

2. (1) description    (4) publicity    ① ② ③ ④ ⑤
   (2) hindrence    (5) no error
   (3) memoir

3. (1) belligerent    (4) decieve    ① ② ③ ④ ⑤
   (2) dearth    (5) no error
   (3) equator

4. (1) bankruptcy     (4) demurrer     ① ② ③ ④ ⑤
   (2) deliberate     (5) no error
   (3) histrionic

5. (1) crystallized     (4) masquerade     ① ② ③ ④ ⑤
   (2) mackeral     (5) no error
   (3) maintenance

6. (1) sandwich     (4) scissors     ① ② ③ ④ ⑤
   (2) peculiar     (5) no error
   (3) neumonia

7. (1) temperment     (4) occur     ① ② ③ ④ ⑤
   (2) summarize     (5) no error
   (3) scripture

8. (1) abundence     (4) colossal     ① ② ③ ④ ⑤
   (2) citation     (5) no error
   (3) clamorous

9. (1) acumulation     (4) adage     ① ② ③ ④ ⑤
   (2) circumstantial     (5) no error
   (3) adoption

10. (1) apparatus     (4) allege     ① ② ③ ④ ⑤
    (2) anceint     (5) no error
    (3) amplify

PRACTICE
XIX

_Directions:_ Blacken the circle that corresponds to the number of the incorrectly spelled word in each group. If there is no error, blacken number 5.

1. (1) consumation     (4) emphasis     ① ② ③ ④ ⑤
   (2) anemia     (5) no error
   (3) corporal

2. (1) crucial     (4) asessment     ① ② ③ ④ ⑤
   (2) disappearance     (5) no error
   (3) eminently

3. (1) impartiality     (4) scissors     ① ② ③ ④ ⑤
   (2) impecable     (5) no error
   (3) indictment

4. (1) maneuver     (4) presumptuous     ① ② ③ ④ ⑤
   (2) preparation     (5) no error
   (3) fasinated

5. (1) rythm     (4) interruption     ① ② ③ ④ ⑤
   (2) pamphlet     (5) no error
   (3) panicky

6. (1) controler     (4) scripture     ① ② ③ ④ ⑤
   (2) labyrinth     (5) no error
   (3) judiciary

7. (1) similar     (4) column     ① ② ③ ④ ⑤
   (2) mediocrity     (5) no error
   (3) emphatically

8. (1) commandant     (4) commemorate     ① ② ③ ④ ⑤
   (2) aquaint     (5) no error
   (3) across

9. (1) demurring     (4) laboratory     ① ② ③ ④ ⑤
   (2) detrimental     (5) no error
   (3) conversent

10. (1) liquidate     (4) medieval     ① ② ③ ④ ⑤
    (2) matinee     (5) no error
    (3) mecanical

**PRACTICE XX**

_Directions:_ Blacken the circle that corresponds to the number of the incorrectly spelled word in each group. If there is no error, blacken number 5.

1. (1) wholly     (4) adjunct     ① ② ③ ④ ⑤
   (2) thorough     (5) no error
   (3) symetrical

2. (1) arouse     (4) proceed     ① ② ③ ④ ⑤
   (2) superceed     (5) no error
   (3) actually

3. (1) accede     (4) arraignment     ① ② ③ ④ ⑤
   (2) succeed     (5) no error
   (3) appellate

4. (1) adjunct     (4) amendment     ① ② ③ ④ ⑤
   (2) advise        (5) no error
   (3) preceed

5. (1) anoyance     (4) actually      ① ② ③ ④ ⑤
   (2) antipathy     (5) no error
   (3) biased

# Commonly Misspelled Words

Give special review to all those words that have given you trouble. Do not try to learn more than 10 new words at one time.

| | | | |
|---|---|---|---|
| abandoned | allege | attendants | candidacy |
| aberration | allies | attorneys | candle |
| abeyance | all right | authentic | cannon |
| abscess | ambassador | aversion | canon |
| absence | amendment | awkward | capital |
| absurd | amplify | axle | capitol |
| abundance | ancient | | (a building) |
| abutting | anecdote | baccalaureate | carburetor |
| academy | anemia | bachelor | carnage |
| accent | angle | bacteria | carriage |
| accede | annoyance | balance | category |
| accessible | annum | banana | caucus |
| acclimate | anticipate | bankruptcy | cauldron |
| accommodate | antipathy | barely | cavalier |
| accumulation | antique | beaker | cavalry |
| accusation | apologetic | beatitude | cease |
| achievement | apparatus | beleaguered | ceiling |
| acknowledge | apparently | belligerent | cemetery |
| acquaint | appellate | benefit | certain |
| acquired | appetite | biased | certified |
| acquisition | appreciation | bigamy | chagrined |
| across | appropriation | bimonthly | chamois |
| actually | apricot | biscuit | chancellor |
| acutely | aquatic | blamable | changeable |
| adage | architecture | blight | character |
| addressee | arduous | bookkeeping | charitable |
| adequate | arguing | border | chauffeur |
| adieu | arouse | bored | chef |
| adjournment | arraignment | bounteous | chisel |
| adjunct | arrest | breeding | Christian |
| adopted | article | brief | circumstantial |
| adoption | artificial | bulletin | citation |
| advise | ascertain | bungalow | clamorous |
| advisable | aspirations | bureau | classified |
| advising | assassination | burglaries | clique |
| affirmative | assessment | business | clothe |
| aggravate | assigned | | colonel |
| aggregate | association | | colossal |
| agitation | assurance | cafeteria | column |
| agreeable | athletic | calendar | comedian |
| agreement | attach | cameos | commandant |
| aisle | attempt | campaign | commemorate |
| alcohol | attendance | cancel | commenced |

committal
committing
community
comparative
compel
competition
competitors
complacency
conciliatory
conclusively
condemned
confectionery
congenial
congestion
conjunction
connoisseur
conquer
conscript
consequently
conservatory
consistent
consummation
contagious
contemptible
continually
control
controller
convenient
conversant
cooperate
coronation
coroner
corporal
corral
  (an enclosure)
correlation
correspondence
correspondent
corrugated
corset
countenance
courtesies
criticism
crochet
cronies
crowded
crucial
crystallized
currency

death
deceive
decision
declaration
deferred
definite
delegate
deliberate
delicious
delinquent
democrat
demurrage
denunciatory
deodorize
derogatory
description
desecration
desert
desirable
despair
dessert (food)
destruction
detrimental
development
digestible
dilapidated
dining room
diocese
diphtheria
dirigible
disappear
disappearance
disapprove
discipline
discretion
diseases
disgust
dispatch
dispensable
dissatisfied
dissatisfy
dissolution
distillery
distinguished
distributor
dizzy
doctor
dormitory
drastically

dual
duchess
duly
dungarees
duped
dyeing

economical
economy
ecstasy
eczema
effects
efficient
elaborate
electrolysis
embarrass
embassies
emergency
eminently
emolument
emphasis
emphasize
emphatically
endurance
enlargement
enormous
enthusiastic
ephemeral
equilibrium
equinoctial
equipped
error
essential
everlasting
exaggerate
exceed
excel
exercise
exhibition
exhortation
existence
extradite
extraordinary
extravagant

facilitation
faculties
fallibility

falsify
falsity
fascinated
fatal
feudal
filial
finally
financial
financier
finely
fireman
flexible
foggy
foliage
forcible
foreign
foretell
forfeit
fortissimo
forty
fragrance
fraternally
freshman
frightfully
frostbitten
function
fundamental
furl

gallery
galvanized
gelatin
glimpse
guaranteed
guardian
gout
government
grammar
grandeur
grapevines
grease
grieve
guidance
guild
guitar

handicapped
harass
hearth

height

heinous

hence

herald

heritage

hideous

hindrance

histrionic

holly

hosiery

humorists

hybrid

hygienic

hysterics

idiomatic

ignoramus

ignorant

illegitimate

illuminate

illustrative

imminent

impartiality

impeccable

impromptu

incongruity

indecent

indictment

individual

ingenuity

ingenuous

inimitable

innocent

innocuous

insulation

insurance

integrity

intelligence

intercede

interruption

irreparably

itemized

jealous

jeopardy

journal

jovial

judgment

judiciary

jurisdiction

kindergarten

kinsman

label

laboratory

labyrinth

laceration

lacquer

ladies

larceny

latter

leased

legend

leggings

legitimate

leisure

libel

lieutenant

ligament

lightning

likeness

likewise

liquidate

literally

logical

loose

loot

lose

losing

lovable

loveliness

loyalty

lucrative

luxury

lynch

macaroni

mackerel

magnificent

maintain

maintenance

malice

maneuver

mania

manual

marital

marmalade

masquerade

massacre

matinee

matrimony

mattress

maturity

mayonnaise

mechanical

medal

medallion

medicine

medieval

mediocrity

melancholy

memoir

mercantile

mercury

merely

midget

midriff

military

millinery

millionaire

misanthrope

mischievous

misdemeanor

mislaid

misspell

misstep

monarchical

monkeys

morale

moribund

mortgage

movable

murmuring

muscle

museum

myriad

necessity

negligible

negotiate

nervous

nevertheless

nickel

niece

ninety

ninth

notary

notoriety

nowadays

nuisance

obedient

obliged

obstacles

occasionally

occur

occurrence

odyssey

official

omissions

omitted

operated

opportunity

option

ordinance

overwhelming

pacifist

pageant

pamphlet

panel

panicky

papal

parachute

paradoxical

parasite

parliament

parole

partisan

partner

patient

patronize

pattern

peculiar

penitentiary

people's

perilous

perjury

permanent

permissible

persevere

pervade

phrenologist

physical

physician
picnicking
piquancy
pitiful
plagiarism
plague
planned
playwright
pneumonia
policy
politician
portable
portend
portiere
possession
possibilities
post office
postpone
potato
poultry
prairie
preceding
precious
predatory
predilection
preferably
preference
premises
preparation
prestige
presume
presumptuous
previous
primarily
primitive
principal
principalship
prisoner
privilege
probably
proffer
profit
proletarian
promissory
promptness
propaganda
proprietor
psychology
publicity

publicly
punctilious

quantities
quartet
questionnaire
queue
quinine

rabid
raisin
realize
reasonable
receipted
receipts
receptacle
recognizable
recommend
recompense
reconcile
recruit
refrigerator
regrettable
regretted
rehearsal
relevant
relieve
religious
remodel
renaissance
renascence
repetitious
requisition
reservoir
resilience
resonance
resources
response
responsibility
responsible
restaurant
rheostat
rhetorical
rheumatism
rhubarb
rhythm
rickety
ridiculous
righteous

roommate
routine

Sabbath
sacrilegious
salable
salaries
salient
sandwiches
Saturn
saucy
scenes
scissors
screech
scripture
scrutiny
secretary
seize
senior
serenity
series
session
sieges
significant
silhouette
similar
sincerely
sitting
sobriquet
society
solemn
soliciting
sophomore
soporific
source
sovereign
specialized
specific
specifically
speech
spiritualist
squalor
squirrels
staid
staunch
standard
stationary (fixed)
statistics
statutes

steak
strengthen
strenuous
stretch
studying
subsidy
suburb
subversive
succeed
successor
suffrage
summarize
superb
surfeit
surgeon
symmetrical
sympathy
systematic

tableaux
 (or tableaus)
taciturn
talcum
tantalizing
tariff
taunt
technical
temperament
temperature
temporarily
tenet
tennis
terse
tetanus
thermometer
thesis
thorough
thought
together
tournament
tragedy
traitor
transaction
transient
transparent
treachery
tremendous
triumph
troupe (theatrical)

| | | | |
|---|---|---|---|
| truce | unfortunately | verbal | wholly |
| tuition | uniform | villain | width |
| turkeys | unify | visible | wield |
| twelfth | universe | vivisection | wiring |
| twins | unnecessary | voluntary | witnesses |
| typewriting | utilize | voucher | woman's |
| typhoid | | | women's |
| tyranny | | | worlds |
| | vacancy | warrant | wrapped |
| unanimous | vacillate | warranted | wretched |
| unauthorized | vacuum | weather | |
| unbearable | vague | Wednesday | |
| unconscious | valuing | weird | yacht |
| undecided | vegetable | welfare | yoke |
| undoubtedly | velvet | we're | |
| undulate | vengeance | whether | zephyr |

# Chapter 18    Spelling

**Practice I** *Page 194.*

1. reinstate
2. disillusion
3. unnecessary
4. cooperate
5. immortal
6. misspell
7. irreverent
8. illegal
9. acclimate
10. overrate
11. malcontent
12. inaccurate

**Practice II** *Page 196.*

1. announcement
2. dyeing
3. snappiness
4. association
5. dispensable
6. definitely
7. economical
8. courageous
9. movable
10. necessarily
11. practically
12. portable
13. rudeness
14. guidance
15. truly

**Practice III** *Page 196.*

1. (**4**) irrational
2. (**2**) happiness
3. (**4**) misspell

4. (**1**) commencement
5. (**1**) safety
6. (**5**) No error
7. (**3**) accumulate
8. (**4**) noticeable
9. (**2**) argument
10. (**5**) No error

**Practice IV** *Page 198.*

1. paint´ • er
2. pri´ • vate
3. of´ • fice
4. e • con´ • o • my
5. ad • vise´
6. bal´ • ance
7. dis • sat´ • is • fy
8. de • vel´ • op • ment
9. in • di • vid´ • u • al
10. pre • fer´
11. pref´ • er • ence
12. psy • chol´ • o • gy
13. vac´ • il • late
14. u • nan´ • i • mous
15. wretch´ • ed

**Practice V** *Page 199.*

1. (**2**) preference
2. (**4**) deterred
3. (**5**) No error
4. (**3**) deterrent
5. (**4**) occurrence

**Practice VI** *Page 199.*

1. n<u>ie</u>ce
2. dec<u>ei</u>ve

3. th<u>ie</u>f
4. rel<u>ie</u>ve
5. n<u>eig</u>h
6. rec<u>ei</u>ve
7. conc<u>ei</u>ve
8. bel<u>ie</u>f
9. n<u>ei</u>ther
10. s<u>ei</u>ze

**Practice VII** *Page 201.*
1. **(2)** mouthfuls
2. **(1)** Chinese
3. **(2)** sons-in-law
4. **(5)** No error
5. **(1)** 8's

**Practice VIII** *Page 202.*
1. **(3)** conclusively
2. **(2)** coronation
3. **(1)** similar
4. **(2)** achievement
5. **(2)** seize
6. **(4)** duped
7. **(3)** pertinent
8. **(5)** No error
9. **(3)** lovable
10. **(5)** No error

**Practice IX** *Page 203.*
1. **(5)** No error
2. **(2)** merciful
3. **(1)** dissolution
4. **(5)** No error
5. **(3)** weird
6. **(2)** government
7. **(3)** cordially
8. **(4)** piece
9. **(5)** No error
10. **(5)** No error

**Practice X** *Page 204.*
1. **(3)** habitually
2. **(4)** deference
3. **(1)** candies
4. **(2)** disappoint
5. **(1)** potatoes
6. **(3)** propelling
7. **(4)** truckfuls
8. **(1)** truly
9. **(5)** No error
10. **(1)** salaries
11. **(5)** No error
12. **(5)** No error

**Practice XI** *Page 205.*
1. **(3)** niece
2. **(4)** relief
3. **(3)** referred
4. **(3)** assessment
5. **(5)** No error
6. **(4)** receipt
7. **(1)** acquired
8. **(4)** lieutenant
9. **(1)** adjournment
10. **(1)** chef

**Practice XII** *Page 206.*
1. **(2)** athletic
2. **(3)** temperature
3. **(3)** incessant
4. **(1)** legitimate
5. **(5)** No error
6. **(5)** No error
7. **(5)** No error
8. **(4)** tetanus
9. **(5)** No error
10. **(1)** fundamental

**Practice XIII** *Page 207.*

1. (**5**) No error
2. (**1**) absence
3. (**3**) discussion
4. (**2**) athletic
5. (**5**) No error
6. (**1**) Wednesday
7. (**5**) No error
8. (**2**) possession
9. (**5**) No error
10. (**4**) library

**Practice XIV** *Page 208.*

1. (**2**) aberration
2. (**5**) No error
3. (**1**) ascertain
4. (**2**) resilience
5. (**5**) No error
6. (**3**) lucrative
7. (**4**) surfeit
8. (**1**) wield
9. (**5**) No error
10. (**1**) psychology

**Practice XV** *Page 209.*

1. (**2**) negligible
2. (**3**) forfeit
3. (**5**) No error
4. (**1**) fallibility
5. (**4**) promissory
6. (**2**) ephemeral
7. (**3**) exhortation
8. (**4**) eczema
9. (**1**) dissatisfied
10. (**1**) deferred

**Practice XVI** *Page 210.*

1. (**2**) resonance
2. (**3**) patient
3. (**1**) secretary

4. (**2**) distinguished
5. (**5**) No error
6. (**2**) chauffeur
7. (**3**) permissible
8. (**3**) recognizable
9. (**2**) mischievous
10. (**2**) sovereign

**Practice XVII** *Page 211.*

1. (**2**) carburetor
2. (**1**) biscuit
3. (**5**) No error
4. (**5**) No error
5. (**3**) relevant
6. (**4**) weather
7. (**1**) exceed
8. (**2**) foreign
9. (**3**) equipped
10. (**2**) corrugated

**Practice XVIII** *Page 212.*

1. (**3**) exercise
2. (**2**) hindrance
3. (**4**) deceive
4. (**5**) No error
5. (**2**) mackerel
6. (**3**) pneumonia
7. (**1**) temperament
8. (**1**) abundance
9. (**1**) accumulation
10. (**2**) ancient

**Practice XIX** *Page 213.*

1. (**1**) consummation
2. (**4**) assessment
3. (**2**) impeccable
4. (**3**) fascinated
5. (**1**) rhythm
6. (**1**) controller
7. (**5**) No error

8. **(2)** acquaint

9. **(3)** conversant

10. **(3)** mechanical

3. **(5)** No error

4. **(3)** precede

5. **(1)** annoyance

**Practice XX** *Page 214.*

1. **(3)** symmetrical

2. **(2)** supersede

# CHAPTER 19

# BUILDING VOCABULARY

Costard: "O, they have liv'd long on the
almsbasket of words. I marvel thy
master hath not eaten thee for a word;
for thou art not so long by the head as
honorificabilitudinitatibus; thou art
easier swallowed than a flapdragon."
—William Shakespeare
from *Love's Labour's Lost*, Act V, Scene 1

## *A Word With You . . .*

Costard, a clown in Shakespeare's comedy, uses one of the longest words in the English language (almost as long as *antidisestablishmentarianism*) in his conversation with Holofernes, the schoolmaster. Not only did Shakespeare know that 27-letter word, but he knew thousands upon thousands of other choice vocabulary words. Youngsters in his time were exposed to Latin and Greek in the schools and were able to develop a mastery of English words through their knowledge of prefixes, suffixes, and roots in those languages.

You may not catch up to Shakespeare, but you can get started in a modest way with the hints offered in this chapter.

## Some Facts About Vocabulary

We use words to think. A large and precise vocabulary leads to clear thinking.

The words we use "talk" about us. They create an impression of intelligence or dullness, success or failure.

The average person stops collecting new words early in life—probably during the twenties. Only by a conscious effort do we continue to add words to our vocabulary. This chapter will show you how to expand your vocabulary.

There are many ways to increase your vocabulary. If you are an avid reader, you've found the most natural way. But what if you're not? You can choose one or more of the following methods to help you. You may find that certain ways appeal to you more than others.

To increase your vocabulary, take advantage of what you like to do. When we like what we're doing, we learn faster. Building vocabulary may not be your idea of fun, but if you start with a topic you like, you might develop an interest.

Are you interested in history? Learn new words by studying their histories. Many English words include Latin, Greek, and other languages in their histories. One of our most frequently used words is an example of this. The word *television* came to English from the French: *télévision*. But television was not originally a French word. In fact, its journey through history includes both Latin and Greek.

*tele* from the Greek *tēle*, meaning at a distance, or far off
*vision* from the Latin *vīsiō*, meaning see

Put the two parts together and you have a good definition of television: pictures taken at a distance that you can see. Let's see how this works with other common words.

PRACTICE

I

*Directions:*   Draw a line from the Latin and Greek word parts in the left-hand column to the English words in the right-hand column.

*Note:* In the dictionary, histories of words follow definitions and are placed in brackets.

| Latin and Greek Word Parts | English Words |
| --- | --- |
| 1. [Greek *teknē*, skill, art + *logos*, word speech] | video |
| 2. [Latin *alere*, to nourish] | computer |
| 3. [Latin *com*, together, jointly + Latin *dominium*, property] | alimony |
| 4. [Latin *com*, together + Latin *putare*, to think, reckon] | technology |
| 5. [Latin *videre*, to see] | condominium |

PRACTICE
II

*Directions:* Use your dictionary to discover the histories of the following words. Notice that a word may have gone through more than one language before it reached English. A word's most recent history is found at the beginning of the bracketed information. Its earliest history is at the end. Copy the earliest history.

1. compress _____
2. vindictive _____
3. pedicure _____
4. manicure _____
5. unique _____

Latin roots are found over and over again in English words. Once you know the meanings of these roots, you can unlock the meanings of many English words. The following are just a few examples:

| Common Latin Roots | English Words |
|---|---|
| *bene* | well |
| *dicere* | to say |
| *facere* | to do, to make |
| *volens* | wishing |
| *unus* | one, single |
| *signum* | sign |
| *portare* | to carry |
| *manu* | by hand |

PRACTICE
III

*Directions:* Can you guess from which Latin root each of the following words was formed? Use the above list to make your decision.

1. united _____
2. factory _____
3. benefit _____
4. insignia _____
5. portable _____
6. dictation _____
7. volunteer _____

Sometimes two roots combine to make another word.

*bene* + *dicere* = benediction = a blessing, or "saying well"
*bene* + *facere* = benefactor = one who does something good for another
*bene* + *volens* = benevolent = wishing others well, kindly

## Building Your Vocabulary With Prefixes

Perhaps you are interested in building your vocabulary. You can build words by learning how prefixes add to the meanings of roots. Below is a partial list of common prefixes that will help you build a larger vocabulary.

**COMMON PREFIXES**

| Prefix | Meaning | Example |
|--------|---------|---------|
| ab- | away, from | absent, absorb |
| ad- | to, toward | advice, adhere |
| ante- | before | antebellum, antecedent |
| anti- | against | antisocial, antihistamine |
| auto- | self | autobiography |
| bi- | two, twice | biannual |
| bio- | life | biology, biography |
| com-, con- | with, together | combine, conflict, confederate |
| contra- | against | contradict, contraband |
| de- | down from | debase, decamp |
| dia- | through, around | diagonal, diameter |
| dis- | not, apart | disapprove |
| en- | put into, on | engrave |
| ex- | out of | except, expel |
| il- | not | illegal |
| im-, in- | not | impossible, inadequate |
| in- | in, into | inward, ingest, insert |
| inter- | between, among | interfere, interject |
| ir- | not | irrational |
| mal- | evil, wrong | malicious, malign |
| mono- | one | monorail, monotone |
| non- | not | nonfiction |
| post- | after | postpone, postdate |
| pre- | before | precede, prescription |

## COMMON PREFIXES

| Prefix | Meaning | Example |
|--------|---------|---------|
| pro- | for, forward | promote, provide |
| re- | again, back | reapply, return |
| semi- | half | semicircle |
| sub- | under | submarine |
| super- | over, above | supervisor |
| trans- | across | transportation |
| tri- | three | triangle |
| un- | not | untied, unbutton |

PRACTICE
IV

_Directions:_   Think about the meaning each prefix adds to these words. The prefixes are underlined. Answer the questions. If you are in doubt about the meanings, check the list above or your dictionary. Prefixes appear in this way: pre-

| Prefixes | Meanings |
|----------|----------|
| predate | 1. Which prefixes make root words negative?_____ |
| impossible | _____ |
| disorganize | _____ |
| return | 2. Which prefix means "evil"? |
| extract | _____ |
| untie | 3. Which prefix means "self"?_____ |
| malodorous | 4. Which prefix means "back" or "again"? |
| postnatal | _____ |
| amoral | 5. Which prefix means "after"?_____ |
| automobile | 6. Which prefix means "out"?_____ |
|  | 7. Which prefix means "before"?_____ |

_Directions:_    Make new words by adding a prefix to each word below. If you need to check the meaning of a prefix, look back at the long list of prefixes on page 228.

| dis- | trans- | un- | sub- | re- | auto- | pre- | bio- |
|------|--------|-----|------|-----|-------|------|------|
| post- | ir- | non- | bi- | im- | ab- | anti- | ex- |

1. _____view
2. _____agree
3. _____biography
4. _____live
5. _____dress
6. _____contract
7. _____continental
8. _____port

9. _____profit
10. _____sent
11. _____biotic
12. _____script
13. _____sphere
14. _____regular
15. _____mortal
16. _____cycle

# Building Your Vocabulary With Action and Descriptive Words

How would you like to enlarge your vocabulary and improve your writing skills—_at the same time?_ You can accomplish both by increasing the number of action and descriptive words you know. Begin by using the word _get_ less frequently and by using precise words more.

| Less Interesting | Precise |
|---|---|
| 1. We should _get_ a new typewriter for the office. | 1. We should (_buy, rent, lease_) a new typewriter for the office. |
| 2. Milton tried to _get_ me to take his side in the debate. | 2. Milton tried to _persuade_ me to take his side in the debate. |
| 3. The first baseman _got_ hit by the pitcher's fast ball. | 3. The pitcher's fast ball _struck_ the first baseman. |
| 4. When he spoke of his war buddies, he _got_ sad. | 4. When he spoke of his war buddies, he _grew_ sad. |

Try to avoid overused words. Learn new descriptive words to replace them. Start with the word _very. Very_ plus an overused word hides a precise word.

| Overused Words | Precise Words |
|---|---|
| very pretty | captivating |
| very new | novel |
| very lazy | indolent |
| very funny | amusing |
| very slow | languid |

PRACTICE
VI

*Directions:*   Replace the italicized word in each sentence with a descriptive one chosen from the list below.

ancient    swift    overjoyed    terrified    craves

1. I am *very afraid* of night noises._____
2. We toured a *very old* ruin in Rome._____
3. A *very fast* runner won the marathon._____
4. My friend, Sheila, *really wants* fame._____
5. I was *very glad* to hear of your good fortune._____

This chapter offers only a few techniques for increasing your vocabulary. There are many more. In fact, entire books have been written on the subject. Now that you have completed a sample improvement program, don't stop building your vocabulary. Be aware of new words. Keep a list of them, define them, and write them in sentences. Try to use them in your everyday conversations, letters, or memos. Your personal gains will make it well worth the effort.

# Chapter 19   Building Vocabulary

**Practice I** *Page 226.*

1. technology
2. alimony
3. condominium
4. computer
5. video

**Practice II** *Page 227.*

1. [Latin: com-, together + premere, to press]
2. [Latin vindicare, to revenge]
3. [French pédicure: pedi + Latin cūrāre, to take care of]
4. [Latin manus, hand + cūra, care]
5. [Latin ūnicus, only]

**Practice III** *Page 227.*

1. unus—one, single
2. facere—to do
3. benefit—well
4. signum—sign
5. portare—to carry
6. dicere—to say
7. volens—wishing

**Practice IV** *Page 229.*

1. im-, dis-, un-, a-
2. mal-
3. auto-
4. re-
5. post-
6. ex-
7. pre-

**Practice V** *Page 230.*

1. preview
2. disagree
3. autobiography
4. relive
5. undress
6. subcontract
7. transcontinental
8. import
9. nonprofit
10. absent
11. antibiotic
12. postscript
13. biosphere
14. irregular
15. immortal
16. bicycle

**Practice VI** *Page 231.*

1. terrified
2. ancient
3. swift
4. craves
5. overjoyed

# WORD USAGE

I was a pretty good student back in Wilberforce in the 1930's but there were a few things that always gave me trouble. I never felt comfortable with *affect* and *effect, capital* and *capitol, beside* and *besides*—and hundreds of others like that with which Miss Conway used to torture us every Friday.

"Now we come to words frequently confused," she would drool, adjusting wig and lorgnette, her eyes brightening with anticipation.

I think what really turned me off on that subject was when old Mr. Wentworth tried to show me the difference between *principal* and *principle,* pontificating that "Your princi*pal* is your *pal*," and spraying me with tobacco juice in the process.

I didn't believe him then, and I still have trouble with those words, forty years later. Traumatic, I guess.

—Oliver L. Kenworthy
*Bluegrass Lawyer*

## *A Word With You . . .*

English seems to have so many more words that sound alike and words that are frequently confused than any other language. The same problems young Oliver Kenworthy found in Wilberforce, Kentucky may have plagued you, too.

In the following pages, you will find some of the more troublesome sets of words. See how well you can handle them.

## Commonly Misused Words

Many words are easily confused. Some words sound the same but are spelled differently and have different meanings. These are *homonyms.*

*Examples:*    1. A full moon *shone* brightly last night.

The film was *shown* on TV.

2. Once we nail up this *board,* the tool shed will be finished.

I was very *bored* during that long, rainy week.

3. The *pain* in my lower back increases during rainy weather.

Could you please replace the cracked *pane* of glass?

Other words are confusing because they sound almost the same.

*Examples:*

1. The legislators had an angry debate before *adopting* a policy on school funding.

Since we moved from the West Coast to the Midwest, we've had to *adapt* to colder weather.

2. The politician's *allusions* to his opponent's past errors in judgment were unnecessary.

In the story *The Christmas Carol,* Scrooge's visitors were *illusions.*

3. How do you think the current job action will *affect* management?

I think the *effect* will be that management will meet labor's demands.

In order to improve your understanding of easily confused words, study the following list. An example of correct usage is given for each commonly confused word.

### accept—except

I *accept* your apology.

Everyone *except* John may leave.

### adapt—adopt

When visiting a foreign country, you must *adapt* yourself to the customs practiced there.

The Grays plan to *adopt* several hard-to-place children.

### advice—advise

Because of Michael's excellent *advice,* Bob completed a successful business deal.

Michael will *advise* Bob to be daring.

### affect—effect

The accident did not *affect* Thomas.

The *effect* on his brother, however, was great.

### aggravate—annoy

If you continue to scratch that rash, you will *aggravate* your condition.

Your constant scratching *annoys* me.

### all ready—already

Call me when you are *all ready* to go.

By the time Sue arrived, we had *already* finished dinner.

### all right

(*Alright* is not an acceptable word.)

Is it *all right* to leave this window open?

### all together—altogether

The four of us were *all together* at the coffee shop.

This book is *altogether* too long.

### allude—refer

In passing, the speaker *alluded* to the new technology in business.

The speaker *referred* to statistics that demonstrated the rise of technology in business.

### allusion—illusion

I resent your *allusion* to my cooking as comparable with MacDonald's.

You have the *illusion* that I enjoy classical music; I don't.

### altar—alter

Many a would-be-bride has been left at the *altar.*

Would it be inconvenient for you to *alter* your plans for this weekend?

### among—between

The campaign director divided the state *among* his *three* most competent assistants.

In many of today's homes, the care of the children is divided *between* the *two* parents.

### amount—number

You would not believe the *amount* of time I have spent on this project.

I wish I could reuse the *number* of hours I have spent on this project.

### angry at—angry with

Ira was *angry at* the thought of working overtime.

Ira was *angry with* his boss for insisting that Ira work overtime.

### anxious—eager

I am *anxious* about the diagnosis.

I am *eager* to see your new car.

### anywhere

(There is no such word as *anywheres*.)

Marlene cannot find her glasses *anywhere*.

### as—like

Paula looks very much *like* her sister.

Rosemary swims *as* well as Pam does.

Carl looks *as* if he needs a nap.

### ascent—assent

The *ascent* to the tower was frighteningly steep.

Because I value his opinion, I will not go ahead with the project without his *assent*.

### awful—very—real

This fish tastes *awful*.

This fish tastes *very* bad.

Are these pearls *real* or imitation?

### because of—due to

*Because of* our tight budget, we're vacationing at home.

We're vacationing at home *due to* our tight budget.

### beside—besides

Linda likes to sit *beside* Ellen at the table.

Who, *besides* Pam, is taking swimming lessons?

### born—borne

Our youngest child was *born* last month.

John has *borne* the burden by himself for long enough.

*borrow from*

(*borrow off* is unacceptable.)

Mickey borrowed the soldering iron from Allen.

*borrow—lend—loan*

May I *borrow* your pocket calculator?

I can *lend* you my mechanical pencil.

I need a $500 *loan*.

*brake—break*

I prefer a bicycle with a foot *brake*.

Because he did not *brake* in time, Herman crashed into the tree.

If you are not careful, you will *break* that dish.

*can—may*

Some fortunate people *can* arrange their time to include work and pleasure.

You *may* hunt deer only during certain seasons.

*capital—capitol—Capitol*

Ricardo has 90 percent of the necessary *capital* for his new business venture.

Trenton is the *capital* of New Jersey.

New Jersey's *capitol* building is in Trenton.

Did you visit the *Capitol* when you were in Washington, D.C.?

*cite—sight—site*

An attorney often *cites* previous cases that support his argument.

One of the most beautiful *sights* in the country is the Grand Canyon.

The alternative school will be built on this *site*.

*coarse—course*

I find this *coarse* fabric to be abrasive.

That is an acceptable *course* of action.

*complement—compliment*

Rice nicely *complements* a chicken dinner.

I'd like to *compliment* you for doing such a thorough job.

### communicate with—contact

I will *communicate with* (call, write, speak) you in May.

*Contact* (call, write, speak) me when you return.

### continually—continuously

Tom is *continually* late.

The river runs *continuously* through several towns.

### council—counsel

Our neighbor has just been elected to the town *council*.

The troubled man sought his friend's *counsel*.

### credible—creditable—credulous

Because the defendant had a good alibi, his story seemed *credible*.

As a result of many hours of hard work, Joe presented a *creditable* report.

Sally is so *credulous* that one could sell her the Brooklyn Bridge.

### currant—current

His unusual recipe called for *currant* jelly.

Because the *current* was swift, the canoe was difficult to maneuver.

### desert—dessert

The *desert* is very hot and dry.

More and more young soldiers have been *deserting* the army.

Apple pie is America's favorite *dessert*.

### die—dye

Eventually, every living thing *dies*.

I'll never *dye* my hair.

### discover—invent

The builders *discovered* oil on our land.

Whitney *invented* the cotton gin.

### disinterested—uninterested

The *disinterested* observer of the accident was certain that the driver of the blue car was at fault.

Because Sheila was *uninterested* in the lecture, she paid no attention.

*draw—drawer*

Marlene *draws* very well.

She keeps her pads and pencils in the top *drawer* of her desk.

*emigration—immigration*

The Harlows *emigrated* from England.

After *immigrating* to the United States, the Harlows settled in Kansas.

*famous—infamous*

John Simpson is a *famous* pianist.

Arthur Jones is an *infamous* car thief.

*farther—further*

My car can run *farther* on this other brand of gasoline.

I cannot continue this discussion any *further*.

*fewer—less*

Gerry invited *fewer* people to her office party this year.

Since she moved from a house to an apartment, she has *less* space.

*formally—formerly*

Please dress *formally* for the wedding.

I was *formerly* employed by a jewelry company, but I am now working in a bank.

*good—well*

Maria performed a *good* job.

Maria performed the job *well*.

Maria doesn't feel *good*.

Maria doesn't feel *well*.

*grate—great*

The continuous harsh and rasping sound *grated* on my nerves.

A *grate* in the sidewalk covered the opening to the sewer.

Ernest Hemingway was considered a *great* writer in his own lifetime.

*healthful—healthy*

Orange juice is *healthful*.

If you eat properly and exercise sufficiently, you will be *healthy*.

### imply—infer

Although he did not state it directly, the candidate *implied* that his opponent was dishonest.

From the mayor's constructive suggestions, the townsfolk *inferred* that he was trying his best to do a good job.

### in—into

Marlene stood *in* the living room.

Wayne came rushing *into* the room.

### it's—its

I think *it's* a fine idea!

The dog wagged *its* tail.

### kind of—sort of—type of

(These expressions can be used interchangeably. They should never be followed by "a.")

Mrs. Peterson always buys that *kind of* meat.

I like that *sort of* book.

This is my favorite *type of* music.

### later—latter

Sue can finish the report *later* this week.

I can meet you Tuesday or Thursday. The *latter* would be more convenient.

### lead—led

I'll need one more *lead* pipe to complete this plumbing job.

I only enjoy a race when I am in the *lead*.

John was unfamiliar with that route, so Jules *led* the way.

### learn—teach

Harriet is having great difficulty with her efforts to *learn* flowcharting.

Leslie is patiently trying to *teach* Harriet how to flowchart.

### leave—let

If the customs officer finds nothing wrong with a traveler's baggage, the officer *lets* the traveler *leave* the area.

### loose—lose

Eric was excited about his first *loose* tooth.

If you step out of line, you will *lose* your place.

### manor—manner

The *manor,* or landed estate, dates back to feudal times in England.

They don't like the *manner* in which you responded to my sincere question.

### miner—minor

The coal *miners* were trapped during the cave-in.

The young man was not allowed to enter the bar because he was a *minor.*

### moral—morale

Because of Ed's high *moral* standards, he returned the wallet to its owner.

The story of *The Boy Who Cried Wolf* has a *moral* that applies to everyone.

Because the war was *immoral,* the *morale* of the troops was low.

### nauseated—nauseous

When we drove past the skunk, the car was filled with a *nauseous* odor.

The odor of the skunk *nauseated* Sara.

### pail—pale

The amount of paint needed to finish the job would fill a one-gallon *pail.*

Because of her long illness, Maria's complexion was very *pale.*

### passed—past

We *passed* the Model T on the parkway.

You cannot always try to recapture the *past.*

### peace—piece

If we work together, perhaps we can end the war and achieve a truly lasting *peace.*

In time, we will be paying an extremely high price for a *piece* of paper.

### persecute—prosecute

Older children frequently *persecute* their younger siblings.

If you do not return the stolen money, you will be *prosecuted.*

### personal—personnel

The items written in a young girl's diary are very *personal.*

When applying for a job at a large company, you must go to the *personnel* office.

### plain—plane

The meaning is quite *plain* and requires no further explanation.

We rode for miles across the open *plains* of Kansas.

The *plane* landed smoothly.

Please *plane* that wood so that I can build a birdhouse with it.

### precede—proceed

A preface always *precedes* the body of a book.

Don't let me interrupt you; *proceed* with your work.

### practicable—practical

Studying computer programming is a *practicable* plan today's job market.

Computerizing payroll is a *practical* business decision.

### principal—principle

A school is as good as the teachers and *principal.*

The *principal* actors in the play remained for a final rehearsal of the second act.

The *principle* upon which many simple machines are based is frequently the lever.

### quiet—quite

As the campers lay down for the night, *quiet* settled over the campsite.

That is *quite* a strong accusation.

### raise—rise

When we *raise* the flag, we'd like everyone in the audience to *rise.*

### sit—set

The chairman requested committee members to *sit* down.

The artist *set* his clay on the workbench and began to create a sculpture.

### stationary—stationery

Theater seats are most often *stationary*.

When I write letters, I always use my personal *stationery*.

### sure—surely

I am *sure* Alice will be at the meeting.

*Surely,* you don't expect me to take notes.

### teach—learn

Miss Smith *teaches* math every Thursday.

Ron Jonas, a student, *learns* math from Miss Smith.

### than—then

New York is smaller than Wyoming, but Wyoming has a much smaller population *than* New York.

First the eastern seaboard was colonized, *then* settlers moved westward.

### their—there—they're

When leaving *their* war-torn country, most of the refugees left all *their* possessions behind.

*There* are no easy answers to the problem of worldwide hunger.

As for the members of Congress, *they're* not always responsible for the wisest decisions.

### through—threw

The special crew worked *through* the night to repair the damaged wires.

When the Little League pitcher *threw* the ball, her teammates cheered.

### to—too—two

United States presidents often travel *to* foreign countries.

Many foreign heads of state visit the United States, *too*.

*Two* visitors were the late Anwar Sadat and Margaret Thatcher.

### vain—vane—vein

The *vain* man peered at his reflection in every window as he strolled down the street.

A rooster is the traditional weather *vane* symbol.

*Veins* are passageways that carry deoxygenated blood to the heart.

### vale—veil

*Vale* is an uncommonly used synonym for valley.

The mourning woman hid her grief behind her *veil*.

### wade—weighed

The smaller children were told to *wade* near the shore.

The clerk *weighed* and priced the fresh vegetables.

### waist—waste

If you measure your *waist* before you go to buy a pattern, you will avoid much confusion.

Don't *waste* precious time gossiping on the phone.

### weather—whether

Tomorrow morning the general *weather* conditions will determine the distance of our first day's hike.

*Whether* or not you wish to pay taxes, you must.

### who's—whose

The teacher asked, "*Who's* responsible for clean-up today?"

We must determine *whose* turn it is.

### writes—rights—rites

Kurt Vonnegut *writes* excellent fiction.

Their attorney explained the family's *rights* in the lawsuit.

The religious *rites* of many Indian tribes are an impressive part of their culture.

***your—you're***

Where is *your* car parked?

*You're* attempting something that's too difficult for you.

PRACTICE
I

*Directions:* Blacken the circle that corresponds to the number of the correct word to complete each sentence.

1. *Your You're* on the right track.          ①②
   1     2

2. I enjoy a cold *bier beer* on a warm day.      ①②
              1    2

3. Please use the main *aisle isle* in the theater.   ①②
                     1   2

4. We left early because we were *bored board.*   ①②
                     1    2

5. The ship traveled through the *straight strait.*  ①②
                       1    2

6. The *sum some* collected was not significant.  ①②
     1   2

7. Please, don't *waist waste* my time.        ①②
            1   2

8. The queen sat gracefully on her *thrown throne.*  ①②
                   1    2

9. Buddy would never *steal steel* from anyone.  ①②
            1   2

10. The wise old Indian knew many interesting *tales tails.*  ①②
                            1   2

PRACTICE
II

*Directions:* Blacken the circle that corresponds to the number of the sentence in each group that contains an incorrectly used word. If there is no error, blacken number 5.

1. (1) The jewel was shown to the prospective  ①②③④⑤
buyer.
   (2) Her hair shown in the bright sunlight.
   (3) The sun shone brightly this morning.
   (4) I have never been shown how to use this machine.
   (5) No error

2. (1) I would like you to cite at least three examples.   ① ② ③ ④ ⑤
   (2) Her husband was cited for contempt.
   (3) For that sight, we're planning a municipal parking lot.
   (4) When the bridge is within your sight, start looking for our street.
   (5) No error

3. (1) The some total of these facts spells disaster.   ① ② ③ ④ ⑤
   (2) Take some cake with you to the picnic.
   (3) I have some clothes that are no longer useful to me.
   (4) That sum of money is to be labeled petty cash.
   (5) No error

4. (1) Since the development of the tape recorder, Braille is no longer the sole method of communicating fine literature to sightless people.   ① ② ③ ④ ⑤
   (2) Lemon sole is one of the many varieties of fish that can enhance a meatless diet.
   (3) Sole music is very popular among people of all ages.
   (4) The concept of the soul does not have the same meaning in all religions.
   (5) No error

5. (1) Napoleon had a great deal at steak when he decided to invade Russia.   ① ② ③ ④ ⑤
   (2) Finally, William hammered the last stake into the ground.
   (3) I would enjoy a steak dinner tonight.
   (4) Sue was upset because her job was at stake.
   (5) No error

6. (1) Please, remain stationary while I draw your picture.  ① ② ③ ④ ⑤
   (2) Irene wrote the letter on her finest stationary.
   (3) I believe you can buy staples at the stationery store.
   (4) This appliance cannot be moved; it is stationary.
   (5) No error

7. (1) Ilene attended a conference there.  ① ② ③ ④ ⑤
   (2) There is the book I've been wanting to read.
   (3) There's is a truly open relationship.
   (4) I have never been to their summer home.
   (5) No error

8. (1) Those two stairs make this house bi-level.  ① ② ③ ④ ⑤
   (2) Hers was hardly a friendly stair.
   (3) We've already swept the stairs today.
   (4) Don't stare at me!
   (5) No error

9. (1) I think it's time that he buys a new suite of furniture.  ① ② ③ ④ ⑤
   (2) We've already eaten our portion of sweets for this day.
   (3) The visiting lecturer's hotel suite was paid for by the university.
   (4) Don't make the chocolate pudding overly sweet.
   (5) No error

10. (1) The boat was taken in toe after its motor failed.  ① ② ③ ④ ⑤
    (2) We were towed all the way to shore.
    (3) At the football game we had a bad case of frozen toes.
    (4) When you go beyond your own authority, you must step on somebody's toes.
    (5) No error

*Directions:* Blacken the circle that corresponds to the number of the incorrect word in each sentence. If there is no error, blacken number 5.

1. The guide *led* us to a *straight* path *through* the
         1        2        3

   woods and to a lovely *veil.* *No error*
               4    5

   ① ② ③ ④ ⑤

2. My neighbor *dies* her *hair* *two* times every
              1      2   3

   *week.* *No error*
     4     5

   ① ② ③ ④ ⑤

3. We had *already* planned our vacation to an
          1

   unknown *isle* when our friends said that they
         2

   were *all ready* to come along *to.* *No error*
       3                4   5

   ① ② ③ ④ ⑤

4. You are *all together* mistaken about *their*
           1                  2

   decision *to write* to the newspaper. *No error*
        3  4              5

   ① ② ③ ④ ⑤

5. Ira Swanson *writes* about the religious *rights*
             1                2

   of the Indians who inhabit the island *right*
                               3

   off the coast *of* Japan. *No error*
             4     5

   ① ② ③ ④ ⑤

6. The *capital* of each state is the *cite* of the
       1                  2

   *capitol building* of that state and main attraction
         3

   for *sightseers.* *No error*
       4     5

   ① ② ③ ④ ⑤

7. Because the *currant* was *strong,* we had
           1        2

   *great* difficulty reaching *shore.* *No error*
    3                4    5

   ① ② ③ ④ ⑤

8. I, for one, <u>*didn't*</u> <u>*appreciate*</u> the <u>*manor*</u> in     ① ② ③ ④ ⑤
              1         2         3

    <u>*which*</u> she answered. <u>*No error*</u>
     4                   5

9. We <u>*truly*</u> felt that the <u>*exorbitant*</u> <u>*expenditure*</u>    ① ② ③ ④ ⑤
       1                2          3

    was a <u>*waist.*</u> <u>*No error*</u>
          4     5

10. We <u>*wade*</u> both <u>*arguments,*</u> and we decided     ① ② ③ ④ ⑤
       1         2

    in <u>*favor*</u> of the <u>*contract.*</u> <u>*No error*</u>
      3          4       5

11. The <u>*nutritious*</u> food, the fine <u>*weather,*</u> and     ① ② ③ ④ ⑤
        1                   2

    the <u>*exercise*</u> made us feel <u>*grate.*</u> <u>*No error*</u>
       3              4    5

12. The <u>*members*</u> of the <u>*panel*</u> were asked to leave    ① ② ③ ④ ⑤
        1         2

    <u>*their*</u> jackets in the <u>*outer*</u> office. <u>*No error*</u>
     3            4       5

13. We <u>*heard*</u> Pete <u>*moan,*</u> and we saw that he     ① ② ③ ④ ⑤
       1         2

    <u>*had become*</u> deadly <u>*pail.*</u> <u>*No error*</u>
      3          4    5

---

**PRACTICE IV**

<u>*Directions:*</u>   Blacken the circle that corresponds to the number of the incorrect word in each passage. If there is no error, blacken number 5.

1. Because I was <u>*anxious*</u> to avoid another     ① ② ③ ④ ⑤
               1

    argument, I <u>*accepted*</u> Roy's apology. His story
              2

    seemed <u>*credible*</u> so there was no point in
           3

    carrying the argument any <u>*further.*</u> <u>*No error*</u>
                    4      5

2. Sue left the elevator and *proceeded* to the    ① ② ③ ④ ⑤
                                1

   *personal* office. The cold, efficient interviewer
      2

   lowered Sue's *morale,* but she was *eager* to
                     3                      4

   obtain the job. *No error*
                        5

3. The *effect* of the unusual visitor on the family    ① ② ③ ④ ⑤
        1

   was startling. Mother *adopted* Mrs. Chuggley's
                              2

   speech habits; father *altered* his smoking habits
                             3

   to suit Mrs. Chuggley's allergy; and I found

   myself *continuously* saying, "Yes, Ma'am."
              4

   *No error*
      5

4. The *course* of action determined by the city    ① ② ③ ④ ⑤
        1

   *counsel* at its last meeting has *already* begun to
      2                                 3

   *affect* us. *No error*
      4          5

5. Family  gatherings  are  *always*  interesting.    ① ② ③ ④ ⑤
                               1

   Grandpa is usually *angry with* Aunt Jean.
                          2

   Rhoda insists upon sitting *besides* Grandma.
                                 3

   Mother tries to divide her attention equally

   *among* all of the guests. *No error*
      4                           5

6. I was <u>altogether</u> shocked when Sam returned
        1

   the ice bucket that he had <u>borrowed from</u> us
                           2

   last spring. When I <u>complemented</u> him for
                       3

   returning it so promptly, Sam's red face told

   me that he understood my <u>implied</u> sarcasm.
                          4

   <u>No error</u>
    5

                                    ① ② ③ ④ ⑤

7. Please put the change <u>into</u> your pocket before
                     1

   you lose it. It's hard enough to keep pace with

   today's prices without carelessly <u>losing</u> money.
                          2

   That <u>kind of</u> carelessness makes me <u>loose</u> my
       3                     4

   temper. <u>No error</u>
        5

                                      ① ② ③ ④ ⑤

8. The <u>minor</u> <u>led</u> his <u>team</u> into the shaft. After
     1   2     3

   several hours of dangerous work, they <u>ascended</u>
                                4

   jubilantly. <u>No error</u>
           5

                                    ① ② ③ ④ ⑤

9. I am <u>formally</u> engaged in a program of good
       1

   nutrition. I always eat a <u>healthy</u> breakfast. I
                       2

   consume <u>fewer</u> sweets and I spend <u>less</u> time
         3                 4

   stalking the refrigerator for snacks. <u>No error</u>
                                5

10.  Sue asked if she <u>might</u> go swimming at the pool.      ① ② ③ ④ ⑤
                          1

Although Sue <u>can</u> swim <u>quite</u> well, her mother
                2              3

refused  permission.  Sue  was  angry  and  said

she was being <u>prosecuted.</u> <u>No error</u>
                   4              5

PRACTICE

V    <u>Directions:</u>    Blacken the circle that corresponds to the number of the
sentence in each group that contains an incorrectly used word. If there
is no error, blacken number 5.

1.  (1)  The damage has all ready been done.         ① ② ③ ④ ⑤
    (2)  Father  was  altogether  too  surprised  to
         speak.
    (3)  Events have borne out my prediction.
    (4)  Perry  is  an  altar  boy  at  Queen  of  Peace
         Church.
    (5)  No error

2.  (1)  The family was all together for the annual      ① ② ③ ④ ⑤
         picnic.
    (2)  Terry's  mother  cautioned,  "If  you  break  a
         window, you will have to pay for it."
    (3)  Paris is the capital of France.
    (4)  My mother was borne in Canada.
    (5)  No error

3.  (1)  Was his work all right?         ① ② ③ ④ ⑤
    (2)  I use old shirts for cleaning cloths.
    (3)  The  dome  on  the  capital  is  lighted  each
         night.
    (4)  Everyone was wearing his best clothes.
    (5)  No error

4.  (1)  I applied the brakes immediately.         ① ② ③ ④ ⑤
    (2)  Cars are borne across the river on a ferry.
    (3)  Are you feeling all right?
    (4)  When you are all ready, I will pick you up.
    (5)  No error

5. (1) John is considered an imminent member of  ① ② ③ ④ ⑤
   congress.
   (2) The duke was received formally at the ambassador's home.
   (3) Out of deference to her loss, we did not resume the music.
   (4) We could hear a vigorous discussion of current problems.
   (5) No error

6. (1) When you give your report, be sure to cite  ① ② ③ ④ ⑤
   as many concrete examples as possible.
   (2) "I am surely not guilty of excessive spending!" he shouted.
   (3) We are not likely to meet again in the near
   future.
   (4) Because of several miner disagreements,
   the discussion came to a halt.
   (5) No error

7. (1) The politician was asked to accede to the  ① ② ③ ④ ⑤
   council's wishes.
   (2) I am opposed to the construction of the
   bridge for two good reasons.
   (3) Do not hire anyone whose personality
   doesn't complement the rest of the staff.
   (4) Prospective homeowners are eager for re-
   duction of the mortgage interest rate.
   (5) No error

8. (1) The attorney set fourth his ideas and told us  ① ② ③ ④ ⑤
   all of the angles of his case.
   (2) Will you sign this senior citizen petition?
   (3) The beauty of the mountains exceeded all
   our expectations.
   (4) Mike is quite an athlete.
   (5) No error

9.  (1) Wayne is likely to be defeated.    ① ② ③ ④ ⑤
    (2) There was nothing to do but accept his plan.
    (3) I am opposed too airing family matters in public.
    (4) The crowd was quiet until the rocket ascended.
    (5) No error

10. (1) After listening with great patience, the    ① ② ③ ④ ⑤
    diplomat listed his objectives.
    (2) No one knew him as well as I.
    (3) Choose your coarse of action and stick to it.
    (4) I think the skirt is too loose on you.
    (5) No error

PRACTICE
VI

_Directions:_   Blacken the circle that corresponds to the number of the incorrect word in each passage. If there is no error, blacken number 5.

1. The _principal_ members of the committee    ① ② ③ ④ ⑤
        1
   decided to _lead_ a discussion about the _peace_
           2                3
   movement and the _type of a_ person attracted
                   4
   to it. _No error_
        5

2. Many of the _minors_ in the audience began to    ① ② ③ ④ ⑤
             1
   _lose_ _there_ tempers because the discussion
     2   3
   _seemed_ partisan. _No error_
      4         5

3. The chairman _tryed_ _to_ explain that the _principle_    ① ② ③ ④ ⑤
              1  2               3
   of freedom to pursue one's beliefs was not the
   _main_ issue. _No error_
    4      5

4. It was not the committee's intention to _persecute_    ① ② ③ ④ ⑤
                                              1

    anyone but rather to make _plain_ the _already_
                                 2         3

    divergent viewpoints and to _precede_ to bring
                                      4

    them together. _No error_
                    5

5. The _main_ effect of the chairman's speech was    ① ② ③ ④ ⑤
         1

    _to quiet_ the audience so that the discussion
    2    3

    could continue _farther._ _No error_
                      4       5

6. The next speaker _waisted_ more time by express-    ① ② ③ ④ ⑤
                    1

    ing anger with the young people _present_ rather
                                    2

    than _formally_ addressing the _issues_ at hand.
           3                    4

    _No error_
        5

7. I am certain that the committee _learned_ a    ① ② ③ ④ ⑤
                                   1

    lesson about discussing _volatile_ issues. Next time
                            2

    it will _altar_ _its_ presentation so that speakers
             3    4

    will be more to the point. _No error_
                            5

8. That way, _less_ misunderstandings will occur.    ① ② ③ ④ ⑤
            1

    The Lakeview Town _Council_ had planned a
                          2

    _similar_ discussion, but changed _its_ program.
      3                               4

    _No error_
       5

9. It will have a speaker on the new <u>*adoption*</u>    ① ② ③ ④ ⑤
                                            1

   laws. Many people need <u>*advise*</u> on this topic.
                              2

   It <u>*plainly*</u> will be less controversial than the
      3

   <u>*peace*</u> movement was. <u>*No error*</u>
      4                           5

10. The council has <u>*all  ready*</u> advertised in    ① ② ③ ④ ⑤
                          1

    local papers and <u>*expects*</u> a large <u>*number*</u> of
                          2                     3

    people to be <u>*eager*</u> to attend. <u>*No error*</u>
                     4                          5

PRACTICE
VII

*Directions:*    Circle the error in each incorrect sentence. If there is no
error, put a "C" next to the sentence. Write the correct word to replace
each error.

1. Sam wants to lend your calculator for a
   few days.                                              _____
2. Please contact me by phone.                           _____
3. The book alluded to the Civil War in
   great depth.                                           _____
4. Company B's continued dumping into
   the stream has aggravated the pollution
   problem.                                               _____
5. His foot-tapping really aggravated me.                _____
6. Please rise your hand if you know the
   answer.                                                _____
7. She gives the allusion of being much
   thinner than she is.                                   _____
8. Bill sure doesn't want to work overtime.              _____
9. John promised to learn Maria English.                 _____
10. José felt awful bad about the accident.              _____

# Words and Phrases to Avoid

Some incorrect words and phrases are used frequently. Because of their common use, we begin to think they are *correct*. No amount of usage will make the following words acceptable as proper English. Just as Eliza Doolittle's dialect labeled her as "lower class," our use of certain words and phrases can label us "uneducated." This may sound unfair, but most employers are looking for people who can give their businesses the best "image." "Ain't" won't do it.

### ain't
We used to be able to say, "Ain't" ain't in the dictionary. Now it is! Most educated people do not accept this word. You would do well to avoid it. *Ain't* is used incorrectly in place of **am not, is not, isn't, are not, aren't.**

### could of
This is incorrect grammar. You mean **could have.** The contraction for **could have** is **could've,** which sounds like **could of** but is not written that way. Example: I *could have* danced all night.

### disregardless, irregardless
There is no such word. The word you want is **regardless.**
Example: *Regardless* of the weather, I plan to wear my new suit.

### graduate (high school or college)
You did not *graduate high school,* you **graduated from** *high school,* or any other school.

### hisself
There is no such word. Use **himself.** Example: The congressman gave *himself* high marks on his voting record.

### nowheres
This is incorrect. Use **nowhere.** Example: This debate is going *nowhere.*

### off of
Incorrect usage. The word *of* is to be omitted. Example: He climbed *off* the bleachers.

### theirselves
There is no such word. Use **themselves.** Example: The employees, *themselves,* decided on office policy.

### you all

This is incorrect grammar. Examples: *All of you* must attend.
*You must all* attend.

### youse

This is not a word. *You* is singular; *you* is plural.

PRACTICE
VIII

*Directions:* Underline the error in each of the following sentences.
Rewrite each sentence correctly.

1. This project is going nowheres.

   _____

2. You all are dressed incorrectly.

   _____

3. He ain't a very good businessman.

   _____

4. Wilma could of had the promotion if she had wanted it.

   _____

5. Please take your feet off of my desk.

   _____

6. I graduated high school in 1979.

   _____

7. Irregardless of your opinion, I plan to hire the person I interviewed Tuesday.

   _____

# Chapter 20 Word Usage

**Practice I** *Page 245.*

1. **(2)** you're (you are)
2. **(2)** beer
3. **(1)** aisle
4. **(1)** bored
5. **(2)** strait
6. **(1)** sum
7. **(2)** waste
8. **(2)** throne
9. **(1)** steal
10. **(1)** tales

**Practice II** *Page 245.*

1. **(2)** shone
2. **(3)** site
3. **(1)** sum
4. **(3)** soul
5. **(1)** stake
6. **(2)** stationery
7. **(3)** Theirs
8. **(2)** stare
9. **(5)** No error
10. **(1)** tow

**Practice III** *Page 248.*

1. **(4)** vale
2. **(1)** dyes
3. **(4)** too
4. **(1)** altogether
5. **(2)** rites
6. **(2)** site
7. **(1)** current
8. **(3)** manner
9. **(4)** waste
10. **(1)** weighed
11. **(4)** great

12. **(5)** No error
13. **(4)** pale

**Practice IV** *Page 249.*

1. **(1)** eager
2. **(2)** personnel
3. **(4)** continually
4. **(2)** council
5. **(3)** beside
6. **(3)** complimented
7. **(4)** lose
8. **(1)** miner
9. **(2)** healthful
10. **(4)** persecuted

**Practice V** *Page 252.*

1. **(1)** already
2. **(4)** born
3. **(3)** Capitol
4. **(5)** No error
5. **(1)** eminent
6. **(4)** minor
7. **(5)** No error
8. **(1)** forth
9. **(3)** to
10. **(3)** course

**Practice VI** *Page 254.*

1. **(4)** type of
2. **(3)** their
3. **(1)** tried
4. **(4)** proceed
5. **(4)** further
6. **(1)** wasted
7. **(3)** alter
8. **(1)** fewer

9. (**2**) advice

10. (**1**) already

**Practice VII** *Page 256.*

1. Sam wants to *borrow* your calculator for a few days.

2. Please *communicate with* me by phone.

3. The book *referred* to the Civil War in great depth.

4. C (correct)

5. His foot-tapping really *annoys* me.

6. Please *raise* your hand if you know the answer.

7. She gives the *illusion* of being much thinner than she is.

8. Bill *surely* doesn't want to work overtime.

9. John promised to *teach* Maria English.

10. José felt *very* bad about the accident. Or, José felt *really* bad about the accident.

**Practice VIII** *Page 258.*

1. This project is going *nowhere*.

2. *You* are dressed incorrectly. *You are all* dressed incorrectly.

3. He *isn't* a very good businessman.

4. Wilma *could have* had the promotion if she had wanted it.

5. Please take your feet *off* my desk.

6. I *graduated from* high school in 1979.

7. *Regardless* of your opinion, I plan to hire the person I interviewed Tuesday.

# CHAPTER 21

# CUMULATIVE REVIEW

This review covers the following concepts:

- Effectiveness of Expression
- Punctuation
- Capitalization
- Spelling
- Vocabulary
- Word Usage

After completing the Cumulative Review exercises, evaluate your ability on the SUMMARY OF RESULTS chart on page 278. Acceptable scores for each practice are given.

To identify your areas for skill improvement, find the question numbers you answered incorrectly on the SKILLS ANALYSIS table. The table will show which of your skills need improvement and the necessary chapters to review.

## Practice Exercises

PRACTICE
I

*Directions:* Blacken the circle that corresponds to the number of the incorrect sentence in each group. If there is no error, blacken number 5.

1. (1) Doctor Smith ordered a mahogany, octagonal-shaped table for his office.  ① ② ③ ④ ⑤
   (2) I wasn't never told to take this highway to your house.
   (3) My aunt baked that cake for me because I'm giving a party for my friend Joan.
   (4) The plumber left the job almost immediately because he did not have the parts he needed.
   (5) No error

2. (1) After the clerk gave the customer his change, he heard the store's closing bell ring.
   (2) We went to a concert at City Center and heard an especially fine pianist, Peter Serkin.
   (3) The best part of our day occurred when we realized we were seated behind Woody Allen.
   (4) The traveling lecturer hardly ever has time for lunch.
   (5) No error

   ① ② ③ ④ ⑤

3. (1) The lecturer prepared slides to accompany his talk.
   (2) Since the hour was late, the Senate adjourned its session.
   (3) Our weekly discussion club, which meets each week on Thursday, invited Bob Woodward to comment on his latest book.
   (4) Although our building was painted last year, it looks as if it needs to be painted again.
   (5) No error

   ① ② ③ ④ ⑤

4. (1) Our group, we visited the museum to see a display of mobiles.
   (2) The supplies included pencils, papers, rulers, and blackboards.
   (3) I have never seen a neater room!
   (4) The president meets with his aides at 11:55 A.M.
   (5) No error

   ① ② ③ ④ ⑤

5. (1) I cancelled the meeting because I expected  ① ② ③ ④ ⑤
to be too busy to attend.
   (2) Do you ever feel pressured by a too-full
schedule?
   (3) Because the plane arrived late, we missed
our connecting flight.
   (4) The resettled Cuban refugees, they finally
got jobs.
   (5) No error

6. (1) The best part of the book occurs when the  ① ② ③ ④ ⑤
brothers meet after a 25-year separation.
   (2) The most exciting event in the movie is the
auto race.
   (3) The reason for his absence is because he has
the flu.
   (4) Richard Robinson hasn't been seen for
weeks.
   (5) No error

7. (1) What the sergeant wanted to know was what  ① ② ③ ④ ⑤
supplies the unit needed.
   (2) Because it's Monday, the stores are open
late.
   (3) The reason for my confusion is that my
notes are incomplete.
   (4) My children left for day camp at 9:00 A.M.
   (5) No error

8. (1) Because the power steering fluid had evapo-  ① ② ③ ④ ⑤
rated, the wheel would not turn.
   (2) An insect, it is difficult to eliminate after it
has become established in an area.
   (3) William the Conqueror and the barons of
Normandy were not in agreement about the
invasion of England.
   (4) His parents said that John was neither too
young nor too busy to hold a part-time job.
   (5) No error

9. (1) If history doesn't repeat itself, why is there never an end to war?      ① ② ③ ④ ⑤

   (2) Why is it that nothing never goes smoothly?

   (3) On the subject of the dangerous effects of depletion of the ozone layer, one cannot hope for scientists' accord.

   (4) An automobile accident occurred when two drivers proceeded into the intersection at the same time.

   (5) No error

10. (1) More and more people are eating fruits and vegetables because they are health conscious.      ① ② ③ ④ ⑤

   (2) There are many solutions to the energy crisis.

   (3) A man, carrying a fishing pole and wearing hip boots, stood knee-high in the flooded street.

   (4) None of Albert Schweitzer's expenses was borne by the Evangelical Mission that had sent him to Lambaréné.

   (5) No error

11. (1) The football team played football well yesterday at the football game.      ① ② ③ ④ ⑤

   (2) Mark's hockey team is the best in the league.

   (3) None of the basketball players was at the victory party.

   (4) Pete Sampras rarely plays tennis with a player who isn't a pro.

   (5) No error

12. (1) Sylvester Stallone's latest movie seems to be a variation on his famous *Rocky* movies.
    (2) The novel that the customer requested was out of print.
    (3) Herbert Hoover, a man of humble beginnings, he was the son of a blacksmith.
    (4) Because the restriction on misleading food labels is vague, the consumer must be vigilant.
    (5) No error

① ② ③ ④ ⑤

13. (1) The reason the ERA was defeated was a lack of understanding of the benefits.
    (2) The reason the primitive people relied on witch doctors was because these people thought they had been attacked by evil spirits.
    (3) Our specialty is good service.
    (4) We feature the finest service in the field.
    (5) No error

① ② ③ ④ ⑤

14. (1) Although I am exhausted, I plan to rest this afternoon.
    (2) Please don't leave early; we are enjoying your company.
    (3) The world's future population is hardly ever discussed without mention of food and other resources.
    (4) If you continue to smoke, I'll continue to ask you to stop.
    (5) No error

① ② ③ ④ ⑤

15. (1) Don't you find talk shows boring?
    (2) Are you not Mary Smith's aunt?
    (3) The business manager, who was ranting uncontrollably, lost the respect of his colleagues.
    (4) Although it isn't none of my business, I'm concerned about your health.
    (5) No error

① ② ③ ④ ⑤

PRACTICE
II     _Directions:_   Blacken the circle that corresponds to the number of the best completion for each sentence

1. The mailman slipped on the steps          ① ② ③ ④
   (1)  because he was wearing boots.
   (2)  even though they were icy.
   (3)  because the steps, they were icy.
   (4)  because they were icy.

2. Jules continues to smoke          ① ② ③ ④
   (1)  because he cannot read the warning.
   (2)  since smoking is hazardous to his health.
   (3)  although smoking is hazardous to his health.
   (4)  when it's hazardous to his health.

3. The camping trip was uncomfortable          ① ② ③ ④
   (1)  in spite of the heat and the bugs.
   (2)  although it was hot and buggy.
   (3)  even though it was hot and buggy.
   (4)  because of the heat and the bugs.

4. The Giants played well          ① ② ③ ④
   (1)  because they feared the fans.
   (2)  because the day was unseasonably hot.
   (3)  even though the day was unseasonably hot.
   (4)  even though the weather was perfect.

5. That man, who speaks at every public meeting,          ① ② ③ ④
   (1)  he is my uncle Joe.
   (2)  he is a town nuisance.
   (3)  never offers an acceptable suggestion.
   (4)  hardly never offers an acceptable suggestion.

6. I'd like draperies made of a transparent fabric          ① ② ③ ④
   (1)  that sees through and is durable.
   (2)  that is durable.
   (3)  that I can see through and is durable.
   (4)  that is durable and I can see through.

7. My favorite scene in *Romeo and Juliet*                ① ② ③ ④
    (1) is when Romeo kills himself.
    (2) is the one where Romeo kills himself.
    (3) is because Romeo kills himself.
    (4) is the one in which Romeo kills himself.

8. Bob Rice, my brother's friend,                ① ② ③ ④
    (1) he's a male chauvinist.
    (2) is a male chauvinist.
    (3) he is a male chauvinist.
    (4) are male chauvinists.

9. The reason for the meeting                ① ② ③ ④
    (1) was that the principal had resigned.
    (2) was because the principal had resigned.
    (3) was when the principal had resigned.
    (4) was to discuss the principal's resignation.

10. The game was dull                ① ② ③ ④
    (1) because the teams were not evenly matched.
    (2) although the teams were not evenly matched.
    (3) in spite of the fact that the teams were not
        evenly matched.
    (4) since both the teams played well.

PRACTICE
III
_Directions:_   Blacken the circle that corresponds to the number of the
error in each sentence. If there is no error, blacken number 5.

1. "Would you like to record the song you                ① ② ③ ④
    1
   wrote? " , the conductor asked the singer.
       2  3 4
   _No error_
       5

2. If you wish, you may pick some flowers—                ① ② ③ ④
                1                                2
   only those along the side of the house—
                                            3
   for your centerpiece." _No error_
                        4    5

3. "My favorite book," said Melissa "is *Animal*    ① ② ③ ④ ⑤
   1                    2                3
   *Farm.*" *No error*
        4    5

4. The show (for which you have tickets) begins    ① ② ③ ④ ⑤
            1                          2
   promptly at 7:45 and ends (believe it or not at
                 3                              4
   11:00. *No error*
          5

5. Last Sunday, I met my *ex* roommate (whom    ① ② ③ ④ ⑤
             1              2          3
   I haven't seen for twelve years) in the super-
                                4
   market. *No error*
           5

6. "After you've practiced writing r's," said Miss    ① ② ③ ④ ⑤
   1                                      2
   Green, go right on to s's." *No error*
        3                  4    5

7. The *Brownies* annual party was at the home    ① ② ③ ④ ⑤
        1
   of Jane *Simpson* on Friday, at *4:15* P.M.
                2            3        4
   *No error*
   5

8. *Two thirds* of the membership voted—despite    ① ② ③ ④ ⑤
      1                              2
   last year's increase—to increase the *dues* for
           3                            4
   the next fiscal year. *No error*
                         5

9. The painter called this morning to say "that    ① ② ③ ④ ⑤
                                          1
   he won't be able *to* begin working until next
         2          3
   *weekend.* *No error*
        4        5

10. Please _take_ that envelope _(the_ one on the hall
      1                          2

   _table)_ across the street to Mrs. _Jones. No error_
      3                                   4

_Directions:_    Blacken the circle that corresponds to the number of the error in each sentence. If there is no error, blacken number 5.

1. _Sue Simpson,_ the lead in _The Glass menagerie,_    ① ② ③ ④ ⑤
      1      2                          3

   is a really competent _actress. No error_
                              4          5

2. _When_ you leave _School_ today, take a _bus_ and    ① ② ③ ④ ⑤
      1              2                    3

   meet me in New York _City. No error_
                           4      5

3. _Our course, history IA,_ will include discussion    ① ② ③ ④ ⑤
      1     2        3

   of the settlement of the _American_ colonies.
                                4

   _No error_
      5

4. _Remember_ that _Ellie_ said we should meet _Her_    ① ② ③ ④ ⑤
      1              2                          3

   for lunch on _Tuesday. No error_
                    4          5

5. _On Twenty-second Street_ there's a charming    ① ② ③ ④ ⑤
      1      2          3

   restaurant called _Lou's. No error_
                         4       5

6. _Mr. Goren_ reminded _us, "all_ lights must be    ① ② ③ ④ ⑤
      1   2              2     3  4

   turned off in the laboratory at the end of the

   work day." _No error_
                  5

7. The *lieutenant* asked *captain* *John Forbes* to    ① ② ③ ④ ⑤
      1                    2            3

   cut the ribbon at the ceremonies marking

   the opening of *Fort Titan.* *No error*
                     4             5

8. *This* *October,* *halloween* falls on a *Tuesday.*    ① ② ③ ④ ⑤
     1       2           3                      4

   *No error*
     5

9. "We can learn much," said *Edith,* *"from* the    ① ② ③ ④ ⑤
    1                           2        3

   cultures of the *east."* *No error*
                     4         5

10. *One* of the earliest and most significant *British*    ① ② ③ ④ ⑤
      1                                            2

    *documents* is the *magna carta.* *No error*
        3                  4               5

PRACTICE
V      *Directions:*    Blacken the circle that corresponds to the number of the
incorrectly spelled word in each group. If there is no error, blacken
number 5.

1. (1) reinstitute          (4) foxes          ① ② ③ ④ ⑤
   (2) overated             (5) No error
   (3) happily

2. (1) dyeing               (4) dice           ① ② ③ ④ ⑤
   (2) dying                (5) No error
   (3) dies

3. (1) truly                (4) duly           ① ② ③ ④ ⑤
   (2) noticable            (5) No error
   (3) famous

4. (1) guidance             (4) edibles        ① ② ③ ④ ⑤
   (2) necessarily          (5) No error
   (3) mispell

5. (1) safely    (4) recede   ① ② ③ ④ ⑤
 (2) proceed   (5) No error
 (3) preceed

6. (1) merrily    (4) theif    ① ② ③ ④ ⑤
 (2) quickly    (5) No error
 (3) niece

7. (1) succeed    (4) wierd    ① ② ③ ④ ⑤
 (2) willingly   (5) No error
 (3) reference

8. (1) canning    (4) radios    ① ② ③ ④ ⑤
 (2) caning    (5) No error
 (3) confering

9. (1) seize     (4) axes    ① ② ③ ④ ⑤
 (2) secede    (5) No error
 (3) skys

10. (1) recede    (4) hunches   ① ② ③ ④ ⑤
 (2) ilegal    (5) No error
 (3) disillusion

11. (1) sheep    (4) exrays    ① ② ③ ④ ⑤
 (2) data     (5) No error
 (3) datum

12. (1) sevens    (4) loosens   ① ② ③ ④ ⑤
 (2) courtisans   (5) No error
 (3) 9s

13. (1) atheletic   (4) mice    ① ② ③ ④ ⑤
 (2) exceed    (5) No error
 (3) supersede

14. (1) vaccinate   (4) height    ① ② ③ ④ ⑤
 (2) mouthsful   (5) No error
 (3) oxen

15. (1) befitting   (4) leisure    ① ② ③ ④ ⑤
 (2) allegiance   (5) No error
 (3) tonage

16. (1) deceive      (4) heroes      ① ② ③ ④ ⑤
   (2) relieve      (5) No error
   (3) ferret

17. (1) contraltoes      (4) duly      ① ② ③ ④ ⑤
   (2) trout      (5) No error
   (3) brothers-in-law

18. (1) crises      (4) seeing      ① ② ③ ④ ⑤
   (2) knifes      (5) No error
   (3) disappoint

19. (1) colonel      (4) concurred      ① ② ③ ④ ⑤
   (2) interceed      (5) No error
   (3) release

20. (1) rheostat      (4) vacuum      ① ② ③ ④ ⑤
   (2) tariff      (5) No error
   (3) trafic

**PRACTICE VI**

_Directions:_ Blacken the circle that corresponds to the number of the incorrect sentence in each group. If there is no error, blacken number 5.

1. (1) Once the bill was defeated, it was too late to argue its merits.      ① ② ③ ④ ⑤
   (2) In this decade of shortages, the large scale waist of paper is outrageous.
   (3) During the 1992 election, Bill Clinton led the Democrats to victory.
   (4) Most American first ladies have been quiet partners.
   (5) No error

2. (1) The headlights of a solitary car shone down the deserted country road.

   (2) All of the museum's newest paintings were shone at the recent exhibition.

   (3) The weather vane is broken again.

   (4) Beneath his unruffled exterior were the falsely arrested gentleman's true feelings of rage.

   (5) No error

① ② ③ ④ ⑤

3. (1) Napoleon would not settle for a small piece of Europe.

   (2) The judge carefully weighed both arguments.

   (3) Crew is a sport in which races with row boats take place.

   (4) Senator Bill Bradley was once a principle player on the New York Knicks.

   (5) No error

① ② ③ ④ ⑤

4. (1) During the summer of 1994, many American families traveled to New England.

   (2) Many immigrants have had difficulty adapting to life in America.

   (3) If you plan to film the entire Thanksgiving Day Parade, you'll need more than one real of film.

   (4) Even an expert fisherman has, on occasion, lost a rod and reel.

   (5) No error

① ② ③ ④ ⑤

5. (1) The United States had overlooked many acts of aggression towards other nations, until the Germans sank the *Lusitania*.

   (2) Mark lifts weights every morning.

   (3) My wait has dropped considerably since I've been on that diet.

   (4) Phil refuses to wait in line for a movie, a show, or dinner.

   (5) No error

① ② ③ ④ ⑤

6. (1) Some people enjoy camping.        ① ② ③ ④ ⑤
   (2) The sum of my camping experience is two days.
   (3) Martha is too vane to travel without a mirror.
   (4) All of our efforts were in vain because the project failed.
   (5) No error

7. (1) A bird flew past the window.        ① ② ③ ④ ⑤
   (2) Ira is home with the flu.
   (3) A squirrel was trapped in the chimney flue.
   (4) Did you bring a flie-swatter?
   (5) No error

8. (1) A female pig is called a sow.        ① ② ③ ④ ⑤
   (2) Jeannette cannot sew well at all.
   (3) That gift is so nice!
   (4) The ball crashed through the pain of glass.
   (5) No error

9. (1) The old man could not walk without his cane.        ① ② ③ ④ ⑤
   (2) Sugar comes from sugar cane.
   (3) Queen Elizabeth had a peaceful rein.
   (4) That sprained ankle caused me great pain.
   (5) No error

10. (1) The bough was full of blossoms.        ① ② ③ ④ ⑤
    (2) Everyone cheered when the pitcher through the third strike.
    (3) I don't like to sit in the bow of the boat.
    (4) Suzy enjoys wearing bows in her hair.
    (5) No error

11. (1) Do you like to walk in the rain?      ① ② ③ ④ ⑤
   (2) Have you ever seen a ewe?
   (3) The canoe floated silently down the straight.
   (4) Please, straighten your tie.
   (5) No error

12. (1) Some girls will not marry because they are    ① ② ③ ④ ⑤
      waiting for nights in shining armor.
   (2) My favorite fish dinner is baked fillet of sole.
   (3) Many poems have been written about the
      journeys of the soul.
   (4) Because I was the sole tennis player in the
      group, I played a great deal of golf.
   (5) No error

13. (1) Do you grate potatoes into that recipe?     ① ② ③ ④ ⑤
   (2) No, but I beet the eggs thoroughly.
   (3) Have you tried beet soup?
   (4) Yes, it's delicious.
   (5) No error

14. (1) I am not fond of that newscaster.       ① ② ③ ④ ⑤
   (2) His manor is very offensive.
   (3) Did you visit the Manor House at Batsto?
   (4) In what manner would you like the idea pre-
      sented?
   (5) No error

15. (1) Since the meat shortage began, I've been    ① ② ③ ④ ⑤
      freezing a great deal of meat.
   (2) Did you see the lovely freeze on the mu-
      seum wall?
   (3) Please meet me at Wendy's.
   (4) Lately, loud noises wear on my nerves.
   (5) No error

276 ENGLISH THE EASY WAY

PRACTICE
VII

*Directions:* Blacken the circle that corresponds to the number of the incorrect word in each sentence. If there is no error, blacken number 5.

1. Please <u>leave</u> Marie go to the movies <u>with</u> me    ① ② ③ ④ ⑤
        1                                 2

   because I <u>may</u> not go to town <u>alone</u>. <u>No error</u>
             3                   4     5

2. If you don't <u>want</u> to <u>build</u> shelves for me,    ① ② ③ ④ ⑤
                1     2

   <u>then</u> <u>learn</u> me how to build them myself.
     3    4

   <u>No error</u>
      5

3. Because this is a <u>real</u> problem in <u>our</u> community,    ① ② ③ ④ ⑤
                 1         2

   we need a <u>real</u> dedicated group of citizens <u>to</u>
            3                    4

   study possible solutions. <u>No error</u>
                   5

4. Many reports indicate that sugar-coated <u>serials</u>    ① ② ③ ④ ⑤
                                  1

   are not <u>healthful</u>; <u>therefore,</u> more nutritious
          2      3

   breakfast foods <u>are</u> appearing on the market.
             4

   <u>No error</u>
      5

5. When Stuart gives the signal, <u>everyone</u> must    ① ② ③ ④ ⑤
                             1

   <u>rise</u> to his feet, <u>raise</u> his hands above his head,
    2          3

   and <u>set</u> down. <u>No error</u>
      4       5

6. Because so <u>many</u> campers had cut down trees,    ① ② ③ ④ ⑤
      1

   <u>there</u> were <u>less</u> trees this year <u>than</u> ever before.
    2        3             4

   <u>No error</u>
    5

7. Mr. Smith <u>taught</u> the science <u>class</u> the <u>affect</u>    ① ② ③ ④ ⑤
          1            2    3

   of radiation <u>upon</u> cells. <u>No error</u>
          4       5

8. That <u>author</u> carries the <u>principle</u> of free will    ① ② ③ ④ ⑤
      1           2

   <u>farther</u> than any <u>previous</u> author. <u>No error</u>
    3        4       5

9. Mrs. Kelly Warren, <u>formally</u> Miss Kelly    ① ② ③ ④ ⑤
               1

   O'Rourke, <u>emigrated</u> <u>from</u> Ireland this <u>past</u>
          2     3          4

   year. <u>No error</u>
      5

10. <u>Its</u> an <u>illusion</u> to expect that <u>course</u> of action    ① ② ③ ④ ⑤
    1    2            3

    to have a positive <u>effect</u> on our long-range plan.
                4

    <u>No error</u>
     5

After reviewing the Answer Key on page 280, chart your scores below for each practice exercise.

**SUMMARY OF RESULTS**

| Practice Number | Number Correct | Number Incorrect *(Including Omissions)* | Acceptable Score |
|---|---|---|---|
| I | | | 11 Correct |
| II | | | 7 Correct |
| III | | | 7 Correct |
| IV | | | 7 Correct |
| V | | | 15 Correct |
| VI | | | 11 Correct |
| VII | | | 15 Correct |

To identify your areas for skill improvement, locate the questions you answered incorrectly and circle the numbers on this Skills Analysis Chart. Wherever you have circled errors, review the chapters listed in the last column.

**SKILLS ANALYSIS**

| Skill | Question Number | Review Chapter |
|---|---|---|
| **Practice I** | | |
| Double Negative | 1, 9, 15 | 15 |
| Unclear Pronoun Reference | 2 | 15 |
| Repetition | 3, 4, 5, 8, 11, 12 | 15 |
| Wordiness | 6, 7, 13 | 15 |
| Coordination of Ideas | 14 | 15 |
| **Practice II** | | |
| Coordination of Ideas | 1, 2, 3, 4, 10 | 15 |
| Repetition | 6, 8 | 15 |
| Wordiness | 7, 9 | 15 |

| Skill | Question Number | Review Chapter |
|---|---|---|
| **Practice III** | | |
| Quotation Marks | 1, 2, 3, 6, 9 | 16 |
| Parentheses | 4 | 16 |
| Hyphen | 5, 8 | 16 |
| Apostrophe | 7 | 16 |
| **Practice IV** | | |
| Capitalization | 1 to 10 | 17 |
| **Practice V** | | |
| Spelling | 1 to 20 | 18 |
| **Practice VI** | | |
| Word Usage | 1 to 15 | 20 |
| **Practice VII** | | |
| Word Usage | 1 to 20 | 20 |

# Chapter 21 Cumulative Review

**Practice I** *Page 261.*

1. **(2)** I wasn't *ever* told to take this highway to your house.
   Never use *not* (n't) and *never* together.

2. **(1)** After giving the customer change, *the clerk* heard the store's closing bell ring.
   Substitute *the clerk* for *he* in order to clarify who *heard*.

3. **(3)** *Our discussion club, which meets each Thursday,* invited Bob Woodward to comment on his latest book.
   Using *weekly* and *each week* in the same sentence is repetitious.

4. **(1)** *Our group visited* the museum to see a display of mobiles.
   *We* refers to *our group* and is, therefore, repetitious.

5. **(4)** The resettled Cuban *refugees finally* got jobs.
   *They* refers to the *Cuban refugees* and is, therefore, repetitious.

6. **(3)** *He is absent* because he has the flu.
   *Is because* is unacceptable form. The sentence reads more smoothly as corrected.

7. **(1)** *The sergeant wanted* to know what supplies the unit needed.
   *What . . . was* is poor form. The sentence reads more smoothly as corrected.

8. **(2)** *An insect is difficult* to eliminate after it has become established in an area.
   The first *it* referred to *insect* and was, therefore, repetitious.

9. **(2)** Why is it that nothing *ever* goes smoothly?
   Never use *nothing* and *never* together.

10. **(5)** No error

11. **(1)** *The football team played well yesterday.*
    *Football* is repetitious.

12. **(3)** Herbert Hoover, a man of humble beginnings, *was* the son of a blacksmith.
    *He* refers to *Herbert Hoover* and is, therefore, repetitious.

13. **(2)** *Primitive people relied on witch doctors because* those people thought they had been attacked by evil spirits.
    *Was because* is unacceptable form. The sentence reads more smoothly as corrected.

14. **(1)** *Because* I am exhausted, I plan to rest this afternoon.
    *Although* contradicts the intended meaning of the sentence. *Because* clarifies the meaning.

15. **(4)** Although it isn't *any* of my business, I'm concerned about your health.
    Never use *not* and *none* together.

**Practice II** *Page 266.*

1. **(4)** The mailman slipped on the steps *because they were icy.*
   *Because they were icy* explains, simply, why the mailman slipped on the steps. The word *because* makes the connection between the mailman's slipping and the icy steps.

CUMULATIVE REVIEW **281**

2. **(3)** Jules continues to smoke *although smoking is hazardous to his health. Although smoking is hazardous to his health* shows that Jules continues to smoke despite the hazards.

3. **(4)** The camping trip was uncomfortable *because of the heat and the bugs. Because of the heat and the bugs* explains, simply, why the camping trip was uncomfortable. The word *because* makes the connection between the discomfort and the heat and the bugs.

4. **(3)** The Giants played well *even though the day was unseasonably hot. Even though the day was unseasonably hot* shows that the Giants played well despite the heat.

5. **(3)** That man, who speaks at every meeting, *never offers an acceptable suggestion. Never offers an acceptable suggestion* is the only grammatically correct completion for this sentence.

6. **(2)** I'd like draperies made of a transparent fabric *that is durable. That is durable* is the only possible completion for this sentence. All other choices are grammatically incorrect and repetitive.

7. **(4)** My favorite scene in *Romeo and Juliet is the one in which Romeo kills himself. Is the one in which Romeo kills himself* is the only completion that conforms to correct style.

8. **(2)** Bob Rice, my brother's friend, *is a male chauvinist. Is a male chauvinist* is the only grammatically and stylistically correct completion for this sentence.

9. **(4)** The reason for the meeting *was to discuss the principal's resignation. Was to discuss the principal's resignation* is the simplest completion for this sentence. *Was that, was when,* and *was because* are poor style.

10. **(1)** The game was dull *because the teams were not evenly matched. Because the teams were not evenly matched* explains, simply, why the game was dull. The word *because* makes the connection between the dull game and the unevenly matched teams.

**Practice III** *Page 267.*

1. **(4)** "Would you like to record the song you wrote?" the conductor asked the singer.
Never place a comma *outside* quotation marks. Never use two marks of punctuation at the end of a sentence.

2. **(4)** If you wish, you may pick some flowers—only those along the side of the house—for your centerpiece.
This sentence is not a quotation; therefore, the quotation mark at the end of the sentence is incorrect.

3. **(3)** "My favorite book," said Melissa, "is *Animal Farm.*"
Use a comma to separate *said Melissa* from the remainder of the quotation.

4. **(4)** The show (for which you have tickets) begins promptly at 7:45 and ends (believe it or not) at 11:00.

   The writer shows by the use of parentheses that *believe it or not* is not necessary to the meaning of the sentence. Once opened, parentheses must be closed.

5. **(2)** Last Sunday, I met my <u>ex</u>-roommate (whom I haven't seen for twelve years) in the supermarket.

   When the prefix *ex-* means former or previously, as in *ex-roommate,* it is followed by a hyphen.

6. **(3)** "After you've practiced writing r's," said Miss Green, "go right on to s's."

   When continuing an interrupted quotation, precede the quoted portion with quotation marks.

7. **(1)** The <u>*Brownies'*</u> annual party was at the home of Natalie Simpson on Friday at 4:15 P.M.

   Use an apostrophe to show possession. The apostrophe follows the *s* in *Brownies* to show that the party belonged to them.

8. **(1)** <u>*Two-thirds*</u> of the membership voted—despite last year's increase—to increase the dues for the next fiscal year.

   *Two-thirds* is an example of two descriptive words brought together to form a new word; therefore, it is hyphenated.

9. **(1)** The painter called this morning to say <u>*that*</u> he won't be able to begin working until next weekend.

   *That* signals the fact that this is a report, or an indirect quotation, of what the painter said. Therefore, no quotation marks are needed.

10. **(5)** No error

**Practice IV** *Page 269.*

1. **(3)** Sue Simpson, the lead in *The Glass Menagerie,* is really a competent actress. Capitalize the complete title of a play, book, or long poem.

2. **(2)** When you leave <u>school</u> today, take a bus and meet me in New York City. *School* is not capitalized because it does not refer to a particular school.

3. **(3)** Our course, <u>*History IA,*</u> will include discussion of the settlement of the American colonies.

   *History IA* is the name of a particular course and, therefore, should be capitalized.

4. **(3)** Remember that Ellie said we should meet <u>*her*</u> for lunch on Tuesday. Never capitalize a pronoun unless it is the first word of a sentence or a quotation.

5. **(5)** No error

6. **(4)** Mr. Goren reminded us, "<u>*All*</u> lights must be turned off in the laboratory at the end of the work day."

   *All* is the first word of the quotation and must be capitalized.

7. **(2)** The lieutenant asked <u>*Captain*</u> John Forbes to cut the ribbon at ceremonies marking the opening of Fort Titan.

   *Captain* refers to a particular captain, *Captain John Forbes,* and must be capitalized.

8. **(3)** This October, <u>*Halloween*</u> falls on a Tuesday.

   *Halloween* is the name of a holiday and, therefore, must be capitalized.

9. (4) "We can learn much," said Edith, "from the cultures of the *East*."

*East* refers to a particular section of the world and, therefore, must be capitalized.

10. (4) One of the earliest and most significant British documents is the *Magna Carta*.

*Magna Carta* is the title of a document and, therefore, must be capitalized.

**Practice V** *Page 270.*

For explanations of the following answers, see spelling rules in Chapter 18.

1. (2) overrated
2. (5) No error
3. (2) noticeable
4. (3) misspell
5. (3) precede
6. (4) thief
7. (4) weird
8. (3) conferring
9. (3) skies
10. (2) illegal
11. (4) x-rays
12. (3) 9's
13. (1) athletic
14. (2) mouthfuls
15. (3) tonnage
16. (5) No error
17. (1) contraltos
18. (2) knives
19. (2) intercede
20. (3) traffic

**Practice VI** *Page 272.*

For explanations of the following answers, see word list and examples in Chapter 20.

1. (2) In this decade of shortages, the large scale *waste* of paper is outrageous.
2. (2) All of the museum's newest paintings were *shown* at the recent exhibition.
3. (4) Senator Bill Bradley was a *principal* player on the New York Knicks.
4. (3) If you plan to film the entire Thanksgiving Day Parade, you'll need more than one *reel* of film.
5. (3) My *weight* has dropped considerably since I've been on that diet.

6. (3) Martha is too *vain* to travel without a mirror.
7. (4) Did you bring a *fly*-swatter?
8. (4) The ball crashed through the *pane* of glass.
9. (3) Queen Elizabeth had a peaceful *reign.*
10. (2) Everyone cheered when the pitcher *threw* the third strike.
11. (3) The canoe floated silently down the *strait.*
12. (1) Some girls will not marry because they are waiting for their *knights* in shining armor.
13. (2) No, but I *beat* the eggs thoroughly.
14. (2) His *manner* is very offensive.
15. (2) Did you see the lovely *frieze* on the museum wall?

**Practice VII** *Page 276.*

For explanations of the following answers, see word list and examples in Chapter 20.

1. (1) Please *let* Marie go to the movies with me because I may not go to town alone.
2. (4) If you don't want to build shelves for me, then *teach* me how to build them myself.
3. (3) Because this is a real problem in our community, we need a *very* dedicated group of citizens to study possible solutions.
4. (1) Many reports indicate that sugar-coated *cereals* are not healthful; therefore, more nutritious breakfast foods are appearing on the market.
5. (4) When Stuart gives the signal, everyone must rise to his feet, raise his hands above his head, and *sit* down.

6. **(3)** Because so many campers had cut down trees, there were *fewer* trees this year than ever before.

7. **(3)** Mrs. Smith taught the science class the *effect* of radiation upon cells.

8. **(3)** The author carries the principle of free will *further* than any previous author.

9. **(1)** Mrs. Kelly Warren, *formerly* Miss Kelly O'Rourke, emigrated from Ireland this past year.

10. **(1)** *It's* an illusion to expect that course of action to have a positive effect on our long-range plan.

# CHAPTER 22

# WRITING RIGHT

May 13, 1987

Golden Oldie Records
WOR-TV
1440 Broadway
New York City, NY 10019

Dear Dumbbells:

What's the matter with you people? I sent you my hard-earned money (I'm a construction worker) for the Lawrence Welk records you advertised, and after waiting eight weeks I received a Rolling Stones album. Can't you get anything right? I hate rock'n roll music. It gives me a splitting headache. I have a good mind to punch you in the nose!

Boiling mad,

*Harry Flowers*

Harry Flowers[1]

## *A Word With You . . .*

Harry Flowers' letter is one of the horrible examples presented in the National Association of Retailers' booklet, *How Not to Get Results*. Mr. Flowers has a legitimate complaint, but he should realize that he will not win friends or influence people by abusing them. Furthermore, a letter of complaint should contain all the necessary information needed to help a merchant redress your grievance.

Homework assignment for Mr. Flowers: Study this chapter . . . and clean up your act!

---

1 National Association of Retailers *How Not to Get Results*

# Thinking Before You Write

Whether you intend to write a letter, memo, report, or essay, one thing is certain. You should make some important decisions before you get started. You could delay making those decisions—as many people do—and end up writing your piece again and again until you hit upon what you want to say. By doing some critical thinking before you write, you could save yourself a great deal of time and frustration. Following are some questions to help you plan your writing.

### SHOULD YOU WRITE?

If you can accomplish your purpose by talking to someone, then talk! During your work day, if you see an associate three, four, perhaps five times, there may be no need to write a memo regarding a simple matter. Say what you want if the issue can be concluded with that conversation, and save time and paper. Do not, however, expect a busy co-worker to carry your request in his or her head for an hour, a day, or a week. Do yourself and the person with whom you are communicating a favor. Put the question, the information, or the request in writing, if the issue cannot be concluded with a brief conversation. If you don't commit your request or message to paper, the person receiving it will have to remember it or write it down. You risk having your message ignored or forgotten.

If you have a complaint about the dangerous cracks in the sidewalk on your block, your request to the town administrator will get faster attention if it arrives on paper. If you are a student with an assignment to write a term paper, of course you have no choice but to put your thoughts down on paper. When you write, you must make those thoughts clear to your reader. You want your message to be understood.

### WHAT DO YOU WANT TO SAY?

Recognizing what you feel and think can still be worlds apart from understanding the "purpose" of your writing. For example, you may feel angry that the dress you bought shrunk when you had it dry-cleaned, but the purpose of your writing a letter to the store will be to persuade them to refund your money. Consider your basic motivation in writing. Are you going to berate your senator for voting against the Clean Air Bill or will you congratulate him for his veto? Will your term paper support the idea that Hamlet had a tragic flaw or will it show him as a victim of circumstance? Before you write, you must know what you want to say.

# Who Is Your Reader?

A first step in writing is determining who will read what you write. Your audience will determine what type of writing you will do. Think of one idea going to two different people. For example, the following two letters describe a job, first to a friend, then to a potential employer. Notice how Jane's tone changes, depending on whether she is writing to someone she knows well or a potential employer.

Dear Judy,

I've finally decided to pack in this dead-end job. I can no longer calmly listen to Mr. B. present my ideas as his accomplishments. He is so convinced they're his, he even brags to me about them. Most recently, I developed a training program for new employees. I sent him a draft. A week later, a manual was circulated with his name on it. He didn't even correct my typing error. I've applied for a comparable position in another company and hope to have good news for you soon.

Love,<br>Jane

16 Sunset Road<br>Boise, Idaho 83701<br>April 3, 1995

Ms. Eunice Munson
General Manager
ABC Corporation
Boise, Idaho 83720

Dear Ms. Munson:

I am writing in response to your ad in Sunday's *Inquirer* for an assistant manager. I believe my experience is directly related to the position offered.

For the past five years, I have assisted the manager of XYZ Corporation. My duties have included drafting speeches, devising company manuals, and providing administrative support. Most recently, we worked together on a training manual for new employees. While I still find my present position challenging, I am seeking employment with greater growth potential.

I enclose a copy of my résumé and look forward to hearing from you at your earliest convenience.

Sincerely,<br>Jane Brody

## HOW DO YOU SAY IT BEST?

Writing takes many forms: letters, memos, reports, notes, lists, and books, to name just a few. Depending on your intention, the form you choose will determine the structure of your writing. We discuss letters, memos, reports, and essays in the following pages.

# Letters

In the age of audiovisual miracles, letter writing has become a forgotten art. When phones were not available to exchange news or greetings, letters were common. Because people wrote often, they wrote well.

We still need letters on occasion in our personal lives: thank you notes, condolence notes, letters to distant friends or relatives, and greetings of all kinds. Letter writing is also helpful when we want to request information, complain about a product, let our congressmen know our views, or apply for a job.

Another type of letter that has not been eliminated by the telephone is the business letter. Anyone who works for a business, large or small, should be able to write a clear business letter. While modern office technology may somewhat reduce the need for letters, it won't eliminate it. Although computer software—spellchecks and grammar-checks—override human error, the machines continue to be only as good as their operators.

This chapter will not attempt to deal with all the skills necessary to write a perfect letter. Elements such as grammar, spelling, and punctuation, covered earlier, play an important role. This chapter provides you with models and helpful hints for form and style.

## HEADINGS

Headings consist of your address, the date, the name and address of the recipient, and the salutation or greeting. Business letters include each of these elements (see Sample Business Letter on page 292). However, when writing to a friend or relative, your address and the recipient's address need not be included. The sample letters later in the chapter will show you the correct formats to use for both informal letters and business letters.

Part of the heading is the salutation or greeting—the "Dear [Somebody]." Changes in language usage and business itself have made "Dear [Somebody]" increasingly complicated. Once upon a time, if you were addressing an unknown group, the term "Gentlemen:" was appropriate. Today, those gentlemen include women who would not take kindly to that greeting. Often, business people sign letters that give no clue to the signator's gender. For example: "T. Warren" or "Terry Smith." "Ladies and Gentlemen:," "Dear T. Warren:," or "Dear XYZ Company:" could replace more conventional salutations. Some sample salutations follow.

| Friendly Salutations | Formal Salutations |
| --- | --- |
| Dear Aunt Sue, | Gentlemen: |
| Dear Rosa, | Dear Sir: |
| Dearest William, | Dear Sirs: |
| | Dear Mr. Wright: |
| | Dear Ms. Smith: |
| | Dear Dr. Schwarz: |
| | Dear Director of Personnel: |
| | Dear Salespeople: |
| | Ladies and Gentlemen: |
| | Dear T. Warren: |
| | Dear XYZ Company: |

## INTRODUCTION, BODY, CONCLUSION

Since your opening paragraph is like a first meeting with your reader, the impression you make is a lasting one. The reader expects to have your purpose revealed. Whether it is to complain, compliment, or inform, it should be clear immediately.

Throughout the letter, say what you want to say as clearly and as briefly as possible. Your letter may be long, but it should not ramble. Every sentence should be a necessary one.

The traditional interviewer-reporter questions help keep a letter clear and concise. Note which questions apply to your letter: *who, what, when, where, why.* If you answer these questions, you will probably give all the necessary information for situations ranging from a party invitation to a complaint about a broken radio.

Just as your first impression is a lasting one, so is your final one. Make sure your reader knows what you expect. If you plan a follow-up phone call, say so and say when. If you want a written or telephone response, ask for it. If you began the letter by thanking the person, reinforce your appreciation in the final paragraph.

## CLOSINGS

Closings range from "Love," to "Very truly yours," depending upon the purpose and audience of your letter. The closing should be in the same style as the salutation. A letter would not begin "Dear Sir:" and end with "Love."

| Friendly Closings | Formal Closings |
|---|---|
| Sincerely, | Very truly yours, |
| Warmly, | Yours very truly, |
| With love, | Yours truly, |
| Love, | Sincerely yours, |
| Fondly, | Yours sincerely, |
| Warmest regards, | Sincerely, |
| (Any other nice thought | Respectfully yours, |
| you may want to use) | Very respectfully yours, |
| | Yours respectfully, |

# Business Letter Format

### Sender's Address:

This is obviously not necessary on printed stationery. If your letter will be on plain paper, place your address in the upper right-hand corner or upper left.

### Date:

Spell out the month in a business letter. Date can be right or left, but it must be aligned with the recipient's address and closing. In this age of personal computers many people keep their letters "flush left." Everything lines up with the left margin.

### Recipient's Address:

On the left-hand side of the page, include the name (and title or position if you know it) of the person to whom you are writing. Then, put the name of the company or organization and, finally, the complete address of the organization.

### Salutation:

See page 289 for examples of formal salutations.

### Introduction:

One short paragraph states the subject or purpose of the letter. Make your purpose clear immediately.

**Body:**

One, two, three or more paragraphs contain the relevant details. Each paragraph should expand on one main point.

**Conclusion**

The conclusion should give direction. One short paragraph finishes the letter with a summary, a recommendation, an instruction, or a thank you.

**Closing:**

See page 290 for formal closings.

**Name and Signature**

Business form dictates typing your name and title beneath your signature. If your title is on your letterhead, do not repeat it. If you are hand writing a business letter as a consumer, print your name beneath your signature. You want the response addressed to you correctly. Name and signature should be aligned with the date and closing.

---

## SAMPLE PERSONAL LETTER

---

*July 15, 1988*

*Dear Aunt Polly,*

*Thank you so much for the leather-bound dictionary. It was a perfect graduation gift. I will treasure it always.*

*My family and I were sorry you couldn't come to Arizona for the graduation and party. We all missed you very much. I'm enclosing some photos for you.*

*Love,*
*David*

---
**SAMPLE BUSINESS LETTER**
---

## ABC Corporation

===

*231 West 53 Street, New York, New York 10022*

July 10, 1995

Ms. Cary Jeffers
66 Columbus Avenue
Tarrytown, New York 10571

Dear Ms. Jeffers:

Thank you for your resume and letter (dated June 25, 1995), asking about employment opportunities at the ABC Corporation. Because we receive so many unsolicited requests each year, we must limit interviews to those with relevant work experience. While your resume indicates a strong manufacturing background, you have no experience with our specialized product.

Thank you for considering ABC Corporation. We wish you every success in your employment search.

Very truly yours,

*David Green*

David Green
Personnel Director
DG/sl

## SAMPLE COMPLAINT LETTER

106 Goodtree Drive
Columbus, Ohio 43201
March 10, 1995

Mr. William Wellington, President
Cool-It, Inc.
738 Second Avenue
New York, New York 10017

Dear Mr. Wellington:

On February 23, 1995, while a local Cool-It, Inc., representative was servicing my air-conditioner, the tank of freon exploded in my basement. The tank was located next to my clothes dryer, so this explosion caused damage to my dryer as well as some clothing that was in the dryer at the time. This event led to an expensive dryer service call and the need to replace a complete load of laundry. I would appreciate full reimbursement for the items listed on the attached bills.

The serviceman who repaired the dryer suggested that the malfunction was mostly caused by the freon. The spilled freon permanently froze the dryer thermostat, preventing the dryer from cooling down. A full load of towels and underwear that were in the dryer at the time became excessively dried out to the point of disintegration. In fact, when I removed the laundry from the dryer, the laundry fell apart in my hands. Prior to the explosion, the load of laundry was fine and the dryer worked perfectly.

I've always had an excellent relationship with your company and look forward to your continuing service. Your representative, by the way, was courteous and thorough in his job of repairing the air-conditioning system. I look forward to your payment within a reasonable amount of time.

Thank you.

Sincerely,

*Mary Edwards*

Mary Edwards

PRACTICE

I    *Directions:*   Read the following facts and write a letter of complaint from Tom Williams based on those facts. You can include your opinion or attitude toward the problem in the letter.

Tom Williams bought a clock radio at Warren's Department Store on May 15, 1995. Tom could not get the alarm to work properly from the start. He brought the clock radio back to the store on May 19, 1995, and was told he would have to mail the item to the manufacturer for repair. Tom lives at 1419 Maple Street, Dayton, Ohio 82050. The clock radio was made by the Wake-Up Corporation located at 2042 Main Street, Chicago, Illinois 60791.

PRACTICE

II    *Directions:*   Rewrite Matthew Manager's letter. Remember to write simply and clearly.

February 10, 1995

Ms. Suzanne Jones
1 Willow Way
Edison, New Jersey 08817

Dear Ms. Jones:

I wish to thank you for choosing to inform me about the incident which occurred at MarketRite last Friday. It is important to us in management to know what is going on when salespeople help—or don't help—as the case may be customers.

John Rich is usually a generally friendly person. He has been under very extreme personal pressure even though that should not enter into it. I have taken the liberty of speaking with John and am assured that what happened to you won't happen again at least from him.

Please be kind enough to accept the enclosed herewith gift certificate as a small token of our regret.

Thank you for shopping at MarketRite.

Sincerely,

*Matthew Manager*

Matthew Manager
Vice President
Customer Relations

# Memoranda

A memorandum is commonly used for interoffice communications, such as sharing information, setting procedures, or asking questions within a company or organization. Every business has its preferred style for memos, but the tips that follow can be applied in most situations. Treat a memo as you would any other kind of writing. Plan ahead and then construct clear and concise sentences that convey your intentions. Either write a brief outline or jot down phrases that will help you organize your thinking. Stick to the subject at hand. State your purpose first, then give all the necessary facts. Tell what you want done or request information. If you are informing the reader, do so simply and clearly, keeping your tone friendly and positive. A memo need not be an edict. Simply answer the question, "What do I want to accomplish?" Again, make sure that what you say is accurate because memos, when filed, become records.

## FORMAT FOR MEMOS

Although a memo is very much like a letter in purpose, its format is different. The memo style sheet that follows is one, common memo format.

---

### MEMO STYLE SHEET

---

MEMO

TO:       The name of the recipient, including the person's title and/or department

FROM:     Your name, title, and department

DATE:     The date you send the memo

SUBJECT:  The subject of the memo

Start with your purpose in writing the memo. Include relevant details, or what the recipient must know, and close with what the recipient must do.

Thank the recipient and offer to answer any questions.

ABC:df

A memo usually is not signed at the bottom the way a letter would be. Instead, the sender initials the memo next to his or her name at the top. Sometimes, for security reasons, companies require full signatures on memos.

Note the structure of the following sample memo. The opening gets right to the point. Helms recalls that he and Sperry have agreed that there is a potential problem. The memo proposes a solution. For emphasis, the solution is set off—highlighted—in its own paragraph. Other ways to visually emphasize ideas include using numbers, letters, headings, or bullets (black dots) at the left-hand margin. The final two sentences tell the reader what to do.

Note also that job titles appear next to the names. These titles can be omitted in very informal memos. However, memos that will be filed for future reference should have the titles included.

---

## SAMPLE MEMO 1

---

MEMORANDUM

TO:            Janice Sperry, Vice President, Marketing
FROM:        Rob Helms, Purchasing Agent
DATE:        July 10, 1995
SUBJECT:    Purchase Agreement #47

When we spoke last Thursday, we agreed that the above purchase agreement #47 was vague and could cause problems with the completed job. I propose the following changes:

1. Delete lines 4–7.
2. Insert the following in place of lines 2–7: "The seller is under no obligation to accept returned merchandise 90 days after delivery."

Let me know by the 15th if you agree with these changes or have another suggestion. Thank you.

RH:cd

The following memo is a very informal one between two co-workers. No last names appear in the heading, and without these names, the memo would be almost useless as a record. Mary gets to the point immediately, however, noting co-responsibility for coordinating the company's calendar and letting Pat know the times during the week that she will be available. Mary then tells Pat what to do—that is, to decide on a convenient time to work together.

---

## SAMPLE MEMO 2

---

MEMO

TO:        Pat
FROM:      Mary
DATE:      November 3, 1994
SUBJECT:   Company Calendar

You and I are responsible for coordinating the company calendar. I'm available any morning next week. Please let me know the day and time convenient for you.

Now read the following memo. Does it meet all the requirements of a well-written memo? Yes. This short memo gets the job done. The subject is clearly stated in the SUBJECT line. In the first sentence, the reader learns the new due date and what has to be done. Sentences 2 and 3 show the writer's concern for Bill Greenway's well-being. There is nothing wrong with a personal touch. One improvement would be to include the job titles and/or department names.

---

## SAMPLE MEMO 3

---

FROM THE DESK OF JOHN SMITH:

TO:        Bill Greenway
DATE:      December 10, 1994
SUBJECT:   Monthly Report

You should be pleased to know that your December monthly report will not be due until January 7, 1995. This extension should make your vacation a little more relaxing. Enjoy the holidays.

## LONG MEMOS

Sometimes you will need to write a longer memo. For example, you may want to provide background information related to the subject, as well as give current information. Read the following memo and note how the need dictates form. In this memo, the introduction explains the background of Dr. Taylor's idea. The first part of the memo tells what the writer intends to do. The memo then asks Martin Atkins, the reader, to do three things: read, select, and estimate. The memo concludes with a due date. It is effective and should result in Dr. Taylor's getting what he wants.

---

### SAMPLE MEMO 4

---

MEMO

TO:         Martin Atkins, Director of Rehabilitation Services
FROM:       Bruce Taylor, M.D., Hospital Administrator
DATE:       June 10, 1994
SUBJECT:    Development of a hortitherapy program for patients

At the recent Hospital Directors' Round Table, Dr. Seymour Watson of the New England Hortitherapy Council gave a speech on the positive results achieved with hospitalized patients who had been taking care of plants. He further explained the long-term benefits of hortitherapy, especially its continued use after the patient's discharge.

Dr. Watson gave me some guidelines on raising funds for such a project. I plan to survey the board to see how much money could be made available for our own hortitherapy program.

I've attached Dr. Watson's studies, "The Use of Hortitherapy in Geriatric Settings," "Hortitherapy in a Psychiatric Setting," and "Outpatient Programs in Hortitherapy." Please study these and decide which approach we could use at Sunnycrest.

After you decide which patients would benefit most from the program, estimate what personnel and supplies would cost for 20 patients. I'll need your cost estimates by July 16, 1994, so that I can review them before presenting my report to the Board of Directors on July 30.

BT:sz

### DISCIPLINARY MEMOS

If you find it necessary to write a disciplinary memo, bear in mind that a disciplinary memo must:

- document inappropriate or unacceptable behavior
- focus on the serious effect of such behavior
- establish guidelines for future behavior
- state consequences of continued inappropriate behavior
- schedule a follow up review of progress

PRACTICE
III

_Directions:_  Rewrite the memo below to conform with the guidelines for a disciplinary memo.

Memo

TO:        Edna Employee
FROM:    Sandy Supervisor
DATE:    March 25, 1995

We talked today about your being late a lot lately. This is not the way we do things around here. It makes it look like you don't care about your job, and other people complain about it.

The next time you're late it could be serious.

PRACTICE
IV

_Directions:_  Write an appropriate memo for each situation below.

1. From a supervisor in the order department to the inventory control manager, noting a shortage in a recent shipment to a key client.
2. From a supervisor, who plans to be away, to an employee designated to cover that supervisor's duties during that time.

# Reports and Proposals

A report is a detailed statement of accomplishments or findings. A proposal is a request for funding or support to solve a recognized problem or to implement a new idea.

Since reports and proposals serve different functions, they take on different forms. Regardless of the format, however, the basics of good writing prevail. You should present your information in a clear, concise style. You need to document your facts, and if you are taking facts from another source, you must give credit to those sources. In a formal report for school, you would use footnotes. For a business report, you would include footnotes where appropriate. Your conclusions should be set off from your facts so the reader is able to distinguish fact from opinion.

## REPORTS

Most reports have a set form, similar to an outline. For example, a business report may follow this format:

| | |
|---|---|
| COVER PAGE: | Title, author, date of report |
| SUMMARY OR ABSTRACT: | A brief overview of the subject covered and conclusions drawn |
| INTRODUCTION: | A beginning section in which you set the scene, giving relevant background information and/or explaining terminology used in the report |
| BODY: | The information you are sharing, which supports the conclusions you have drawn |
| APPENDIX: | All additional relevant data, such as sources of information, additional charts and graphs, and supporting statistics |

In preparing reports for business, check for company style by referring to previous reports. If you ask, you may even find a company manual with clear guidelines for report writing. For school reports, ask your teacher what particulars are important to him or her. No one form is correct, but you should use the form preferred.

A lengthy report should have a cover page indicating the purpose of the report, the person or persons to whom it is submitted, the person or persons by whom it is submitted, and the date. The table of contents indicates the scope of the report and the organization of the body of the report. Lengthy reports include a summary at the beginning so that the reader can know at the start the scope and breadth of the report without having to first read the entire report. In the following sample, note the cover page, table of contents, and excerpt from the introduction of a report.

REPORT

OF THE

JOINT STATEWIDE TASK FORCE ON

SOLID WASTE DISPOSAL SITES

Submitted to:

John Doe

Commissioner of Environmental Protection

by:

The Joint Statewide Task Force on Solid Waste Disposal

March, 1995

TABLE OF CONTENTS

I.   INTRODUCTION AND OVERVIEW

This report assesses the condition of existing solid waste disposal sites in New Jersey. While landfills are closing, the amount of solid waste produced continues to rise. Faced with this crisis, government must make hard choices based on an accurate appraisal of those few remaining sites.

At the turn of the century, refuse was taken to a nearby "dump," of which there may have been a thousand. The focus was then on repelling flies, dissipating odor, and avoiding fires. The remedy was the use of a "sanitary landfill," which meant nothing more than regularly covering the refuse with layers of soil or sand.

Over the years, the nature of the waste stream has changed. Toxic materials have entered those landfills. Often, hazardous waste from manufacturers has been accepted along with household waste. This has contaminated rainwater on the site. The tainted water, leachate, has become part of the groundwater and contaminates nearby wells.

Currently, ten landfills accept household waste, and eighty accept industrial waste. Each presents problems. Their continued use is necessary because we have not yet reduced the waste stream or employed alternative technologies that would neutralize that waste. While an in-depth discussion of those aspects is beyond the scope of this report, they raise questions in the assessment of existing landfills: May existing landfills safely continue in use? If so, for how long and under what conditions? This report provides answers to those questions.

## PROPOSALS

Proposals follow the same general approach as reports, although most proposals have their own form. Among different companies or agencies, the requested format will vary; one typical form follows.

---

### TYPICAL PROPOSAL FORMAT

---

*Background:*

Describe in one short paragraph the history of the operation you plan to change.

*Example:*   MarketRite has been offering one express lane to customers with ten or fewer items for the past twelve years. The express shopper used to be the exception, but is now the rule. Many working men and women stop in for three or four items on their way home.

*Present Conditions:*

What goes on now? Why is it inadequate?

*Example:*   Express lanes defy the term. The lanes are exceptionally long and customers often choose to forego buying the one or two items to avoid the lines. This is demonstrated by the merchandise left on the magazine racks near the express lanes.

*Proposed Solution:*

What changes will you make? What new equipment will be needed? What personnel changes will be needed? How will other operations be affected?

*Example:*   Open two lanes for express purchases during peak times. In order to maintain regular service in other lines, additional part-time help must be hired. Encourage respecting the item limit for express lanes. Have the store manager periodically check for bottlenecks during assumed "slow times" and reassign someone from a regular line to express. This step will be difficult at first, but will become easier as patterns are noted.

*Benefits:*

What long- and short-term benefits will result?

*Example:*   MarketRite will attract the new breed of shopper. Working people will find shopping at MarketRite is as convenient, more cost effective, and more versatile than the convenience stores. We will retain the traditional shopper by continuing to provide quality check-out for them while eliminating the disgruntled "fast shopper" who "just has six items" and would like to cut into the regular line.

*Alternatives:*

What are some possible alternatives?

*Examples:*   Do not hire additional part-time help for peak times. This would mean closing a regular register to open the additional express lane and would reduce service to the traditional shopper.

Do not try to monitor during assumed "slow times." Nothing will be gained by not trying.

Hire additional full-time help to keep the extra express lane open. This may not be cost effective. Relieving the problem during peak times may be sufficient.

# Essays

Essays, written for school, for publication, or for yourself, present your own ideas, views, or conclusions. Essays, as well as other writing, benefit from careful planning. Follow these steps to good essay writing.

---
### EASY WRITING STEPS
---

### Plan
Establish a controlling idea by defining your topic and major points.

### Outline
Think through your writing from beginning to end. A perfect, final outline is not necessary; outlining serves to order your thoughts and ideas and to subordinate supporting details to major points.

### Draft

Fast and furious. Get it down on paper. Don't agonize over grammar, structure, and word choice.

### Edit

Fine tuning. Now is the time to agonize over organization, grammar, structure, and word choice. Begin with the end. If you want your audience to continue reading, say immediately why you are writing; you are not writing a mystery. Don't keep your audience in suspense.

Follow with relevant details. Include facts that support the point you want to make. If you lead your readers down an unrelated side road, they may not return to the main issue.

### Rewrite

The final product. Make sure that editing did not destroy the flow of writing. One change often necessitates others. Follow through. Simplify reading with subheadings, capitalization, underlining, bulleting, and spacing.

## Editing and Rewriting

As you begin editing, ask yourself some important questions.

1. Does your letter, memo, report, proposal, or essay follow your original plan? If not, why not? You may have followed your plan but find that the ideas could be arranged more effectively now. Move those misplaced paragraphs or sentences. Don't hesitate to change the order, even though, at the beginning, it seemed the right way to arrange things. On second look, you may have found a better way of saying what you want to get across to the reader.

2. Are your ideas well supported? If not, you may need to expand on an idea and add evidence to your argument. On the other hand, if you've gone beyond the subject matter when you've defended a point, you may need to shorten that paragraph or delete an entire section.

3. Is the tone of your writing appropriate? Some people answer this question by reading the report or letter aloud. You can read to a friend—real or imagined—and ask yourself along the way, "Is this the way I would talk?" "Is my idea stated in a conversational way?" "Is the letter overwritten and stiff?" Remember: informal does not mean substandard, and substandard does not mean informal.

4. Have you accomplished your purpose? Find a friend who is not an expert in the subject at hand. Have that person read your letter or report. If your friend is honest, you'll soon know if you've accomplished your purpose for writing.

## CHECKING YOUR LANGUAGE

### *Wordiness*

Have you avoided repeating words or thoughts? You can expect your first draft to suffer from wordiness and repetition. Remember, though, that no reader wants to waste time cutting through sentences filled with repetition. When you force your readers to struggle, you try their patience. As you read the examples below, remember to go back and take two or three more words out of every sentence after you've finished editing your work.

Here are some examples of wordiness and repetition with their corrected forms:

No: Today in our modern world we can offer new products at competitive prices.

Yes: Today we can offer new products at competitive prices.

Note that "today" means the same as "modern world."

No: These are the basic essentials of our plan.

Yes: These are the essentials of our plan.

Note that by definition, "essentials" are basic.

PRACTICE
V

*Directions:* In the following sentences, eliminate the words that are not necessary to the meaning of the sentence.

1. Even after the machine stopped, smoke was visible to the eye.
2. We'll rent a conference room midway between our two offices.
3. If you don't understand an abbreviation, refer back to the index.
4. Rewrite the introduction again before you go on.
5. First and foremost, I want to commend your department.
6. Our study group reached a consensus of opinion.
7. Advanced planning was credited with saving the company.
8. Our product is totally unique.
9. The reason is because it would cost too much to replace the old equipment.
10. The battle produced gains that were small in size.

### Stilted Phrases

Have you avoided words that writers seem to *save* for letters, memos, and reports? Business letters are frequently filled with legal language as well as archaic words and phrases, even though they add no meaning. Ask yourself "Would I use this in conversation or at any other time?" If the answer is no, strike that heavy phrase from your work.

Here are some examples of stilted, out-of-date, and overly formal phrases that creep into business and report writing.

| Don't Use | Substitute |
|---|---|
| Due to the fact | Because |
| Attached herewith | Here is |
| In receipt of | Have received |
| In reference to | Concerning |
| At the present time | Now |
| Under separate cover | Separately |
| Thanking you in advance | Thank you |

PRACTICE
VI

*Directions:* Substitute plain English for the stilted language used in the following sentences.

1. In the process of checking your account, we have found that your bill is overdue.
2. Attached please find my check for $42.37.
3. I will take your plan under advisement.
4. We beg to advise you that our product will be on sale in May.
5. I am in receipt of your letter and its contents are noted.

### Clichés and Pretension

Did you use words that everyone has already used many times before? Are those words stilted and stuffy? You'll improve your writing if you choose a simpler, more precise term.

| Don't Use | Substitute |
|---|---|
| Utilize | Use |
| Maximize | Increase |
| Finalize | Finish |

| Don't Use | Substitute |
|-----------|------------|
| Prioritize | Rank |
| Optimize | Cut the cost, improve |
| Bottom line | Profit |
| Interface | Meet or work together |
| Facilitate | Help |
| Profitwise | Profit |

PRACTICE VII

_Directions:_  Substitute a precise word or a simpler word for the underlined word or words in each sentence.

1. We need to <u>systematize</u> our files so that we can <u>utilize</u> them easily.
2. <u>Size-wise,</u> these bookcases are a better choice for our office.
3. The way you use your time affects the <u>bottom line</u> figure for the company.
4. A larger sales force will <u>maximize</u> our profits.
5. Absenteeism <u>impacts</u> on production schedules.
6. Your report <u>legitimizes</u> our need for monthly meetings.
7. The personnel and production departments will <u>interface</u> to solve the problem.

## KEEPING SEXISM OUT OF YOUR WRITING

Follow these guidelines to avoid sexism in your writing.

1. Do not add _ess_ to words that do not require that suffix. For example, _actor_ means male actor and _actress_ means female, _manager_ means male or female _manager._
2. Where the word is comfortably modified to be unisex, modify it. _Chairperson_ sounds as legitimate as _chairman._
3. Try to avoid situations that require a singular pronoun. For example, instead of the following:

   > Each member of the management team took his place (or his/her place) at the conference table.

   Use:

   > Members of the management team took their places at the conference table.

## PROOFREADING

Proofreading is an important part of editing what you have written. It assures you that careless errors in grammar, punctuation, and sense have been caught and corrected. Proofreading must be done in several steps:

1. Read through for content. Do not expect to pick up technical errors. Do expect to pick up missing or transposed words or sentences and errors in information.
2. Read for grammar, spelling, punctuation, and sense. Force yourself to read *each* word.
3. Read one more time to ensure that changes did not alter consistency or sense.
4. Have another person proofread your work after you have proofread it yourself.

# Summary of Steps to Simplify and Clarify Your Writing

1. Use action words. Write so that your performers act and are not acted upon. (Unless you do not want to assign responsibility.)

   INSTEAD OF: A new check-cashing policy will be introduced this spring.

   USE: General Markets will introduce a new check-cashing policy this spring.

2. Limit your use of descriptive phrases.

   INSTEAD OF: We scheduled a meeting of supervisors of MIS for January 12.

   USE: We scheduled an MIS supervisors' meeting for January 12.

3. Eliminate unnecessary words and phrases.

   INSTEAD OF: When a new spa opens, all of the spas in the Wonder Woman chain take part in the grand opening of that spa.

   USE: All Wonder Woman spas take part in the grand opening of a new spa in the chain.

4. Use names rather than pronouns as often as possible.

   INSTEAD OF: When he gives the report to him, make sure he understands the ramifications.

   USE: When Tom gives the report to Jason, make sure Jason understands the ramifications.

5. Focus on concrete word choice rather than abstract.

   INSTEAD OF: In order to create a holiday atmosphere, we want to encourage spirit and festivity throughout the store.

   USE: In order to create a holiday atmosphere, we want managers to develop special displays, provide holiday music, and remind cashiers to say, "Happy holidays" to customers.

6. Avoid using performers as action words.

   INSTEAD OF: Please Federal Express the report to Michael.

   USE: Please send the report to Michael by Federal Express.

7. Use positive words; avoid negative words.

   INSTEAD OF: Only fifty some odd residents turned out for the opening of the Middletown Bank.

   USE: Over fifty residents participated in the opening of the Middletown Bank.

PRACTICE VIII

_Directions:_ Correct each sentence below according to the rules.

1. Use action words.

   The order was placed too late.

2. Limit your use of prepositional phrases.

   We arranged a meeting with the manager of data processing at the location in East Brunswick.

3. Eliminate unnecessary words and phrases.

   There are two possible approaches that we are considering.

4. Use names rather than pronouns as often as possible.

   When he delivers the papers to him, be sure he gets a signature.

5. Focus on concrete word choice rather than abstract.

   Contributions help many people.

6. Avoid using nouns as verbs.

   Please overnight mail the report to Michael.

7. Use positive words.

   If it's not inconvenient for you now, perhaps we could talk.

---

# Writer's Block

Any adult who has ever had reason to write more than three words at a time has experienced writer's block. What is writer's block? Think of it as the "empty paper syndrome"—the fight between the need to Get Something Down on a blank piece of paper and the desire to Get It Down Correctly on the first try—an impossible task.

To a great extent, writer's block occurs because we refuse to admit—or we haven't been taught—that no one can produce perfect written work on the first try. Writer's block results from thinking that you can put an idea on paper AND edit it at the same time. This creates unreasonable pressure. You can't. I can't. Well-known writers can't. You say you need proof? Read on.

Recently, the editors of *Writer's Digest* asked several authors of fiction to write articles using the title, "How I Write My Books." Their articles revealed different approaches to their craft, but one idea remained constant: there are two aspects to writing—creating and revising.

You may be wondering if this applies to you—after all, you don't write fiction. It does. Whether writing fiction or fact, you are dealing with two things: creating and revising.

What can be done to circumvent writer's block? Without knowing it, you have probably just taken the first step simply by thinking about the idea that creating and revising are two different tasks. If you accept that as a fact, you can go on to attack the first half of the process—creating.

Educators have developed techniques to help the writer get the creator working. Whether called brainstorming, improvisational writing, mapping, or clustering, these techniques have one idea in common: each writer is a combination of creator and editor. Each technique requires that your editor leave the room while your creator writes. The creator must work unhampered by concerns of spelling, word choice, and sentence structure. Each technique asks that, as you think about your subject, you jot down your thoughts in single words, phrases, or brief sentences, no matter how or in what order they occur to you. DON'T JUDGE YOUR THOUGHTS. JUST WRITE THEM DOWN. The result will be many related ideas (and a few unrelated, but that doesn't matter) that are not in logical order. That's fine. That proves you are part of the human race in which minds do not work in outline form.

Once you have your thoughts on paper, you can open the door and let the editor in. The editor will help you put your thoughts in order and polish your grammar, structure, and word choice. Finally, the editor will increase the readability of your essay by adding necessary subheadings, listing points where appropriate, and using white space creatively.

---

### Some Tools for Better Writing

*100 Ways to Improve Your Writing,* Gary Provost. New York: Mentor Books, 1995.

*Better Letters,* Jan Venolia. California: Ten Speed Press, Periwinkle Press, 1995.

*The Chicago Manual of Style,* Illinois: University of Chicago Press, 1993.

*The Elements of Style,* William Strunk, Jr. and E. B. White. New York: Macmillan Publishing Company, Inc. 1995.

*English the Easy Way,* Harriet Diamond and Phyllis Dutwin. New York: Barron's Educational Series, Inc., 1996.

*The Gregg Reference Manual,* William A. Sabin. Ohio: McGraw Hill, 1992.

*Style: Toward Clarity and Grace,* Joseph M. Williams. Chicago: University of Chicago Press, 1990.

*Write Right!* Jan Venolia. California: Ten Speed Press, Periwinkle Press, 1988.

*Writing the Easy Way,* Phyllis Dutwin and Harriet Diamond. New York: Barron's Educational Series, Inc., 1991.

Any good dictionary and thesaurus, online and on the shelf.

# Chapter 22    Writing Right

**Practice I** *Page 294.*

1419 Maple Street<br>
Dayton, Ohio 82050<br>
May 20, 1995

Service Manager
Wake-Up Corporation
2042 Main Street
Chicago, Illinois 60791

Dear Service Manager:

I bought the enclosed clock radio at Warren's Department Store in Dayton, Ohio, on May 15, 1995. The alarm did not work properly from the start.

On May 19, I brought the clock radio back to Warren's to exchange it for a new model or to have it repaired. The salesman would not accept the clock radio. He insisted that I return it to you. This is a great inconvenience. I never even used this appliance.

Please send me a new clock radio immediately. I also would encourage you to work out a fairer arrangement with your distributors. I know I would never buy a Wake-Up product again because of the inconvenience.

Very truly yours,

*Tom Williams*

Tom Williams

**Practice II** *Page 294.*

February 10, 1995

Ms. Suzanne Jones
1 Willow Way
Edison, New Jersey 08817

Dear Ms. Jones:

Thank you for informing me about the unfortunate experience you had at MarketRite last Friday. You clearly understand the importance of sharing such information with management. We do want to make our shopping environment pleasant.

The treatment you received was inexcusable. John Rich surprised and embarrassed himself by yelling at you. Although that behavior was not typical, it never should have occurred at all. Of course, I have spoken with John and extend his personal apology.

Please accept the enclosed gift certificate and my apology. You are our valued customer. When you are in MarketRite again, please ask for me. I would like to thank you personally for helping us improve our service.

Sincerely,

*Matthew Manager*

Matthew Manager
Vice President
Customer Relations

MM:er
enc.

**Practice III** *Page 299.*

MEMO

TO:        Edna Employee
FROM:    Sandy Supervisor
DATE:    March 25, 1995

As we discussed in our meeting today, you have been 30 minutes late for work on three occasions in the last two weeks. These incidents follow two earlier discussions we had regarding your tardiness.

In our talk today, we went over the Company's policy on tardiness and agreed that when you are late it creates problems for other employees who must cover for you. It also results in filling orders late, which can affect our customer relations. Repeated tardiness also causes resentment among co-workers who are consistently on time. As we agreed, you will purchase a new alarm clock and get a bus schedule so you have an alternative mode of transportation if your car will not start. As I pointed out, further incidents of tardiness could result in withholding your upcoming wage increase or, if sustained improvement is not seen, termination.

We will meet again in two weeks to review your record.

**Practice IV** *Page 299.*

1. TO:        Jack Barnes, Inventory Control Manager
   FROM:    Sally Farmer, Supervisor, Order Department
   DATE:    October 10, 1994
   SUBJECT: ORDER #67-8850/October 1, 1994

Please note that the above order was shipped short of 50 copies of WRITING THE EASY WAY. This customer is one of our key buyers and expects a replacement shipment within 2 days. Can you look into this and assure me that the shipment will go out immediately via Federal Express?

2. TO:        William
   FROM:    Rita
   DATE:    February 16, 1995
   SUBJECT: My upcoming vacation—2/23–2/30

Please read the attached outline of duties in its entirety before I leave on Tuesday. I will be available to answer any questions you might have regarding materials, personnel, etc. Please maintain a log of messages, and note which ones will not have been answered. John should be available to assist you when necessary. Thank you for taking on the extra load; I'll be available for same when your vacation comes along.

**Practice V**  *Page 307.*

1. Even after the machine stopped, smoke was visible.
2. We'll rent a conference room between our two offices.
3. If you don't understand an abbreviation, refer to the index.
4. Rewrite the introduction before you go on.
5. First, I commend your department.
6. Our study group reached a consensus.
7. Planning was credited with saving the company.
8. Our product is unique.
9. It would cost too much to replace the old equipment.
10. The battle produced gains that were small.

**Practice VI**  *Page 308.*

1. Checking your account, we have found that your bill is overdue.
2. Here's my check for $42.37.
3. I will consider your plan.
4. We want you to know that our product will be on sale in May.
5. I've received your letter.

**Practice VII**  *Page 309.*

1. We need to <u>organize</u> our files so that we can <u>use</u> them easily.
2. These bookcases are a better <u>size</u> for our office.
3. The way you use your time affects our <u>profits.</u>
4. A larger sales force will <u>increase</u> our profits.
5. Absenteeism <u>affects</u> production schedules.
6. Your report <u>demonstrates</u> (shows) our need for monthly meetings.
7. The personnel and production departments will <u>meet</u> (<u>work together</u>) to solve the problem.

**Practice VIII**  *Page 311.*

1. Henry placed the order too late.
2. We arranged a meeting in East Brunswick with the data processing manager.
3. We are considering two approaches.
4. When Smith delivers the papers to Caldwell, be sure Smith gets a signature.
5. Contributions provide food and clothing for the homeless.
6. Please send the report to Michael by overnight mail.
7. If it's convenient for you now, let's talk.

# FINAL REVIEW

This review covers all of the concepts presented in *English the Easy Way*, Chapters 1–22.

- Spelling
- Usage
- Effectiveness of Expression
- Punctuation and Capitalization

After completing the Final Review exercises, evaluate your ability on the SUMMARY OF RESULTS chart on page 337. Acceptable scores for each practice are given.

To identify your areas for skill improvement, find the question numbers you answered incorrectly on the SKILLS ANALYSIS table. The table will show which of your skills need improvement and the necessary chapters to review.

## SPELLING

*Directions:*   Blacken the circle that corresponds to the number of the incorrectly spelled word in each group. If there is no error, blacken number 5.

1. (1) belief          (4) changeable     ① ② ③ ④ ⑤
   (2) reference       (5) No error
   (3) caucas

2. (1) temperture     (4) absence        ① ② ③ ④ ⑤
   (2) exceed         (5) No error
   (3) misspell

3. (1) quantity        (4) libary         ① ② ③ ④ ⑤
   (2) probably       (5) No error
   (3) warrant

4. (1) subversive     (4) queue          ① ② ③ ④ ⑤
   (2) lucritive      (5) No error
   (3) psychology

5. (1) hygenic        (4) salient        ① ② ③ ④ ⑤
   (2) currency       (5) No error
   (3) eczema

6. (1) Wednesday      (4) contemptible   ① ② ③ ④ ⑤
   (2) biscuit        (5) No error
   (3) efemoral

7. (1) corrugated     (4) unecessary     ① ② ③ ④ ⑤
   (2) diphtheria     (5) No error
   (3) voucher

8. (1) wierd          (4) duly           ① ② ③ ④ ⑤
   (2) tuition        (5) No error
   (3) capital

9. (1) illustrative   (4) receits        ① ② ③ ④ ⑤
   (2) laboratory     (5) No error
   (3) judiciary

10. (1) though        (4) voluntary      ① ② ③ ④ ⑤
    (2) simular       (5) No error
    (3) surgeon

11. (1) preference    (4) deterrent      ① ② ③ ④ ⑤
    (2) economical    (5) No error
    (3) prefered

12. (1) psychology    (4) argument       ① ② ③ ④ ⑤
    (2) cooperation   (5) No error
    (3) rationally

13. (1) generally     (4) portable       ① ② ③ ④ ⑤
    (2) improbable    (5) No error
    (3) dispensible

14. (1) truely        (4) occurrence     ① ② ③ ④ ⑤
    (2) niece         (5) No error
    (3) neighbor

15. (1) cunning      (4) crushs      ① ② ③ ④ ⑤
    (2) tomatoes      (5) No error
    (3) mouthfuls

16. (1) sheep      (4) thiefs      ① ② ③ ④ ⑤
    (2) pianos      (5) No error
    (3) Z's

17. (1) men-of-war      (4) precede      ① ② ③ ④ ⑤
    (2) supersede      (5) No error
    (3) succeed

18. (1) misunderstand      (4) cancellation      ① ② ③ ④ ⑤
    (2) achevement      (5) No error
    (3) condemned

19. (1) acquire      (4) character      ① ② ③ ④ ⑤
    (2) assessment      (5) No error
    (3) Thursday

20. (1) churches      (4) realize      ① ② ③ ④ ⑤
    (2) wield      (5) No error
    (3) category

## USAGE—PART A

_Directions:_ Blacken the circle that corresponds to the number of the error in each sentence. If there is no error, blacken number 5.

1. No _two_ _cities_ in _this_ country _is_ identical.    ① ② ③ ④ ⑤
      1    2      3      4
  _No error_
    5

2. _Any_ of the local merchants _are_ _willing_ to    ① ② ③ ④ ⑤
  1                      2    3
  _support_ the United Fund. _No error_
    4                    5

3. This CD _has_ _been_ _laying_ on the table _all_    ① ② ③ ④ ⑤
            1    2    3                  4
  week. _No error_
    5

4. <u>*Either*</u> of those two congressmen <u>*will*</u> <u>*vote*</u>
  1           2  3
 against the President's <u>*proposed*</u> bill. <u>*No error*</u>
         4     5

             ① ② ③ ④ ⑤

5. <u>*One*</u> of the <u>*necessary*</u> prerequisites for change
  1    2
 <u>*are*</u> <u>*open-mindedness.*</u> <u>*No error*</u>
  3    4    5

             ① ② ③ ④ ⑤

6. Manuel and <u>*me*</u> <u>*travel*</u> to <u>*work*</u> together each
      1  2   3
 <u>*weekday*</u> morning. <u>*No error*</u>
  4     5

             ① ② ③ ④ ⑤

7. Taxes and <u>*laughter*</u> <u>*is*</u> always <u>*present*</u> in our
      1  2   3
 <u>*American*</u> way of life. <u>*No error*</u>
  4     5

             ① ② ③ ④ ⑤

8. Everyone must <u>*realize*</u> <u>*their*</u> own potential
       1  2
 and <u>*try*</u> to <u>*achieve*</u> it. <u>*No error*</u>
   3  4   5

             ① ② ③ ④ ⑤

9. Mario <u>*is*</u> a much <u>*more*</u> <u>*efficient*</u> bartender
    1   2  3
 than <u>*him.*</u> <u>*No error*</u>
   4  5

             ① ② ③ ④ ⑤

10. Elissa <u>*types*</u> <u>*much*</u> <u>*quicker*</u> <u>*than*</u> any <u>*other*</u>
    1   2   3   4
 person in the office. <u>*No error*</u>
        5

             ① ② ③ ④ ⑤

11. <u>*Each*</u> of the choices <u>*are*</u> <u>*equally*</u> unappealing
  1      2  3
 to <u>*me.*</u> <u>*No error*</u>
  4  5

             ① ② ③ ④ ⑤

12. Before the alarm <u>*had*</u> <u>*stopped*</u> <u>*ringing,*</u> Vera
        1    2
 <u>*had*</u> <u>*pulled*</u> up the shade. <u>*No error*</u>
  3  4      5

             ① ② ③ ④ ⑤

13. One of *those* women *speak* *as* well *as* a profes-
           1           2  3     4

    sional lecturer. *No error*
                   5
    ① ② ③ ④ ⑤

14. The dishes in the box *is* *on* sale this week
                    1 2

    only *and* will be *sold* for more next week.
           3         4

    *No error*
      5
    ① ② ③ ④ ⑤

15. The Township Committee *had* not *realized*
                         1      2

    that so many residents *were* *concerned* about
                      3     4

    the new zoning law. *No error*
                5
    ① ② ③ ④ ⑤

16. *Either* the subway or the *buses* *is* *crowded* at
     1                2   3  4

    this time of day. *No error*
              5
    ① ② ③ ④ ⑤

17. I *noticed* that older women *walk* *more* *graceful*
     1               2   3    4

    than teen-age girls. *No error*
              5
    ① ② ③ ④ ⑤

18. *Each* of the contestants *hope* to *win* the *grand*
     1             2     3     4

    prize. *No error*
        5
    ① ② ③ ④ ⑤

19. When I must *speak* to a *large* group of people,
           1       2

    I always speak *too* *soft.* *No error*
             3  4    5
    ① ② ③ ④ ⑤

20. The mail carriers *each* *has* *their* own *personal*
                 1  2  3      4

    gripes. *No error*
         5
    ① ② ③ ④ ⑤

21. *Any* of the women in that office *may* express
     1                     2

    *their* opinion at *any* time. *No error*
     3         4      5
    ① ② ③ ④ ⑤

22. Either the executive _or_ members of his staff   ① ② ③ ④ ⑤
                               1

    _was responsible_ for _breaking_ the law. _No error_
     2     3        4            5

23. Before they _signed_ the treaty, both parties   ① ② ③ ④ ⑤
                1

    _agreed_ to _uphold_ the terms _provided. No error_
     2      3            4     5

24. Reagan _was_ president before Bush _was,_ and   ① ② ③ ④ ⑤
         1                         2

    Clinton _served_ after Bush _had. No error_
          3          4   5

25. Either Charlie or _I_ will _call_ you or _he_ when   ① ② ③ ④ ⑤
                 1    2       3

    the order _is_ ready. _No error_
          4      5

26. _Romeo and Juliet are_ one of my favorite plays,   ① ② ③ ④ ⑤
               1

    but _I've_ never _seen it_ performed. _No error_
       2       3 4          5

27. _Was it_ Mr. Farrar _whom called_ you? _No error_   ① ② ③ ④ ⑤
    1 2           3    4       5

28. I _am always_ at the bus stop _earlier_ than _him._   ① ② ③ ④ ⑤
     1    2             3       4

    _No error_
     5

29. Eileen and _me are working_ on the night shift   ① ② ③ ④ ⑤
            1 2   3

    with _them. No error_
       4     5

30. Fifteen minutes _are_ all that I _can spare_ to   ① ② ③ ④ ⑤
              1        2   3

    listen to _your_ problems. _No error_
         4         5

31. The problem of _too_ many people _require_   ① ② ③ ④ ⑤
              1            2

    _immediate_ attention by world leaders _as well_
     3                       4

    _as_ scientists and environmentalists. _No error_
                        5

32. After many months *of arguing,* Congress finally     ① ② ③ ④ ⑤
                       1    2

   *adapted* the bill *into* law. *No error*
      3          4        5

33. Because his lawyer *strongly advised* him     ① ② ③ ④ ⑤
                     1       2

   to do *so,* Mr. Rodriguez *offered* his wife a
          3             4

   generous settlement. *No error*
                5

34. The *principle* reason for *my* not borrowing     ① ② ③ ④ ⑤
        1           2

   *your* credit card is that I'm afraid I'll *lose* it.
     3                        4

   *No error*
      5

35. *Your* supervisor *does* not appreciate *you*     ① ② ③ ④ ⑤
   1            2              3

   walking in *consistently* at 9:10. *No error*
          4              5

## USAGE—PART B

*Directions:* Blacken the circle that corresponds to the number of the error in each sentence. If there is no error, blacken number 5.

1. My brother *he* never *calls* before *visiting us.*     ① ② ③ ④ ⑤
              1         2         3  4

   *No error*
      5

2. Great men *throughout* history *hardly never*     ① ② ③ ④ ⑤
                 1             2    3

   avoided some minor *scandal. No error*
                  4      5

3. If you *had* called ahead *of* time, I could     ① ② ③ ④ ⑤
          1            2

   *of been* ready when you arrived. *No error*
     3 4                  5

4. George Burns *scarcely* *never* *missed* a *scheduled*
        1  2  3   4

   performance. *No error*
         5

   ① ② ③ ④ ⑤

5. The *sightseeing* trip on the sightseeing bus *was*
      1          2

   *one of* the highlights of our *much* deserved
    3         4

   vacation. *No error*
       5

   ① ② ③ ④ ⑤

6. Manny *was* shocked when Alfred *raised* his
      1        2

   voice; no one had *never* *spoken* to him in that
          3  4

   tone of voice. *No error*
         5

   ① ② ③ ④ ⑤

7. The sun *it* *is* 865,000 miles in diameter and
      1 2

   *has* a surface temperature of *about* 10,000°F.
    3        4

   *No error*
    5

   ① ② ③ ④ ⑤

8. A wise consumer *carefully* *reads* the labels and
         1   2

   doesn't *never* *buy* unmarked products. *No error*
      3  4       5

   ① ② ③ ④ ⑤

9. If you really *had* *wanted* to, you could *of*
        1  2       3

   *prevented* that misunderstanding. *No error*
    4          5

   ① ② ③ ④ ⑤

10. Some scientists *they* believe *that* one of the long-
          1    2

    range *effects* of food additives *is* hyperactivity
       3        4

    in children. *No error*
        5

    ① ② ③ ④ ⑤

## EFFECTIVENESS OF EXPRESSION—PART A

*Directions:* Blacken the circle that corresponds to the number of the correct completion for each sentence below. Choice 1 is always the same as the underlined portion and is sometimes the right answer.

1. In today's all-volunteer U.S. Army, *the recruit he starts* his two-year enlistment in a different atmosphere.  ① ② ③ ④ ⑤
   (1) the recruit he starts
   (2) the recruit starts
   (3) the recruit starting
   (4) a recruit he is starting
   (5) the recruits they start

2. *The reason that the former soldier would not recognize living conditions in today's army is because* the facilities are more home-like and less barracks-like.  ① ② ③ ④ ⑤
   (1) The reason that the former soldier would not recognize living conditions in today's army is because
   (2) The reason is that the former soldier would not recognize living conditions in today's army because
   (3) The former soldier would not recognize living conditions in today's army because
   (4) Being that the former soldier would not recognize living conditions in today's army is because
   (5) Because the former soldier would not recognize living conditions in today's army is because

3. Today's soldier enjoys *not only more comfort but also better pay.*   ① ② ③ ④ ⑤

   (1) not only more comfort but also better pay.

   (2) not only more comfort and better pay.

   (3) no more comfort and also better pay.

   (4) not only more comfort and, in addition, better pay.

   (5) not only more comforts and, in addition, better pay.

4. Nowadays employers can afford to be choosy *although the period of slow economic growth has increased* the number and the quality of the applicants.   ① ② ③ ④ ⑤

   (1) although the period of slow economic growth has increased

   (2) despite the period of slow economic growth has increased

   (3) in addition to the period of slow economic growth having increased

   (4) since the period of slow economic growth has increased

   (5) but the period of slow economic growth has increased

5. The recruits get *tough, demanding, and training that is useful* under the command of their drill sergeants.   ① ② ③ ④ ⑤

   (1) tough, demanding, and training that is useful

   (2) tough, demanding, useful training

   (3) tough, demanding, usefully training

   (4) tough, demanding, and usefully trained

   (5) tough, demanding, and useful in their training

6. Carl Williams is an excellent basketball coach and *he makes friends with the team members.*   ① ② ③ ④ ⑤

   (1) he makes friends with the team members.

   (2) a good friend to the team members.

   (3) the team members are his friend.

   (4) the team members liking him.

   (5) liking the team members.

7. Every Thursday night the Morgan family watches TV and *TV dinners are served.*    ① ② ③ ④ ⑤
   (1) TV dinners are served.
   (2) they ate TV dinners.
   (3) eats TV dinners.
   (4) eat TV dinners.
   (5) are eating TV dinners.

8. The City Council meets every Wednesday evening in private and *publicly on Thursdays.*    ① ② ③ ④ ⑤
   (1) publicly on Thursdays.
   (2) Thursdays meets publicly.
   (3) every Thursday in public.
   (4) also Thursdays in public.
   (5) has public meetings on Thursdays.

9. Carlos Battaglia has a good historical perspective *since he understands* current events.    ① ② ③ ④ ⑤
   (1) since he understands
   (2) because he understands
   (3) however, he understands
   (4) ; therefore, he understands
   (5) so he doesn't understand

10. I am not in agreement with most of the policies of the present administration, *but I can't change them.*    ① ② ③ ④ ⑤
    (1) but I can't change them.
    (2) so I don't want to change them.
    (3) so I can't change them.
    (4) since I can't change them.
    (5) therefore, I can't change them.

## EFFECTIVENESS OF EXPRESSION—PART B

_Directions:_ Blacken the space beneath the number that corresponds to the number of the group of words that correctly completes each sentence.

1. The boundaries of science have expanded significantly,    ① ② ③ ④ ⑤
   (1) and two distinct fields of science have emerged: pure and applied.
   (2) even though two distinct fields of science have emerged: pure and applied.
   (3) whenever two distinct fields of science have emerged: pure and applied.
   (4) and two fields of science, they have emerged: pure and applied.
   (5) despite two distinct fields of science have emerged: pure and applied.

2. The British pound was devalued    ① ② ③ ④ ⑤
   (1) and the reason was because of an inflationary spiral.
   (2) and the reason was because of inflation.
   (3) and it was because of an inflationary spiral
   (4) because of an inflationary spiral.
   (5) and it was when the inflation spiraled.

3. The Food Guide Pyramid provides a guide to daily food choices,    ① ② ③ ④ ⑤
   (1) although it will help people build a healthful diet.
   (2) thereby helping people build a healthful diet.
   (3) however they will help people build a healthful diet.
   (4) and in addition it will also help people build a healthful diet.
   (5) and then if you use it it will help people build a healthful diet.

4. Many people believed that the recent product "shortages"    ① ② ③ ④ ⑤
   (1) were because manufacturers wanted to raise prices.
   (2) resulted from manufacturers wanting to raise prices.
   (3) happened because of the manufacturers wanted to raise prices.
   (4) were because of the manufacturers, they wanted to raise prices.
   (5) resulted from manufacturers, they wanted to raise prices.

5. Viewers find it difficult to reach agreement on whether    ① ② ③ ④ ⑤
   (1) or not television, it encouraged violent behavior.
   (2) or not television, it does or doesn't encourage violent behavior.
   (3) or not television encourages violent behavior.
   (4) television hardly never encourages violent behavior.
   (5) or not television encourages violent behavior by viewing television.

6. One member of the Surgeon General's Scientific Advisory Committee on Television and Social Behavior felt that    ① ② ③ ④ ⑤
   (1) there is scarcely no question about whether television has a negative effect on its viewers.
   (2) there isn't no question about whether television has a negative effect on its viewers.
   (3) there isn't hardly any question about whether television has a negative effect on its viewers.
   (4) there is no question about whether television has a negative effect on its viewers.
   (5) there really isn't no question about whether television has a negative effect on its viewers.

7. Some TV viewers express their resentment toward anyone else censoring their viewing
choices,            ① ② ③ ④ ⑤

    (1) saying it's their job to censor the TV pro-
grams their children see.

    (2) saying it's the parents' job to censor the TV
programs their children see on television
programs.

    (3) saying it's the parents' job to censor the TV
programs their children see.

    (4) saying parents, they should censor the TV
programs their children see.

    (5) saying TV it should be censored by no one
but parents.

8. An environmental protection agency should            ① ② ③ ④ ⑤

    (1) set automobile pollution standards, oversee
stripmining, and prohibit dumping in public
waterways.

    (2) set automobile pollution standards, oversee
stripmining, and they will prohibit dumping
in public waterways.

    (3) set automobile pollution standards, do the
overseeing of stripmining, and they will prohibit dumping in private waterways.

    (4) set automobile pollution standards, oversee-
ing stripmining, and prohibiting dumping in
private waterways.

    (5) set automobile pollution standards, and they
will oversee stripmining, and prohibit
dumping in private waterways.

9. Many people who formerly drove to work are now taking buses

    ① ② ③ ④ ⑤

   (1) in order to conserve gas, preventing air pollution, and saving money.

   (2) and by the way, they conserve gas, prevent air pollution, and they're saving money.

   (3) in order to conserve gas, and they'll be preventing air pollution, and to save money.

   (4) in order to conserve gas, to prevent air pollution, and to save money.

   (5) in order to conserve gas, do air pollution prevention, and save money.

10. In order to encourage the commuter not to drive to work, some communities have installed park-and-ride facilities

    ① ② ③ ④ ⑤

   (1) where the commuter can leave his car and board a bus for the trip to work.

   (2) where they can leave his car and board a bus for the trip to work.

   (3) where they can leave their cars and board a bus for the trip to work.

   (4) and then they can leave their car and board a bus for the trip to work.

   (5) so that they can leave their car and board a bus for the trip to work.

11. The new employee is very organized;

    ① ② ③ ④ ⑤

   (1) even if she is always late.

   (2) so she is always late.

   (3) however, she is always late.

   (4) despite her always being late.

   (5) although she is always late.

12. The year 1995 showed a marked decline in ① ② ③ ④ ⑤
Americans traveling abroad
   (1) in spite of increasing terrorism.
   (2) inasmuch as there were increased inci-
      dences of terrorism.
   (3) due to increased terrorism.
   (4) because terrorism decreased.
   (5) even though there were increasing inci-
      dences of terrorism.

13. The French Revolution did not occur when the ① ② ③ ④ ⑤
peasants had no rights whatsoever;
   (1) rather, the Revolution occurred when the
      peasants began to taste the better life.
   (2) but it happened when they began to taste
      the better life.
   (3) so it did when they got some rights.
   (4) rather, the Revolution occurred when the
      peasants, they began to taste the better life.
   (5) instead they made the Revolution when
      they became rich.

14. Modern China has eliminated serious conta- ① ② ③ ④ ⑤
gious diseases
   (1) because they use trained nonprofessionals
      to aid their country's limited number of doc-
      tors.
   (2) since using trained nonprofessionals to aid
      their limited number of doctors.
   (3) therefore it uses trained nonprofessionals to
      aid the country's limited number of doctors.
   (4) by using trained nonprofessionals to aid the
      country's limited number of doctors.
   (5) for using trained nonprofessionals to aid the
      country's limited number of doctors.

15. During the first half of the eighteenth century, ① ② ③ ④ ⑤
    the Carter family built a mansion at Williams-
    burg where the family
    (1) it grew its own food, rode to hounds on
        horses from their own stables, and shipped
        its tobacco to England from its private dock.
    (2) they grew their own food, rode to the
        hounds on horses from their own stables,
        made equipment in their own craft shops,
        and shipped their tobacco to England from
        their private dock.
    (3) grew its own food, rode to the hounds on
        horses from its own stables, made equip-
        ment in its own craft shops, and shipped its
        tobacco to England from its private dock.
    (4) grew its own food, rode to the hounds on
        horses from their own stables, made equip-
        ment in its own craft shop, and shipped
        their tobacco to England from its private
        dock.
    (5) grew their own food, rode to the hounds on
        horses from their own stables, made equip-
        ment in their own craft shop, and shipping
        tobacco from their own private dock.

## PUNCTUATION AND CAPITALIZATION

_Directions:_ Blacken the circle that corresponds to the number of the
error in each sentence. If there is no error, blacken number 5.

1. According to historians, when the people in ① ② ③ ④ ⑤
                          1
   power cannot keep the governed content, revolu-
                          2        3 4
   tion is a possibility. _No error_
                          5

2. The *Declaration of Independence* states, "...that
                            2

   all men are created equal, that they are endowed
                   2

   by their Creator with certain inalienable rights;

   that among these are Life, Liberty, and the
                          3

   pursuit of Happiness". *No error*
           4     5

① ② ③ ④ ⑤

3. Great literature, as well as great art is a part of
             1             2

   the American tradition. *No error*
      3     4      5

① ② ③ ④ ⑤

4. The pioneers were a hardy brave group of
                      1

   people who would look in disbelief on the
       2

   comforts of today's middle class. *No error*
           3       4   5

① ② ③ ④ ⑤

5. During their first few years on the American

   continent, the pioneers lived off the animals
   1      2

   in the woods, and stole corn from the natives.
            3                 4

   *No error*
     5

① ② ③ ④ ⑤

6. They traveled with the bare necessities; food,
                              1   2

   water, warm clothing, tools, and weapons.
     3              4

   *No error*
     5

① ② ③ ④ ⑤

7. The <u>Virginians</u> needed their own <u>leader,</u>  ① ② ③ ④ ⑤
       1                               2

   <u>Jefferson,</u> <u>S</u>am Adams was not their type.
       3  4

   <u>No error</u>
     5

8. Many say George Washington was a competent  ① ② ③ ④ ⑤

   <u>general,</u> and a good <u>president;</u> <u>however,</u> <u>some_</u>
        1                      2      3     4
   historians would disagree. <u>No error</u>
                                5

9. There are those who would say that <u>"John</u>  ① ② ③ ④ ⑤
                                           1

   Kennedy was the greatest <u>president</u> to <u>date,</u>
                            2           3

   and others would say that he has been <u>idealized.</u>
                                        4

   <u>No error</u>
     5

10. A <u>flower_consists</u> of a <u>calyx,</u> a <u>corolla,</u> a <u>stamen</u>  ① ② ③ ④ ⑤
           1                2        3      4
    and pistils. <u>No error</u>
                  5

After reviewing the Answer Key on page 339, chart your scores below for each practice exercise.

## SUMMARY OF RESULTS

| Practice Number | Number Correct | Number Incorrect *(Including Omissions)* | Acceptable Score |
|---|---|---|---|
| Spelling | | | 15 Correct |
| Usage—Part A | | | 26 Correct |
| Usage—Part B | | | 7 Correct |
| Effectiveness of Expression— Part A | | | 7 Correct |
| Effectiveness of Expression— Part B | | | 11 Correct |
| Punctuation and Capitalization | | | 7 Correct |

To determine your areas for skill improvement, locate the questions you answered incorrectly and circle the numbers on this Skills Analysis chart. Wherever you have circled errors, review the chapters listed in the last column.

## SKILLS ANALYSIS

| Skill | Question Number | Review Chapter |
|---|---|---|
| **Spelling** | 1 to 20 | 18 |
| **Usage: Part A** Agreement of Subject and Linking Word | 1, 7, 14, 26, 30 | 7 |
| Agreement: Special Problems | 2, 4, 5, 11, 16, 18, 20, 22 | 8 |
| Correct Form of Irregular Action Word | 3 | 1 |
| Correct Use of Pronouns | 6, 8, 9, 21, 25, 27, 28, 29, 35 | 10 |

**SKILLS ANALYSIS**

| Skill | Question Number | Review Chapter |
|---|---|---|
| **Usage: Part A (continued)** | | |
| Time: Special Problems | 12, 15, 23, 24 | 9 |
| Agreement of Performer and Action Word | 13, 31 | 2 |
| Word Usage | 32, 33, 34 | 20 |
| Correct Use of Descriptive Words: -ly ending | 10, 17, 19 | 3 |
| **Usage: Part B** | | |
| Repetition | 1, 5, 7, 10 | 15 |
| Double Negative | 2, 4, 6, 8 | 15 |
| Word Choice | 3, 9 | 20 |
| **Effectiveness of Expression: Part A** | | |
| Repetition | 1 | 15 |
| Wordiness | 2 | 15 |
| Coordination of Ideas | 4, 9, 10 | 15 |
| Balance | 5, 6, 7, 8 | 12 |
| **Effectiveness of Expression: Part B** | | |
| Coordination of Ideas | 1, 3, 11, 12, 13, 14 | 15 |
| Wordiness | 2, 4, 5 | 15 |
| Double Negative | 6 | 15 |
| Unclear Pronoun Reference | 7, 10 | 15 |
| Balance | 8, 9, 15 | 12 |
| **Punctuation and Capitalization** | | |
| Quotation Marks | 2, 9 | 16 |
| Comma | 3, 4, 5, 8, 10 | 13 |
| Semicolon | 7 | 13 |
| Colon | 6 | 16 |

# Chapter 23    Final Review

**Spelling** *Page 318.*

1. **(3)** caucus
2. **(1)** temperature
3. **(4)** library
4. **(2)** lucrative
5. **(1)** hygienic
6. **(3)** ephemeral
7. **(4)** unnecessary
8. **(1)** weird
9. **(4)** receipts
10. **(2)** similar
11. **(3)** preferred
12. **(5)** No error
13. **(3)** dispensable
14. **(1)** truly
15. **(4)** crushes
16. **(4)** thieves
17. **(5)** No error
18. **(2)** achievement
19. **(5)** No error
20. **(5)** No error

**Usage—Part A** *Page 320.*

1. **(4)** No two cities in this country *are* identical. See Chapter 7.
2. **(2)** Any of the local merchants *is* willing to support the United Fund. See Chapter 8.
3. **(3)** This CD has been *lying* on this counter all week. See Chapter 1.
4. **(5)** No error. See Chapter 8.
5. **(3)** One of the necessary prerequisites for change *is* open-mindedness. See Chapter 8.

6. **(1)** Manuel and *I* travel to work together each weekday morning. See Chapter 10.
7. **(2)** Taxes and laughter *are* always present in our American way of life. See Chapter 7.
8. **(2)** Everyone must realize *his* or *her* own potential and try to achieve it. See Chapter 10.
9. **(4)** Mario is a much more efficient bartender than *he*. See Chapter 10.
10. **(2)** Elissa types much *more quickly* than any other person in the office. See Chapter 4.
11. **(2)** Each of the choices *is* equally unappealing to me. See Chapter 8.
12. **(1)** Before the alarm *stopped* ringing, Vera had pulled up the shade. See Chapter 9.
13. **(2)** One of those women *speaks* as well as a professional lecturer. See Chapter 8.
14. **(1)** The dishes in the box *are* on sale this week only but will be sold for more next week. See Chapter 7.
15. **(5)** No error. See Chapter 9.
16. **(3)** Either the subway or the buses *are* crowded at this time of day. See Chapter 8.
17. **(4)** I noticed that older women walk more *gracefully* than teen-age girls. See Chapter 4.
18. **(2)** Each of the contestants *hopes* to win the grand prize. See Chapter 8.

19. **(4)** When I must speak to a large group of people, I always speak too *softly*. See Chapter 4.

20. **(2)** The mail carriers each *have* their own personal gripes. See Chapter 8.

21. **(3)** Any of the women in that office may express *her* opinion at any time. See Chapter 10.

22. **(2)** Either the executive or members of his staff *were* responsible for breaking the law. See Chapter 8.

23. **(2)** Before they signed the treaty, both parties *had agreed* to uphold the terms provided. See Chapter 9.

24. **(1)** Reagan *had been* president before Bush was, and Clinton served after Bush had. See Chapter 9.

25. **(3)** Either Charlie or I will call you or *him* when the order is ready. See Chapter 10.

26. **(1)** *Romeo and Juliet is* one of my favorite plays, but I've never seen it performed. See Chapter 7.

27. **(3)** Was it Mr. Farrar *who* called you? See Chapter 10.

28. **(4)** I am always at the bus stop earlier than *he*. See Chapter 10.

29. **(1)** Eileen and *I* are working on the night shift with them. See Chapter 10.

30. **(1)** Fifteen minutes *is* all that I can spare to listen to your problems. See Chapter 7.

31. **(2)** The problem of too many people *requires* immediate attention by world leaders as well as scientists and environmentalists. See Chapter 2.

32. **(3)** After many months of arguing, Congress finally *adopted* the bill into law. See Chapter 20.

33. **(2)** Because his lawyer strongly *advised* him to do so, Mr. Rodriguez offered his wife a generous settlement. See Chapter 20.

34. **(1)** The *principal* reason for my not borrowing your credit card is that I'm afraid I'll lose it. See Chapter 20.

35. **(3)** Your supervisor does not appreciate *your* walking in consistently at 9:10. See Chapter 10.

**Usage—Part B** *Page 324.*

1. **(1)** *My brother never* calls before visiting us.

2. **(3)** Great men throughout history *hardly ever* avoided some minor scandal.

3. **(3)** If you had called ahead of time, I could *have* been ready when you arrived.

4. **(2)** George Burns *scarcely ever* missed a scheduled performance.

5. **(1)** The trip on the *sightseeing* bus was one of the highlights of our much deserved vacation.

6. **(3)** Manny was shocked when Alfred raised his voice; no one had *ever* spoken to him in that tone of voice.

7. **(1)** The *sun is* 865,000 miles in diameter and has a surface temperature of about 10,000°F.

8. **(3)** A wise consumer carefully reads the labels and *doesn't buy* unmarked products.

9. **(3)** If you really had wanted to, you could *have* prevented that misunderstanding.

10. **(1)** Some *scientists believe* that one of the long-range effects of food additives is hyperactivity in children.

**Effectiveness of Expression—**

**Part A** *Page 326.*

1. **(2)** In today's all-volunteer U.S. Army, *the recruit starts* his two-year enlistment in a different atmosphere.

2. **(3)** *The former soldier would not recognize living conditions in today's army because* the facilities are more home-like and less barracks-like.

3. **(1)** Today's soldier enjoys *not only more comfort but also better pay.*

4. **(4)** Nowadays employers can afford to be choosy *since the period of slow economic growth has increased* the number and the quality of the applicants.

5. **(2)** The recruits get *tough, demanding, useful training* under the command of their drill sergeants.

6. **(2)** Carl Williams is an excellent basketball coach and *a good friend to the team members.*

7. **(3)** Every Thursday night the Morgan family watches TV and *eats TV dinners.*

8. **(3)** The City Council meets every Wednesday evening in private and *every Thursday in public.*

9. **(4)** Carlos Battaglia has a good historical perspective; *therefore, he understands current events.*

10. **(1)** I am not in agreement with most of the policies of the present administration, *but I can't change them.*

**Effectiveness of Expression—**

**Part B** *Page 329.*

1. **(1)** The boundaries of science have expanded significantly, *and two distinct fields of science have emerged: pure and applied.*

2. **(4)** The British pound was devalued *because of an inflationary spiral.*

3. **(2)** The Food Guide Pyramid provides a guide to daily food choices, *thereby helping people build a healthful diet.*

4. **(2)** Many people believed that the recent product "shortages" *resulted from manufacturers wanting to raise prices.*

5. **(3)** Viewers find it difficult to reach agreement on whether *or not television encourages violent behavior.*

6. **(4)** One member of the Surgeon General's Scientific Advisory Committee on Television and Social Behavior felt that *there is no question about whether television has a negative effect on its viewers.*

7. **(3)** Some TV viewers express their resentment toward anyone else censoring their viewing choices, *saying it's the parents' job to censor the TV programs their children see.*

8. **(1)** An environmental protection agency should *set automobile pollution standards, oversee strip-mining, and prohibit dumping in public waterways.*

9. **(4)** Many people who formerly drove to work are now taking buses *in order to conserve gas, to prevent air pollution, and to save money.*

10. **(1)** In order to encourage the commuter not to drive to work, some communities have installed park-and-ride facilities *where the commuter can leave his car and board a bus for the trip to work.*

11. **(3)** The new employee is very organized; *however, she is always late.*

12. **(3)** The year 1995 showed a marked decline in Americans traveling abroad _due to increased terrorism._

13. **(1)** The French Revolution did not occur when the peasants had no rights whatsoever; _rather, the Revolution occurred when the peasants began to taste the better life._

14. **(4)** Modern China has eliminated serious contagious diseases _by using trained nonprofessionals to aid the country's limited number of doctors._

15. **(3)** During the first half of the eighteenth century, the Carter family built a mansion at Williamsburg where the family _grew its own food, rode to the hounds on horses from its own stables, made equipment in its own craft shops, and shipped its tobacco to England from its private dock._

## Punctuation and Capitalization
_Page 334._

1. **(5)** No error

2. **(4)** The _Declaration of Independence_ states "...that all men are created equal, that they are endowed by their Creator with certain inalienable rights; that among these are Life, Liberty, and the pursuit of Happiness."

3. **(2)** Great literature, as well as great art, is a part of the American tradition.

4. **(1)** The pioneers were a hardy, brave group of people who would look in disbelief on the comforts of today's middle class.

5. **(3)** During their first few years on the American continent, the pioneers lived off the animals in the woods_and stole corn from the natives.

6. **(1)** They traveled with the bare necessities: food, water, warm clothing, tools, and weapons.

7. **(3)** The Virginians needed their own leader, Jefferson; Sam Adams was not their type.

8. **(1)** Many say George Washington was a competent general_and a good president; however, some historians would disagree.

9. **(1)** There are those who would say that_John Kennedy was the greatest president to date, and others would say that he has been idealized.

10. **(4)** A flower consists of a calyx, a corolla, a stamen, and pistils.

# MOVE TO THE HEAD OF YOUR CLASS
# THE EASY WAY!

Barron's presents THE EASY WAY SERIES—specially prepared by top educators, it maximizes effective learning while minimizing the time and effort it takes to raise your grades, brush up on the basics, and build your confidence. Comprehensive and full of clear review examples, **THE EASY WAY SERIES** is your best bet for better grades, quickly!

0-8120-9409-3 **Accounting the Easy Way, 3rd Ed.**—$14.95, Can. $21.00
0-8120-9393-3 **Algebra the Easy Way, 3rd Ed.**—$12.95, Can. $16.95
0-8120-1943-1 **American History the Easy Way, 2nd Ed.**—$14.95, Can. $19.95
0-7641-0299-0 **American Sign Language the Easy Way**—$14.95, Can. $21.00
0-8120-9134-5 **Anatomy and Physiology the Easy Way**—$14.95, Can. $19.95
0-8120-9410-7 **Arithmetic the Easy Way, 3rd Ed.**—$13.95, Can. $19.50
0-7641-1358-5 **Biology the Easy Way, 3rd Ed.**—$13.95, Can. $19.50
0-7641-1079-9 **Bookkeeping the Easy Way, 3rd Ed.**—$13.95, Can. $19.50
0-8120-4760-5 **Business Law the Easy Way**—$13.95, Can. $19.50
0-7641-0314-8 **Business Letters the Easy Way, 3rd Ed.**—$12.95, Can. $17.95
0-7641-1359-3 **Business Math the Easy Way, 3rd Ed.**—$14.95, Can. $21.00
0-8120-9141-8 **Calculus the Easy Way, 3rd Ed.**—$13.95, Can. $19.50
0-8120-9138-8 **Chemistry the Easy Way, 3rd Ed.**—$13.95, Can. $18.95
0-7641-0659-7 **Chinese the Easy Way**—$13.95, Can. $18.95
0-8120-9144-2 **Electronics the Easy Way, 3rd Ed.**—$13.95, Can. $18.95
0-8120-9142-6 **English the Easy Way, 3rd Ed.**—$13.95, Can. $19.50
0-8120-9505-7 **French the Easy Way, 3rd Ed.**—$13.95, Can. $18.95
0-7641-0110-2 **Geometry the Easy Way, 3rd Ed.**—$12.95, Can. $16.95
0-8120-9145-0 **German the Easy Way, 2nd Ed.**—$13.95, Can. $18.95
0-8120-4798-2 **Immigration the Easy Way**—$14.95, Can. $19.95
0-8120-9146-9 **Italian the Easy Way, 2nd Ed.**—$13.95, Can. $19.50
0-8120-9627-4 **Japanese the Easy Way**—$14.95, Can. $21.00
0-7641-0752-6 **Java™ Programming the Easy Way**—$18.95, Can. $25.50
0-8120-9139-6 **Math the Easy Way, 3rd Ed.**—$11.95, Can. $15.95
0-8120-9601-0 **Microeconomics the Easy Way**—$13.95, Can. $19.50
0-7641-0236-2 **Physics the Easy Way, 3rd Ed.**—$13.95, Can. $18.95
0-8120-9412-3 **Spanish the Easy Way, 3rd Ed.**—$13.95, Can. $19.50
0-8120-9852-8 **Speed Reading the Easy Way**—$13.95, Can. $19.50
0-8120-9143-4 **Spelling the Easy Way, 3rd Ed.**—$12.95, Can. $16.95
0-8120-9392-5 **Statistics the Easy Way, 3rd Ed.**—$14.95, Can. $21.00
0-7641-1360-7 **Trigonometry the Easy Way, 3rd Ed.**—$14.95, Can. $21.00
0-8120-9147-7 **Typing the Easy Way, 3rd Ed.**—$18.95, Can. $26.50
0-8120-9765-3 **World History the Easy Way, Vol. One**—$14.95, Can. $19.95
0-8120-9766-1 **World History the Easy Way, Vol. Two**—$12.95, Can. $16.95
0-7641-1206-6 **Writing the Easy Way, 3rd Ed.**—$12.95, Can. $17.95